Accounting Essentials for Hospitality Managers

For non-accountant hospitality managers, accounting and financial management is often perceived as an inaccessible part of the business, yet understanding it is crucial for success. Using an "easy-to-read" style, this book provides a comprehensive overview of the most relevant accounting information for hospitality managers. It demonstrates how to organise and analyse accounting data to help make informed decisions with confidence.

With its highly practical approach, this third edition:

- quickly develops the reader's ability to adeptly use and interpret accounting information to further organisational decision making and control;
- demonstrates how an appropriate analysis of financial reports can drive your business strategy forward from a well-informed base;
- develops mastery of the key accounting concepts through financial decision making cases that take a hospitality manager's perspective on a range of issues;
- sets financial problems in the context of a range of countries and currencies;
- includes two new chapters concerning managerial finance issues and revenue management;
- includes accounting problems at the end of each chapter, to be used to test knowledge and apply understanding to real-life situations;
- offers extensive web support for tutors and students, providing explanation and guidelines for instructors on how to use the textbook and examples, PowerPoint slides, solutions to end of chapter problems, and student test bank and additional exercises.

This book is written in an accessible and engaging style, and is structured logically with useful features throughout to aid students' learning and understanding. It is an essential resource for all future hospitality managers.

Chris Guilding is Professor of Hotel Management in the Department of Tourism, Leisure, Hotel and Sport Management at Griffith University, Australia. His teaching specialism is in management accounting and he has taught on the MBA, Masters in Hospitality Management, Professional Golfers Association, Australian Institute of Company Directors Course and undergraduate programmes.

Accounting Essentials for Hospitality Managers

Third edition

Chris Guilding

Routledge
Taylor & Francis Group

LONDON AND NEW YORK

First published 2014
by Routledge
2 Park Square, Milton Park, Abingdon, Oxon OX14 4RN

and by Routledge
711 Third Avenue, New York, NY 10017

Routledge is an imprint of the Taylor & Francis Group, an informa business

British Library Cataloguing in Publication Data
A catalogue record for this book is available from the British Library

Library of Congress Cataloging in Publication Data
Guilding, Chris.
  Accounting essentials for hospitality managers / Chris Guilding.
     pages cm
  Includes bibliographical references and index.
  1. Hospitality industry—Accounting.   2. Hospitality industry—Management.
  I. Title.
  HF5686.H75G848 2013
  657'.837—dc23
                                                                    2013023756

ISBN: 978–0–415–84107–8 (hbk)
ISBN: 978–0–415–84109–2 (pbk)
ISBN: 978–0–203–76666–8 (ebk)

Typeset in Sabon and Frutiger
by RefineCatch Limited, Bungay, Suffolk

MIX
Paper from responsible sources
FSC
www.fsc.org   FSC® C013056

Printed and bound in Great Britain by
TJ International Ltd, Padstow, Cornwall

To Dawne, Logan and Matthew

Contents

Contents

A range of further resources for this book are available on the
Companion Website: www.routledge.com/cw/guilding

Figures

Tables

Boxes

Schedules

Exhibits

Financial decision making and control in action cases

Preface

Welcome to *Accounting Essentials for Hospitality Managers*. This is the third edition of the book, although the book's first edition was entitled *Financial Management for Hospitality Decision Makers*. The re-titling of the book resulted from a concern that the words "financial management" convey a particular meaning to many accounting and finance academics. This meaning suggests a curriculum that encompasses corporate finance topics such as the cost of capital and capital structure. Such topics would be of interest to finance specialists working in the corporate head office of large hotel chains. They are not particularly pertinent, however, to managers operating at the hotel property level. This book is concerned with the key accounting tools and techniques that facilitate effective management in a hotel property. Hence the words "accounting" and "essentials" are included in the new title.

This edition of the book contains two new chapters: Chapter 15, which is concerned with financial management topics not addressed elsewhere in the book, and Chapter 16, which provides an accounting perspective on revenue management, which has become an increasingly important facet of hotel management in recent years. The number of problems appearing at the end of each chapter has also been expanded to a minimum of 12. For each chapter, solutions for the first three problems are provided at the back of the book. This is a self-help feature designed to further facilitate learning and enable students to review their understanding of concepts covered by the book.

The current era of growth and dynamic change in hospitality signifies that it is an exciting time to be involved with the industry. Like many other industries, the hospitality sector is experiencing heightened levels of competition and a growing need to apply appropriate management techniques to ensure commercial success. These factors increasingly signify that a hotel manager needs a working knowledge of accounting tools, techniques and procedures.

From my experience as an instructor of accounting generally, and hospitality management accounting in particular, I have found students tend to approach their first class with a degree of trepidation and an expectation that the subject will be dry and difficult to master. Through this book, I endeavour to make the subject material accessible and to demonstrate the relevance of accounting to all hotel managers in all but the smallest hotels. Recognition of the way that accounting can be usefully applied by the modern manager is a critical factor that can stimulate a student's desire to master the material covered. Once relevance is appreciated, the student starts to explore the range of ways in which accounting can serve the hospitality manager.

The approach to topics covered has been designed to maximise the reader's sense that they are quickly mastering key accounting concepts. Such mastery will help the reader develop the courage to demand excellence of the hotel's accounting department where he or she works. This is a key step in the design of a quality accounting system. Too frequently, managers are "turned-off" by accounting jargon and the way accounting reports are presented. It is an unfortunate reality that accounting reports frequently appear to be designed by accountants for accountants. This problem is partially attributable to the fact that most qualified accountants have gained their qualification through demonstrating their understanding of the rules of external reporting (i.e., financial accounting, which is the branch of accounting concerned with the preparation of annual accounts for external parties, such as shareholders). When providing accounting information to managers within the hotel, however, reports should be designed with the decision making needs of the managers in mind. Hotel accounting systems can be greatly improved if managers play an active role in ensuring that accounting reports developed for their use are designed to be of maximum relevancy and are structured in a format that facilitates easy interpretation and use.

The book has been written with two specific audiences in mind. Firstly, it can serve as a valuable self-help tool for the practising hospitality manager interested in improving their appreciation of accounting techniques and procedures. Secondly, it has been designed to serve as a text that can be used in an accounting course in a hospitality-related programme of study. While the depth of the material covered signifies it would serve well as a stage two text, it can certainly be used in a first year of study, as no prior study of accounting is presumed.

In my view, not only can a well-designed book meet the needs of both the practitioner and student audiences, a well-balanced book is likely to result from addressing the needs of both audiences. Addressing the practising manager audience ensures that the book imparts information that is relevant to today's hospitality manager in a direct and readily accessible style. The reader will be able to quickly see the wood from the trees and gain an early appreciation of how concepts introduced can be applied in practice. Addressing a student audience ensures that the material covered provides a broad foundation. The problems provided at the end of each chapter give students the chance to practice applying issues raised in the chapters and also to gain exposure to the type of problems that can be encountered in examination situations. A review of these problems will also prove extremely beneficial to the practising manager, as deeper understanding of the material covered in the text will result from exposure to a range of real world decision making scenarios.

A distinctive aspect of the book is its international orientation. The hospitality industry is becoming increasingly international with large multi-national chains dominating the 5 and 4 star market segments. This factor, together with the drawing together of countries to form economic alliances such as the European

Economic Union signifies that a hotel manager's career path can involve some international work experience. Further, the clientele base of hotels is becoming more international as a result of increased international business and tourist travel. In combination, these factors highlight the need for a book that views hospitality accounting in a globalised context. Scenarios introduced and problems posed will draw on a range of international settings. This will develop the reader's familiarity with addressing financial problems in the context of a range of countries and currencies.

A second distinctive aspect of the book is its hospitality decision makers' orientation. This theme will be apparent from the problem solving approach used throughout the text. In each chapter this approach is reinforced by the inclusion of a case that takes a particular hospitality manager's perspective on an issue raised. Each of these cases is headed "Financial decision making in action" or "Financial control in action" and has a sub-heading relating to the hotel function and also the aspect of accounting in question.

The book can be viewed as comprising four main parts. After the introductory chapter, Chapters 2 to 5 focus on financial accounting. Chapters 6 to 12 focus on management accounting, Chapters 13 to 15 focus on financial management issues and Chapter 16 concerns revenue management. Each part can be approached independently of the other parts, i.e., if the reader is exclusively interested in management accounting, they can commence their reading at Chapter 6 or Chapter 7.

In Chapter 1, in the course of providing an overview of the nature of accounting, the contents of the book are introduced. Chapters 2, 3 and 4 build on one another to provide a grounding in financial accounting. While financial accounting does not represent the primary orientation of the book, a basic understanding of the workings of the financial accounting system can be highly beneficial to the hospitality manager, due to the importance of financial statements such as the balance sheet and income statement. It is difficult to overstate the importance of these statements as they represent a key resource used by outsiders to gauge an organisation's performance. The need for management to understand the mechanisms by which they are judged externally is clearly important. Chapter 5 provides a structured approach that can be taken to analysing the statements produced by the financial accounting system.

Chapters 6–16 have more of an internal (i.e., within a hotel) orientation. Chapter 6 outlines significant internal control challenges that arise in hotels and describes procedures that can be implemented to counter these challenges. Chapters 7–16 consider hospitality management decision making from the following perspectives:

- Classifying costs in order to facilitate decision making,
- Using cost-volume-profit analysis,
- Applying budgeting and responsibility accounting,
- Applying flexible budgeting and variance analysis,
- Designing appropriate performance measurement systems,

- Drawing on cost information to inform pricing decisions,
- How optimal decisions can be made with respect to working capital (i.e., cash, accounts receivable, inventory and accounts payable management),
- What financial techniques can be used in investment appraisal,
- How operating and financial leverage can be manipulated to increase net profit,
- What revenue management steps can be taken in an effort to increase total revenue.

The book has been designed to facilitate a flexible teaching and learning approach. While the sequencing of the chapters results from my view of the most appropriate order in which to present the material covered, many of the chapters can be read out of sequence. The only chapters that build on one another to such a degree that they should be read consecutively are Chapters 2, 3 and 4 and Chapters 9 and 10.

Should you have any suggestions in connection with how the book could be further strengthened in the next edition, it would be a pleasure to hear from you. Please contact me at my email address noted below.

I hope you find this book to be a stimulating read and that your career benefits from you gaining an enhanced appreciation of the merits of applying appropriately chosen accounting techniques and procedures in hospitality management.

Finally, I would like to thank the publisher, *John Wiley and Sons* for allowing me to draw some of Chapter 6's material from the following book:

The Key Elements of Introductory Accounting, Guilding C., Auyeung, P. and Delaney, D.; John Wiley and Sons Australia Ltd; © 2006, 3rd edition; Reprinted with permission of John Wiley & Sons Australia.

Chris Guilding
c.guilding@griffith.edu.au

Chapter 1

Introduction: hospitality decision makers' use of accounting

Learning objectives

After studying this chapter, you should have developed an appreciation of:

1. the accounting implications of key hospitality industry characteristics,
2. the nature of accounting and financial management,
3. some of the ways hospitality managers become involved in accounting,
4. what is meant by the "*Uniform System of Accounts for the Lodging Industry*",
5. the basic differences between sole proprietorships, partnerships and companies,
6. the focus of this book.

1) Introduction

This book describes accounting and financial management procedures and analytical techniques in the context of hospitality decision making. The purpose of this introductory chapter is to set the scene for the remainder of the book.

The first section of this chapter describes key characteristics relating to the hospitality industry and outlines accounting implications associated with these characteristics. Then, an overview of the nature of accounting is provided. In the course of describing the nature of accounting, the overall structure of the book will be introduced. We will see that Chapters 2–5 provide a grounding in hospitality financial accounting. Chapters 6–12 introduce a range of topics relating to management accounting and will show how management accounting techniques and procedures are critically important to a host of hospitality decision making situations. Chapters 13–15 focus on managerial finance issues and Chapter 16 provides a financial perspective on revenue management.

This chapter's subsequent section highlights some of the many ways that different hospitality managers can apply accounting techniques and procedures to inform their decision making. The following section introduces an important accounting report: the income statement. This statement is introduced in the context of a description of the *Uniform System of Accounts for the Lodging Industry*. This system was developed in the US and is being increasingly used in large hotels internationally. This signifies increased standardisation of the classification scheme used by hotels to record their financial transactions, and also greater standardisation of the financial performance reports produced by hotels. The chapter's final section describes the three main types of commercial organisation: sole proprietorship, partnership, and company.

2) Key characteristics of the hospitality industry

The hospitality industry encompasses a broad range of activities and types of organisation. Some of the industry's particularly visible players include restaurants and bars that provide dining and beverage services and also lodging operations that offer accommodation facilities. Restaurant organisations range from multinational companies to small street corner cafés. Similarly, lodging operations range from multinational hotels offering thousands of rooms worldwide to bed and breakfast operations offering a single guest room. At the bed and breakfast extreme, we have small family-run concerns with a limited service range, while at the other extreme we have multinational companies offering a range of services that include accommodation, dining and frequently conference, sports and leisure facilities. The hospitality industry's heterogeneity becomes apparent when we recognise that its diversity encompasses the following:

- Hotels
- Motels
- Restaurants
- Fast food outlets
- Pubs and bars
- Country and sport clubs
- Cruise liners.

This book is primarily focused on hotel management. This focus has been taken because the majority of large hotels provide most of the service elements offered by the hospitality organisations listed above. In addition, as many large hotels have to co-ordinate provision of a range of hospitality services under one roof, they confront a degree of management complexity not encountered in many other hospitality organisations that offer a narrower range of services. For example, a large hotel's organisational structure and accounting system must be designed with due regard given to co-ordinating a range of disparate functions that, in most cases, will at least include the provision of accommodation, restaurant and bar facilities. The disparity of these functions is apparent when we recognise that the sale of rooms can be likened to the sale of seats in the airline or entertainment industries, a parallel exists between food preparation in restaurant kitchens and production activities in the manufacturing industry, and bar operations can be likened to retailing. In addition to managing this disparate range of services, a hotel needs to co-ordinate a set of distinct support activities such as laundry, building and grounds maintenance, information systems, training, marketing, transportation, etc.

This disparate range of hospitality activities is housed within a single site (i.e., building and surrounds), that we refer to as a hotel. This creates a degree of site complexity which is exacerbated when we recognise that the location of the service provider is also the place where the customer purchases and consumes the services offered. While this is patently obvious to anyone who has been to a hotel, we should not forget that it is not the case in many other service industries (e.g., banking, transportation, telecommunications, law, accounting), or the manufacturing industry. This factor highlights a further dynamic of the hotel industry. Not only is a hotel site the place where a broad range of activities are undertaken, it is the focal point of extensive and continual vigilance with respect to cleaning, maintenance and security. We can thus see that a hotel represents a complex site where distinct activities are conducted in close proximity to one another. Where the performance of one functional activity (e.g., cleaning) can be affected by the way another is conducted (e.g., maintenance), high interdependency is said to exist. Such high interdependency can create problems when attempting to hold one functional area (e.g., cleaning) accountable for its performance.

Not only is functional interdependency an issue when trying to hold a manager accountable for costs, it can be a problem when attempting to hold a manager responsible for a particular department's level of sales. For example, through no fault of her own, a food and beverage (F&B) manager may see her profits plummet as a result of a relatively low number of rooms sold by the rooms division. Such cross-functional interdependency needs to be recognised when identifying what aspect of a hotel's performance a particular manager should be held accountable for.

Sales volatility

The hotel industry experiences significant sales volatility. The extent of this volatility becomes particularly apparent when we recognise it comprises at least four key dimensions:

- economic cycle volatility,
- seasonal sales volatility,
- weekly sales volatility,
- intra-day sales volatility.

These dimensions of sales volatility and the implications they carry for hotel accounting are elaborated upon in Box 1.1.

Box 1.1

Dimensions of sales volatility in the hospitality industry

1) **Economic cycle volatility**: Hotels are extremely susceptible to the highs and lows of the economic cycle. Properties with a high proportion of business clients suffer during economic downturns due to significantly reduced corporate expenditure on business travel. Hotels offering tourist accommodation also suffer during economic downturns due to families reducing discretionary expenditure on activities such as holidays and travel. This high susceptibility to the general economic climate highlights the importance of hotels developing operational plans only once careful analysis has been made of predicted economic conditions.

2) **Seasonal sales volatility**: Many hotels experience seasonal sales volatility over the course of a year. This volatility can be so severe to cause off-season closure for some resort properties. The decision whether to close

should be informed by an appropriately conducted financial analysis such as that described in Chapter 7. Seasonal sales volatility can also pose particular cash management issues. During the middle and tail-end of busy seasons, surplus cash balances are likely to result, while in the off-season and the build up to the busy season, deficit cash balances are likely to arise. The need for careful cash planning and management is discussed in Chapter 13.

3) *Weekly sales volatility*: Hotels with a high proportion of business clients will experience high occupancy (i.e., a high proportion of rooms sold) from Monday to Thursday, and a relatively low occupancy from Friday to Sunday. By contrast, many resort hotels have relatively busy weekends. As will be seen in Chapter 16, accurate forecasting of demand will inform management's decision making with respect to the amount and timing of room rate discounting. Forecasting is also discussed in the context of budgeting in Chapter 9.

4) *Intra-day sales volatility*: Restaurants experience busy periods during meal times, while bars tend to be busiest at night times. This intra-day demand volatility has led to widely-used pricing strategies such as "early bird specials" in restaurants and "happy hours" in bars. Hotel pricing issues are discussed in Chapters 12 and 16. In addition to these dimensions of intra-day sales volatility, staffing needs have to be considered in light of issues such as the front desk experiencing a frenetic early morning period processing check-outs and a second, more protracted, busy period in the late afternoon processing check-ins.

High product perishability

Relative to many other industries, there can be limited scope to produce for inventory in food-service operations. A significant proportion of food inventory is purchased less than 24 hours prior to sale, and much food preparation is conducted within minutes of a sale. There is thus a very short time span between order placement, production and sale. Many menu items cannot be produced in advance of sales due to their high perishability.

Perishability is even more apparent with respect to room and banquet sales. In these contexts, perishability can be described as "absolute", as, if a room is not occupied on a particular night, the opportunity to sell that room that night is lost forever. No discounting of a room's rate the following day can reverse this loss. This situation also applies to conference and banqueting activities. The high perishability associated with rooms, conferencing, banqueting and food underlines the importance of accurate demand forecasting. With respect to food, an accurate forecast of the mix and level of demand can result in the maintenance of all options on a menu during high demand periods, and minimal cost of food scrapped during low demand periods. With respect to rooms, an accurate forecast of room demand can enable appropriate pricing decisions to be made as part of an attempt to maximise revenue. Appropriate room demand management is particularly important, as room sales can be the prime driver of sales of many of a hotel's other services (e.g., restaurant, bar, etc.).

High fixed component in cost structure

A high proportion of a hotel's costs do not vary in line with sales levels. These costs are referred to as "fixed". The high fixed cost structure of hotels results from rent (a significant investment is required to buy land and build a hotel), as well as fixed salary costs associated with administrative and operational staff needed to manage, operate and maintain a hotel. The high proportion of fixed costs signifies that an important issue in hotels concerns the determination of the level of sales necessary to achieve breakeven (i.e., cover all fixed costs).

A considerable proportion of fixed costs result from periodic refurbishment of rooms and also investment in the hotel's physical infrastructure such as kitchen and laundry equipment. In accounting, we refer to such long-held assets of the organisation as "fixed assets". In Chapter 4 we will see how the purchase of a fixed asset results in depreciation (the allocation of a fixed asset's cost over its useful life), and in Chapter 14 techniques that can be used to appraise fixed asset investment proposals are described.

Labour intensive activities

If you visit the typical modern factory, you are likely to be struck by the highly automated and capital-intensive nature of the production process. Procedures are scheduled by computers and robotic engineering is used extensively in physical processing. This capital intensity in the conduct of work lies in stark contrast to what you see when entering a hotel. Major hotel activities include room housekeeping, restaurant food preparation and service as well as bar service. Despite the advent of the machine and computer age, the physical conduct of all of these activities has changed little over the last fifty years. They continue to have a high labour component. Relative to many other industries, we can conclude that activities conducted in the hotel industry are still highly labour intensive.

This high labour intensity highlights the need to develop performance measures that monitor labour productivity. Performance indicators such as restaurant sales per employee hour worked are described in Chapters 5 and 11. In addition, the need to analyse the difference between the actual cost of labour and the budgeted cost of labour can represent a significant dimension of labour cost management. In Chapter 10 we will see how differences between budgeted and actual labour cost can be segregated into labour rate and labour efficiency variances.

The distinctiveness of these hotel characteristics that have just been described underlines the degree to which hotel accounting systems need to be tailored to the particular needs of hotel management. In combination, these characteristics signify that a hotel represents a fascinating arena in which to consider the application of accounting. Box 1.2 provides a summary of accounting implications associated with each of the hospitality industry characteristics just described.

Box 1.2

The accounting implications of distinctive hospitality industry characteristics

Hospitality Industry Characteristic	Accounting Implication
1. Disparity and interdependency of functions	Care must be taken when determining a functional area's scope of accountability. Due to their influence on sales and expenses, some managers can be held profit accountable (e.g., a restaurant manager). Due to no direct influence on sales, others can only be held cost accountable (e.g., a training manager). Factors affecting departmental performance can be complex in hotels, however. If room occupancy affects F&B sales, care must be taken if attempting to hold an F&B manager profit accountable.
2. High sales volatility	Hotel activity can be highly volatile over the course of an economic cycle, a year, a week, and a day. As noted in Box 1.1, this issue highlights the importance of accurate budgeting and forecasting systems to aid discounting decisions with respect to room rates and restaurant menu prices.
3. High product perishability	The absolute perishability of rooms, conference and banquet services and the relative perishability of food underlines the importance of accurate hotel demand forecasting as part of the budgeting process. Generally, the most important aspect of forecasting is room occupancy, as room sales drive the sales levels of other hotel activities. Accurate restaurant forecasting provides the basis for maintaining a full menu of options and minimising the cost of food wastage. With respect to rooms, forecasting accuracy can enable appropriate room rate discounting decisions.
4. High fixed costs	Hotels involve considerable investment in fixed assets such as buildings on prime land as well as extensive furnishings, fittings and equipment. This investment generates high rent and depreciation cost (discussed in Chapter 4), which, together with significant salary costs, result in hotels having a high fixed cost structure. High investment highlights the importance of using appropriate financial analysis when appraising the relative merits of proposed investments.
5. Labour-intensive activities	The high labour intensity apparent in many hotel activities highlights the importance of monitoring differences between actual labour cost and budgeted labour cost and also using performance measures that focus on labour productivity.

3) Accounting and business management

Accounting is often referred to as the "language of business". Accounting concerns information systems that record business activities in financial terms and consolidate the information recorded to produce reports that convey a business's financial achievements to decision makers such as managers and shareholders. Two distinct arms are evident in accounting: financial accounting and management accounting.

Financial accounting concerns the preparation of financial reports for external users such as shareholders, banks and government authorities. In order for these financial reports to be meaningful, it is important that they are produced in a standardised way and are seen to be reliable. Consider the implications arising if investors lost faith in the reliability of accounting reports produced by companies. As financial accounting reports represent a key source of information used by the investing community when deciding whether to buy a company's shares, a lack of confidence in accounting systems would translate into a sense of deficient information and a reluctance to invest. This would inhibit the ability of economically viable companies to expand, which in turn would carry negative implications for employment, availability of goods and services, and our standard of living. For the sake of a healthy economy, it is therefore critically important that a reliable financial accounting system that engenders trust in reported data is established. The importance of reliability in financial reporting is a significant factor that lies behind the considerable resources expended in connection with auditing company accounts. This book provides an introduction to the basics of financial accounting, to provide hotel managers with an appreciation of the financial accounting reporting process and the ability to conduct an informed analysis of the statements produced by the process.

Management accounting concerns the provision of financial information to internal management. This information is designed to help managers in their decision making and control of businesses. Financial information sought by hotel managers includes determining the cost of providing a meal to inform the menu pricing decision, determining how many delegates need to attend a conference in order to achieve breakeven, and determining what level of profit is made by each selling unit of a hotel to inform any rationalization decision to close down a unit. The provision of all these types of financial information falls within the scope of management accounting. In addition to introducing the basics of financial accounting, this book describes management accounting and tools and techniques that can aid hospitality managers in their efforts to ensure efficient and effective management of resources.

For most organisations, the accounting system represents the most extensive and all-encompassing information system. This is because accounting information is based primarily on the most fundamental common denominator in business, i.e., money. A front office manager might talk of the number of check-ins processed, a restaurant manager may talk of the number of covers served, a laundry manager may talk of the weight of linen processed and a housekeeping manager may talk of the number of rooms cleaned. While each manager refers to different operational factors when talking of their respective activities, they are all familiar with the terms "cost" and "profit". Cost and profit are denominated in monetary terms and this underlines the degree to which the accounting system is the organisation's most pervasive and all-encompassing information system. It is also the only information system that measures the economic performance of all departments within an organisation. When we recognise the pervasive nature of the accounting information system and the fact that we are living in a time that is frequently described as "the information age", we begin to appreciate the critically significant role of accounting in promoting effective business management.

Individuals from different functional areas should play an active accounting role by demanding excellence in the design of accounting systems. We sometimes need to remind ourselves that accounting system design is too important to be left solely to accountants. Specific accounting information needs that fall outside the scope of conventional accounting system design will have to be flagged by managers with decision making and control responsibilities. There is boundless scope for tailoring an accounting information system, however the onus is on managers to inform the accounting service providers how the information provided should be tailored to meet their decision making needs.

In the last few years, there appears to have been a strong movement away from accounting's traditional "command and control" philosophy to more of an "inform and improve" philosophy. Despite this, some question the appropriateness of using financial measures to direct and control businesses. Criticisms include:

- Financial measures focus on symptoms rather than causes. Profit may decline because of declining customer service. It might therefore be more helpful for management to focus on monitoring the quality of customer service delivery, rather than profit.
- Financial measures tend to be oriented to monitoring past short-term performance. This can hinder forward-looking, longer-term initiatives such as a quest to develop a strong hotel chain image amongst customers.

Some of these criticisms have led to greater importance being attached to a breadth of financial and non-financial performance indicators, e.g., Kaplan and Norton talk of the "Balanced Scorecard" (Kaplan and Norton 1996). Developing a mix of financial and non-financial performance measures in the context of a balanced scorecard management approach is discussed in Chapter 11. Despite such developments, given the importance attached to published financial statements by the investing community, continued management emphasis on financial controls is to be expected.

Chapters 2, 3, 4 and 5 provide a progressive introduction to the workings of financial accounting systems. In Chapter 2 we will see how, like a coin, a financial transaction has two sides. These two sides signify that all financial transactions have a double impact on the business. In Chapters 3 and 4 we will see how the two sides of the "financial transaction coin" are referred to as debits and credits. It is important that you gain an understanding of the double entry bookkeeping system as it is a fairly fundamental aspect of accounting. An analogy can be drawn between the manner in which knowing the alphabet serves reading and writing and the way in which an appreciation of the double entry accounting system will aid your capacity to exercise appropriate financial management. Once you have mastered the basics of double entry accounting, you will have a grounding that will allow you to begin considering how accounting information can be tailored to the specific financial decision making needs that arise in a hotel. It is from the information stored in the double entry accounting system that an income statement (profit and loss statement) and balance sheet are periodically prepared. These statements, which represent key indicators of an organisation's financial health and performance, are also described in Chapters 2 and 3. Chapter 5 provides an overview of how year end financial accounts can be analysed.

The book's subsequent chapters have more of a management decision making and control orientation. The management issues addressed concern: the importance of internal control in hotels and what steps can be taken to strengthen internal control (Chapter 6), facilitating decision making and control through cost analysis and management (Chapters 7 and 8), responsibility accounting and budgetary control (Chapters 9 and 10), performance measurement (Chapter 11), using cost information to inform pricing decisions (Chapter 12), managing elements of working capital such as cash, accounts receivable, inventory and accounts payable (Chapter 13), and conducting financial analyses of investment proposals (Chapter 14). Chapter 15 reviews a range of managerial finance issues and Chapter 16 provides a financial perspective on revenue management.

4) Accounting and hospitality decision makers

A theme of this book concerns viewing accounting from a range of different hospitality management functional perspectives. This theme will be evident from the book's many worked examples that show how particular accounting applications are pertinent to a broad array of hospitality management decision making situations that can arise. To underline the theme still further, however, each chapter contains a particular case that shows how an accounting issue raised in the chapter can be considered from a particular hotel function's perspective. Each case is headed "Financial Decision Making in Action" or "Financial Control in Action" and has a sub-heading relating to the hotel function and also the aspect of accounting in question.

To provide you with an early sense of the importance of accounting to a range of hospitality decision makers, an overview of these cases is provided in Box 1.3. The particular hospitality functions identified are based on Burgess' (2001) listing of the typical membership of an executive committee in a large leisure hotel.

Box 1.3

Perspectives of hospitality decision makers on aspects of accounting

Hotel Function	Accounting aspect or tool	Significance of the accounting aspect or tool
General Manager	A general manager needs to understand the nature and workings of the main financial statements. Many managers incorrectly believe that asset values recorded in the balance sheet represent the assets' worth (see Chapter 2).	Senior managers are increasingly benchmarking the performance of hotels within chains. Real estate inflation rates need to be considered if conducting an analysis using asset values of hotels bought in different time periods. This is because balance sheets report historical cost and not current value of assets.
	Senior managers with no accounting training also sometimes incorrectly believe that the retained earnings account in the balance sheet represents cash that can be accessed (Chapter 3).	Retained earnings is frequently a large account appearing in a balance sheet. It represents the accumulation of all profits reinvested in the hotel since its inception. Poor cash planning will occur if senior management believe it represents cash.

Hotel Function	Accounting aspect or tool	Significance of the accounting aspect or tool
Rooms Division Manager	The Rooms Division Manager can use cost-volume-profit analysis to determine occupancy levels necessary to achieve breakeven (Chapter 8).	Appreciating the dynamics of breakeven will help a Rooms Division Manager take steps to ensure that sales do not fall below the breakeven level.
	Variance analysis is a tool that can help a range of managers, including the Rooms Division Manager, when investigating differences between budget and actual performance (Chapter 10).	Appraising the efficiency of activities such as room cleaning represents an important and on-going aspect of management. Variance analysis is a technique that helps a manager determine the factors causing room cleaning costs to be above or below budget.
F&B Manager	What type of inventory recording system should be used? (Chapter 4).	If stock loss represents a problem in F&B, a perpetual rather than a periodic system may be warranted.
	Appropriately using cost information to support decision making such as whether to outsource (Chapter 7).	Hotels are increasingly outsourcing, and managers need to know how to correctly draw on cost data when making such decisions.
Small hotel owner	Periodic preparation of bank reconciliation statements (Chapter 6).	An important step in seeking internal control over cash involves reconciling the difference between a bank account balance per a bank statement and the balance per a business's records.
Human Resource Manager	Determining staffing needs from budgeted sales levels (Chapter 9).	In light of the hospitality sector's volatility, matching labour supply with hotel activity is an important aspect of human resource management.
Financial Controller	Analysing return on investment (ROI) to identify poor performing areas of a hotel (Chapter 5).	As ROI is a comprehensive indicator of performance, it is key that managers understand what factors drive ROI.

	Applying an appropriate financial analysis when deciding whether to take a supplier's offer of a discount for early payment (Chapter 13).	Many suppliers offer a discount for early settlement of an account. In light of this, it is important that the accounts payable department is appropriately informed on when to make an early payment.
	Use of debt financing to lever up returns to shareholders (Chapter 15).	Appropriate use of debt finance can have a significant impact on returns earned by shareholders.
Senior Management	Performance measurement system design (Chapter 11).	It is often said that what gets measured is what gets managed. This highlights the importance of carefully determining what should be measured in a hotel's performance measurement system.
Sales & Marketing Manager	The use of revenue management in pricing (Chapters 12 and 16).	Demand volatility highlights the importance of sales staff varying room rates charged through the year as part of a strategy to maximise profit.
Chief Engineer	Financial analysis of investment proposals (Chapter 14).	Chief Engineers are key players in building equipment investment decisions. Appropriate investment analysis is vital, as these decisions often involve large amounts of money.

5) Uniform system of accounts

There is a uniform accounting system for the hotel industry that has been developed in the US. It was initiated in 1925 by the Hotel Association of New York City. Application of this uniform system has grown in the US and it is now increasingly used across the world. The current version of the uniform system, entitled the "*Uniform System of Accounts for the Lodging Industry*" (*USALI*), was produced in 2006 by the American Hotel & Lodging Educational Institute. The following significant benefits derive from this uniform system:

● it represents an "off the shelf" accounting system that can be adopted by any business in the hotel industry,

● the system can be viewed as "state of the art" as it benefits from the accumulated experience of the parties that have contributed to the system's development over many years,

- by promoting consistent account classification schemes as well as consistent presentation of performance reports, it facilitates comparison across hotels,
- it represents a common point of reference for hotels within the same hotel group.

A profit report for Canberra's KangarooLodge Hotel is presented in Exhibit 1.1. This statement is presented in a format consistent with *USALI*. While increased accounting international standardization has resulted in this statement being officially titled an "income statement", in much of the English-speaking world, many managers continue to refer to the statement as a "profit and loss (P&L) statement".

Exhibit 1.1

Summary Income Statement prepared in *USALI* format

KangarooLodge Hotel
Summary Income Statement
For the year ended 30 June 20X1

	Net Revenue	Cost of Sales	Payroll and Related Expenses	Other Expenses	Income (loss)
Operated Departments					
Rooms	$ 1,232,000	$ 0	$ 193,000	$ 101,000	$ 938,000
Food	404,000	171,000	159,000	48,000	26,000
Beverage	221,000	54,000	58,000	27,000	82,000
Telecommunications	64,000	59,000	4,000	2,000	(1,000)
Total Operated Departments	1,921,000	284,000	414,000	178,000	1,045,000
Undistributed Operating Expenses					
Administrative and General			51,000	28,000	79,000
Sales and Marketing			25,000	36,000	61,000
Property Operation and Maintenance			29,000	6,000	35,000
Utilities (energy, water, etc)			0	79,000	79,000
Total Undistributed Operating Expenses			105,000	149,000	254,000
Gross Operating Profit					791,000
Rent, Rates and Insurance					182,000
Depreciation					123,000
Net Operating Income					486,000
Interest Expense					102,000
Income Before Tax					384,000
Tax					110,000
Net Income					$ 274,000

The income statement provided in Exhibit 1.1 shows the sources of a hotel's revenue and also the nature of its expenses. By deducting expenses from revenue, we find a hotel's profit, which is referred to as "income" in the statement (see the statement's last line). To be consistent with international accounting standards, in income statements presented in this book, the term "income" will be used when referring to profit. However, to reflect the reality of language used by many managers in everyday business settings, the word "profit" will also be used extensively in the text.

The *USALI* income statement comprises three sections. In the top section, net revenue (i.e., net sales) for each functional area is identified in the first data column. This is followed by three columns that identify expenses that can be directly related to the departmental areas listed, i.e., cost of sales, payroll and related expenses, and other expenses. Cost of sales refers to the cost of items that are sold, e.g., the cost of wine sold through a restaurant. Each department's income (profit) is determined by deducting the sum of the three expense items from net revenue. The statement's middle section is headed "undistributed operating expenses". In this section the expenses relating to a hotel's service departments (e.g., administrative and general, sales and marketing, etc.) are identified. The distinction between a hotel's service departments and the departments listed in the top section of the statement is that no revenue can be traced directly to the service departments. The statement's lower section includes expenses that are generally not traceable to a hotel's operating management. Expenses such as rent, insurance and interest on debt are generally traceable to a tier of management that lies above a hotel's operational staff. The last line of the statement presents the net income (profit), i.e., all hotel revenue minus all hotel expenses.

It is apparent from Exhibit 1.1 that an income statement presented in accordance with the *USALI* provides much profitability information at the hotel department level (e.g., rooms, food, beverage department, etc.). This format supports financial management, as it allows a hotel's managers to consider the relative profitability levels of its different functional areas, e.g., from Exhibit 1.1, it can be determined that following the deduction of expenses directly related to rooms, 76.14 per cent of room revenue remains as a contribution to covering general hotel expenses and then providing a profit ($938,000 ÷ $1,232,000 × 100).

The *USALI* has been introduced in this first chapter in order to give you an early appreciation of a typical hotel's income statement. Your understanding of the nature of the income statement will be reinforced in the next chapter which, amongst other things, focuses on the relationship between the income statement and the balance sheet.

6) Organisational forms

There is some variation in accounting terminology used across different forms of commercial organisation. As shown in Exhibit 1.2, there are three main types of commercial organisation: (1) sole proprietorship, (2) partnership, and (3) company. An appreciation of each type of organisation will help you develop your understanding of how accounting terms are used in different business forms.

> ### Exhibit 1.2
>
> ## Key differences across organisational forms
>
> | Characteristics | Sole proprietorship | Partnership | Company |
> | --- | --- | --- | --- |
> | Number of owners | One | Two or more | Generally many |
> | Business size | Small | Generally small | Larger and can be very large |
> | Key decision makers | Owner | Partners | Board of directors |
> | Owner liability | Unlimited | Unlimited | Limited |
> | Organisation life | Limited | Limited | On-going |

Sole proprietorships

A sole proprietorship (sometimes called a "sole trader"), is owned by one person. In most cases, the owner also manages the business. Sole proprietorships are the most common type of business, especially in those areas of the economy where we see many small businesses, such as in the restaurant sector.

In legal terms, a sole proprietorship is not really distinct from its owner. This signifies that the owner of a sole proprietorship will report the profit of his or her business as part of their taxable income. It also signifies that a sole proprietorship's owner has to take personal responsibility for all debts of his or her business. This responsibility is generally referred to as "unlimited liability", as if a sole proprietorship has large debts outstanding, the owner must draw on their personal assets to pay off their business debts. This means that if a sole proprietorship becomes insolvent (has more debts than assets), the owner may lose more than the amount that they originally invested in the business.

Exhibit 1.2 indicates that the life of a sole proprietorship is limited. This is because the sole proprietorship's existence ends at the time that the owner decides to stop operating the business. If the sole proprietorship owner is able to sell their business, the sole proprietorship's life comes to an end, and it will be up to the new owner to decide under what organisational form they will operate their newly acquired business.

Partnerships

A partnership arises when two or more people decide to run a business together. Although partnerships tend to be larger than sole proprietorships, it is not the case that all partnerships are bigger than sole proprietorships. The size of partnerships varies greatly, from a small coffee shop owned by a husband and wife team, right through to large multinational accounting partnerships, such as KPMG or PricewaterhouseCoopers.

Exhibit 1.2 shows that business partnerships have many characteristics similar to sole proprietorships. Like a sole proprietorship, it is the owners (the partners) of a partnership that tend to be the business's decision makers. Like a sole proprietorship, the life of a partnership is limited, as in most situations, a new partnership is formed every time a new partner is created, or whenever a partner retires from the organisation. Also like sole proprietorships, the owners of a partnership have unlimited liability with respect to the debts of their business. If your partnership is sinking under a weight of debt, you, as a partner, are liable for all of the debts of the business, regardless of what proportion of the business you own. If your partner, who originally invested 75 per cent of the start up funds (widely referred to as "capital") for your partnership, has become personally bankrupt, you will need to pay off all debts of the partnership, even though you only invested 25 per cent of the partnership's initial capital.

A decision to enter a business partnership can be likened to the decision to get married. Just as in a marriage, business partners have to interact extensively with one another. Most successful partnerships are built on the bedrock of a solid and trusting relationship. It can make a lot of sense to team up with a business partner who has a set of complimentary skills. For instance, you may be a great chef with poor business skills and your partner may have great marketing and organisational skills appropriate for running a restaurant. However, just as many marriages that were initially blessed with a happy honeymoon period finish up in a divorce court, experience indicates that business partnerships can quickly turn pear shaped and acrimonious. Be very careful if going into a business, as business partnerships can be like marriage partnerships; they often break down.

Companies

A company is often referred to as a "corporation" in the USA. A company is an artificial entity that is created by law. Unlike sole proprietorships and partnerships, a company is legally distinct from its owners. Companies are run by boards of directors and their existence continues independently of changes in their ownership.

Company ownership works in the following way. The capital raised by a company from its owners is broken into units that we call shares (the word "share" signifies a share in the ownership of a company). It could be that a company originally raised $1,000,000 of capital from its original owners through the issuance and sale of 500,000 shares that were each initially priced at $2 each. If you bought 5,000 of these shares for $10,000, you would in effect own 1 per cent of the company as you would be the owner of 1 per cent of its 500,000 shares. Two years following your purchase of 1 per cent of the initial share offering, you might sell your 5,000 shares on the stock market for $3 each. You would receive $15,000 for the sale of your shares and will have made a 50 per cent profit on your original $10,000 investment. Note, however, that the company will be unaffected by your share sale, as it is really not involved in your second-hand market (that's what a stock market is) sale of your 1 per cent stake in the company.

This description of the sale of a company's shares highlights one of the principle advantages of a company. Owners of a company can relatively easily liquidate their company ownership investment by selling their shares on the stock market. It is much harder to liquidate your business ownership if the business in question is a sole proprietorship or a partnership.

A further distinguishing feature of companies concerns the fact that the liability of owners is limited. Following your purchase of 5,000 shares for $10,000 that was just referred to, if the company you have invested in were to go bankrupt, the shares that you own might well become worth nothing. So you would lose your $10,000 invested, but, unlike an owner of a sole proprietorship or a partnership, you would not be required to pay any more money to satisfy any outstanding debts of the business. This signifies that your liability is limited to losing no more than your original investment. For this reason, for those companies where this limited liability feature applies, in many countries the company name must conclude with the word "Limited" (widely abbreviated to "Ltd.").

7) Summary

This chapter has set the scene for the remainder of the book. We have reviewed the particular characteristics of the hospitality industry and considered their implications for accounting. We have also considered the nature of accounting in general and also its relevance to a range of hospitality decision makers. The chapter provided a short introduction to financial accounting by outlining the nature of an income statement presented according to the standard that is generally referred to as the "*Uniform System of Accounts for the Lodging Industry*". Finally distinctions between the three basic organisational forms were described. The three organisational forms are sole proprietorships, partnerships and companies. All three types of business are well represented in the hotel industry. The small English hotel depicted in the BBC TV comedy series *Fawlty Towers* that is run (perhaps "run" is the wrong word to use given Basil Fawlty's manic behaviour) by a husband and wife team would likely be a sole proprietorship or a partnership. Large hotel companies such as Hilton Worldwide and the Hyatt Hotels Corporation represent classic examples of American-based international hotel companies. Accor is a company based in France that owns well-known hotel brands such as Novotel and the Mercure.

Having read this chapter you should now know:

- some of the hospitality industry's particular characteristics and their accounting implications,
- what is meant by accounting and how it relates to financial management,
- some of the ways that different hotel functional areas draw on accounting information and analyses in decision making and control,
- the nature of information provided in an income statement,
- the basic differences between sole proprietorships, partnerships and companies.

References

Burgess, C. (2001) *Guide to Money Matters for Hospitality Managers*, Oxford: Butterworth Heinemann: Chapter 1.

Harris, P. (1999) *Profit Planning*, 2nd edition, Oxford: Butterworth Heinemann: Chapters 1 & 2.

Jackling, B., Raar, J., Wines, G. and McDowall, T. (2010) *Accounting: A Framework for Decision Making*, McGraw-Hill: Chapter 1.

Kaplan, R.S. and Norton, D.P. (1996) *The Balanced Scorecard – Translating Strategy into Action*, Boston, MA: Harvard Business School Press.

Schmidgall, R.F. (2011) *Hospitality Industry Managerial Accounting*, 7th edition, East Lansing, MI: American Hotel & Lodging Educational Institute: Chapter 3.

Weygandt, J., Kieso, D., Kimmel, P. and DeFranco, A. (2009) *Hospitality Financial Accounting*, Hoboken, NJ: John Wiley & Sons: Chapter 1.

Problems

Problem 1.1

a) Describe what is meant by functional interdependency.
b) Describe why functional interdependency is an issue that needs to be considered when designing a hotel's system of accountability.

Problem 1.2

a) What are the four main dimensions of sales volatility in the hotel industry?
b) What are the accounting implications arising from these four dimensions of sales volatility?

Problem 1.3

Identify six examples of business decisions requiring the use of accounting information.

Problem 1.4

a) Describe what is meant by high perishability of the hotel product.
b) Describe the accounting implications arising from high product perishability.

Problem 1.5

Describe the factors causing hotels to have a high proportion of fixed costs.

Problem 1.6

a) Describe the manner in which hotel activities tend to be labour intensive.
b) Describe the accounting implications arising from the high labour intensity of hotel activities.

Problem 1.7

What is the difference between financial accounting and management accounting?

Problem 1.8

Who are the main users of accounting information?

Problem 1.9

Why is it important that financial accounting systems are seen to be reliable?

Problem 1.10

Give one example of how a particular accounting tool or technique might be drawn upon in the context of a particular hospitality management function.

Problem 1.11

Identify three advantages that derive from using the "*Uniform System of Accounts for the Lodging Industry*" (*USALI*).

Problem 1.12

List the three main forms of commercial organisation and identify the main differences between the forms.

Problem 1.13

In the context of a new business starting up, what is meant by the term "capital raised".

Chapter 2

Analysing transactions and preparing year-end financial statements

Learning objectives

After studying this chapter, you should have developed an appreciation of:

1. how there is a double financial implication arising from every financial transaction undertaken by an organisation,
2. the nature and format of the balance sheet,
3. the nature and format of the income statement,
4. how profit computed in the income statement flows into the owners' equity section of the balance sheet via the statement of owners' equity.

1) Introduction

This is the first of the three chapters concerned with **financial accounting**. Financial accounting concerns the preparation of **financial reports** that are made available to external users such as shareholders. This chapter provides an overview of the main financial accounting statements that appear in annual reports prepared by publicly listed companies (i.e., companies with shares listed on a stock exchange). Although this is not a long chapter, the material presented is fairly concentrated. A considered review of this material will provide you with a good basic appreciation of the nature of the year-end financial statements. To achieve this appreciation you will need to carefully follow through the chapter's worked example that illustrates how a set of financial transactions impact on the year-end accounts. Once you have gained an appreciation of the nature of the year-end financial statements, the next chapter will introduce the "debit/credit" double entry record keeping process that underlies the financial accounting system. Finally, Chapter 4 introduces some more advanced aspects of double entry record keeping by reviewing year-end adjustments that need to be made to the financial records in order to recognise time-related issues such as asset depreciation.

It may appear a little strange that a book concerned with hospitality decision making has devoted three chapters to financial accounting. There are, however, several reasons why a hotel manager should have a basic familiarity with financial accounting. Of particular significance is the fact that most professional accounting courses of study have a bias towards financial accounting, rather than management accounting, which is the branch of accounting concerned with the provision of accounting information for management decision making and control. Once qualified, many accountants secure jobs working in industries such as the hospitality sector, with the result that a financial accounting mentality frequently prevails in organisations' internal accounting departments. It is important that all managers appreciate the potential for this tendency and have an ability and willingness to "think outside the square" by asking for accounting information and analyses to be presented in a way that **supports management decision making rather than the needs of external reporting.**

An example of "thinking outside the square" might be a marketing manager who feels that a customer profitability analysis would help management deliberations concerned with allocating a promotion budget. The manager might feel reluctant to ask for such information, however, as the accounting system has never provided it in the past. If you review the material presented in Chapter 4, it will become apparent that a key concern of financial accountants is the accurate allocation of profit earned to particular periods of time. The financial accounting system does not require, however, that profit be allocated across customer segments. As the impetus for allocating profit across customer segments is unlikely to come from an accounting department, it will have to be initiated by the manager needing the information. A second reason why a hotel manager should understand the basics of financial accounting is that two outputs of the financial accounting system, the **balance sheet** and the **income statement**, represent important sources of information that can further management control of the company. The manner in which these statements can be used to facilitate management control will be extensively explored in Chapter 5.

2) The balance sheet and income statement

In most Western countries, four financial statements are presented in the published annual reports of publicly listed companies. These reports are the balance sheet, the income statement, the statement of owners' equity and the statement of cash flows.

The elements comprising the balance sheet, income statement and statement of owners' equity are described in this section. Following this, the worked example in the next section will show the extent to which these statements can be seen as direct outputs of the financial accounting record keeping process. No detailed review will be undertaken of the statement of cash flows which classifies cash inflows and outflows and identifies the net change in cash held by the firm over the reporting period. Relative to the balance sheet and income statement, this statement is not used as much for decision making and control purposes. Although it will not be considered further in this book, if you see a cash flow statement you will have an immediate rudimentary understanding of it, due to its resemblance to an aggregated version of your monthly bank statement.

The balance sheet is a schedule summarising what is owned and what is owed by a company at a particular point in time. Its three main sections which comprise assets, liabilities and owners' equity, are described in Box 2.1.

Box 2.1

The main sections of a balance sheet

- **Assets** are "things" that are owned (most usually purchased) by the organisation. They are assets if the organisation can derive some future value from ownership. Typical hotel assets include: cash, accounts receivable, prepayments, inventory (sometimes referred to as "stock"), cars, china, silver, glass, linen, uniforms, equipment, land and buildings. Assets are generally recorded in the accounting system at their cost, although in some countries such as Australia, New Zealand and the UK, asset revaluations can be made (asset revaluation is not permitted under the generally accepted accounting principles of Canada and the US).
- **Liabilities** may be seen as the opposite of assets. They reflect financial obligations of the organisation. Typical liabilities include: wages and salaries payable, accounts payable and bank loans.
- **Owners' equity** reflects the financial investment of the owners in the organisation. It includes the owners' original investment plus all profits not paid out to the owners (i.e., profits retained in the business). For financial accounting purposes, profit is typically determined on an annual basis. This computation is achieved through the **income statement**. In the income statement, **expenses** for the year (which represent resources consumed such as housekeeping wages and cost of beer sold through a bar) are deducted from **revenue** earned during the year to give profit for the year. Money earned from selling room nights and also sales made in a restaurant and bar represent some of the main examples of revenue in a hotel. If expenses are greater than revenue, a loss results. Some profit may be withdrawn from the business by the owners. That portion of profit that the owners choose not to withdraw is effectively a further contribution to the business by the owners. It is therefore treated as an addition to owners' equity (at the end of the accounting year), and is generally termed "retained earnings" or "retained profit". Computation of the year-end owners' equity balance is achieved through the **statement of owners' equity**. The first line of this statement identifies the owners' equity balance at the beginning of the accounting year. To this we add net profit for the year as well as any new equity capital raised. Finally, any profits distributed to the owners during the year (termed "drawings" or "dividends") are deducted to give the closing owners' equity balance.

From Box 2.1 it is apparent that profit earned increases owners' equity. It is also evident that the profit computed through the income statement can be seen to feed into the owners' equity section of the balance sheet via the statement of owners' equity. For this reason, at the year-end we need to prepare the income statement and statement of owners' equity in advance of preparing the balance sheet.

One key difference between the income statement and the balance sheet pertains to time. The income statement (like the statement of owners' equity) always relates to a period of time, i.e., the time taken to make the profit reported in the income statement. The balance sheet, however, relates to a particular moment in time.

Let's draw on the analogy of your own financial situation to highlight this important time distinction. If you were asked "How much do you earn?" you can only respond in the context of a time period, i.e., you could talk of your earnings last month or your earnings last year. Your earnings are analogous to the profit of a firm, in fact, a firm's profit represents what the business has earned for the owners of the firm (note how a time period is referred to in the heading of the income statement presented in Exhibit 2.2 below). If you were asked "what is your wealth", however, your answer would have to be in the context of a particular moment in time, as the value of your assets are constantly changing, i.e., you might receive weekly payments for work rendered, you buy and consume things such as food on a daily basis, etc. To determine your wealth you would have to identify everything you own (your assets) and deduct everything that you owe (your liabilities) at a particular point in time. The issue of determining personal wealth is analogous to the preparation of a company's balance sheet which can be seen as a representation of the wealth of the firm, i.e., it summarises assets and liabilities. Like the wealth of an individual, the wealth of a firm can only be conceived in the context of a particular moment in time (note how a point in time is referred to in the wording of the balance sheet heading presented in Exhibit 2.2 below).

A balance sheet can be presented in one of the following two basic formats:

Assets – Liabilities = Owners' Equity

or

Assets = Liabilities + Owners' Equity

As both formats represent an equation, some people talk of "the balance sheet equation". Underlying the first equation is the notion that the value of the owners' equity (the owners' stake) in the company equals the surplus assets that would remain after the acquittal of all liabilities. Underlying the second equation is the notion that money raised by a business is invested in various assets. The "money raised" notion is on the right-hand side of the equation as liabilities include sources of finance such as bank loans, while owners' equity refers to money invested in the business by the owners. With respect to the left-hand side of the second equation, the money raised finances the purchase of assets and any money raised but not used to purchase assets must be held as cash, which is itself an asset.

3) Classifying transactions according to assets, liabilities and owners' equity

Like a coin, a financial transaction has two sides. These two sides signify that all financial transactions have a double impact on a business. We will now consider a set of transactions and see how, as a result of their double impact, the balance sheet equation is always left intact. In this worked example the balance sheet equation is stated as "assets = liabilities + owners' equity". The same exercise could be performed using a format based on the alternative balance sheet equation, however.

Exhibit 2.1

Illustration of how transactions affect the balance sheet equation

May

1. Owner contributes $30,000 cash to commence business.
2. Purchased a van for $12,000, paying $3,000 in cash and obtaining a loan for the balance.
3. Purchased non-perishable food stock including a large maple syrup shipment on credit for $800.
4. Billed clients $19,000 for use of conference facilities.
5. Received $6,000 from customers billed in (4) above.
6. Paid $500 to trade creditors to reduce amount owing for inventory stock purchased.
7. Owners withdrew $1,500 from the business.
8. The accountant has determined that $600 of inventory stock has been used.
9. Paid $250 for miscellaneous expenses (telephone, electricity, etc.).
10. Repaid $5,000 of the loan taken out for the van.

Balance Sheet Equation

	Assets				=	Liabilities		+	Owners' Equity	
May	**Cash at Bank**	**Accounts Receivable**	**Inventory**	**Vehicles**		**Accounts Payable**	**Loan Payable**		**Capital**	**Profit or Loss**
1	+30,000								+30,000	
2	−3,000			+12,000			+9,000			
3			+800			+800				
4		+19,000								+19,000
5	+6,000	−6,000								
6	−500					−500				
7	−1,500								−1,500	
8			−600							−600
9	−250									−250
10	−5,000						−5,000			
Total	$25,750	$13,000	$200	$12,000		$300	$4,000		$28,500	$18,150
	$50,950				=	**$4,300**		+	**$46,650**	

In Exhibit 2.1, transactions undertaken in the first ten days of trading for Joe Blow, a small sole proprietorship hotel offering seminar facilities close to Montreal's Ile Notre-Dame Formula One Grand Prix circuit, are summarised. Following this, the way in which each of the transactions affect the balance sheet are noted in the "account" columns appearing under the main balance sheet headings: assets, liabilities and owners' equity. In the interests of capturing all of the transactions in one matrix, transactions that affect profit (i.e., a sale or the incurrence of an expense) appear in the final column headed "profit or loss". As profit affects owners' equity, this column appears under the owners' equity heading. Investments in the business by the owners are recorded in the "capital" column which also appears under the owners' equity heading.

Following the steps undertaken in Exhibit 2.1 represents a learning activity designed to develop your appreciation of the fact that every transaction has a double impact on the balance sheet equation. As will be seen later in Exhibit 2.2, in reality transactions affecting profit flow first into the income statement and then flow into the balance sheet via the statement of owners' equity.

Following through the steps involved in Exhibit 2.1 is an important exercise. Not only do they clearly demonstrate how every transaction has a double impact on the balance sheet, the exercise also lays the basis for your appreciation of the workings of the balance sheet. You should approach Exhibit 2.1 by considering each transaction in turn and noting its double impact on the balance sheet in a manner that leaves assets equal to the sum of liabilities and owners' equity. A description of how each transaction results in a double impact is provided in Schedule 2.1.

Schedule 2.1

The impact of Exhibit 2.1's ten transactions on the balance sheet

Transaction date	Description of balance sheet impact
1 May	The business now has $30,000 in cash (increase cash account). The capital account records all financial investments in the business made by the owners (increase capital account).
2 May	This transaction is slightly awkward as it affects three accounts. The business now has a motor vehicle which is an asset that cost $12,000 (increase vehicles account). It paid for the van by using $3,000 cash (reduce the cash account) and by borrowing $9,000 (increase loan payable account).

3 May	The business now has $800 in inventory (increase inventory account). It owes money for this purchase (increase accounts payable account).
4 May	The business is now owed $19,000 for services rendered (increase accounts receivable account). The business has now made a sale (increase the revenue account – treated in this exercise as positively affecting owners' equity by increasing profit).
5 May	The business now has a further $6,000 in cash (increase cash account). The money it was owed with respect to the sale made on 4th May is now $6,000 less (reduce accounts receivable account).
6 May	Cash has now declined by $500 (reduce cash account). The amount owing with respect to the purchase made on 3rd May is now $500 less (reduce accounts payable account).
7 May	The business cash balance has now declined by a further $1,500 (reduce cash account). The net investment in the business made by the owners has declined by $1,500 (reduce capital account).
8 May	The cost of stock held in the business has declined by $600 (reduce inventory account). This decline in stock signifies that resources have been consumed (increase cost of sales account – treated in this exercise as negatively affecting owners' equity by reducing profit).
9 May	Cash has declined by $250 (reduce cash account). The use of telephone and electricity signifies resources have been consumed (increase miscellaneous expense account – treated in this exercise as negatively affecting owners' equity by reducing profit).
10 May	Cash has declined by $5,000 (reduce cash account). The amount owing on the loan taken out for the van is now $5,000 less (reduce loan payable account).

We can present the results of the ten transactions described in Exhibit 2.1 in a more conventional accounting format by compiling Joe Blow's income statement and statement of owners' equity for the first ten days of May and also Joe Blow's balance sheet as at 10th May. These statements are presented as Exhibit 2.2. Note how the column totals in the balance sheet equation matrix appearing at the bottom of Exhibit 2.1 feed into the statements compiled in Exhibit 2.2. Also note how the profit determined in the income statement feeds into the balance sheet via the statement of owners' equity.

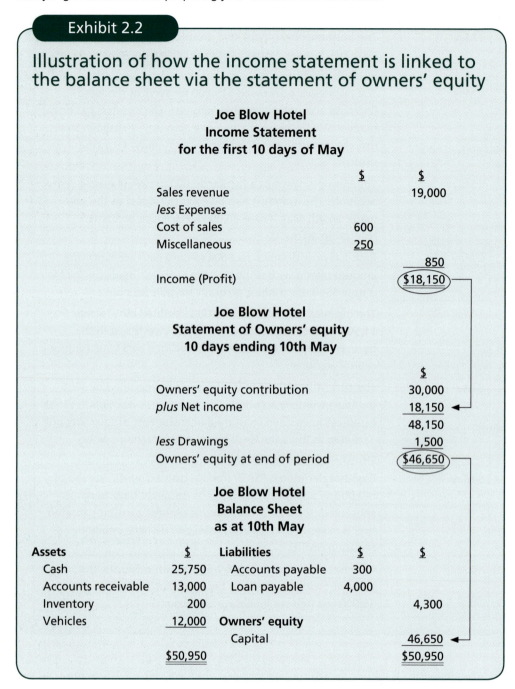

Exhibit 2.2

Illustration of how the income statement is linked to the balance sheet via the statement of owners' equity

Joe Blow Hotel
Income Statement
for the first 10 days of May

	$	$
Sales revenue		19,000
less Expenses		
Cost of sales	600	
Miscellaneous	250	
		850
Income (Profit)		$18,150

Joe Blow Hotel
Statement of Owners' equity
10 days ending 10th May

	$
Owners' equity contribution	30,000
plus Net income	18,150
	48,150
less Drawings	1,500
Owners' equity at end of period	$46,650

Joe Blow Hotel
Balance Sheet
as at 10th May

Assets	$	Liabilities	$	$
Cash	25,750	Accounts payable	300	
Accounts receivable	13,000	Loan payable	4,000	
Inventory	200			4,300
Vehicles	12,000	**Owners' equity**		
		Capital		46,650
	$50,950			$50,950

The balance sheet presented in Exhibit 2.2 has been compiled according to a horizontal format whereby assets appear on one side and liabilities and owners' equity appear on the other. You may also encounter balance sheets presented using a vertical format in which the totals of assets, liabilities and owners' equity appear one above another (see, for example, the balance sheet presented later in the book as Exhibit 5.2).

While both the horizontal and vertical balance sheet formats are widely used within the same countries, some different balance sheet formatting conventions do exist internationally. Relative to other English-speaking countries, some distinct conventions are evident in the United Kingdom. In Australia, Canada, New Zealand and the US, the convention is to present assets in order of liquidity, i.e., the assets that are closest to cash are presented first. If a business has cash, marketable securities, accounts receivable and inventory, then cash is presented first, marketable securities are second (marketable securities are readily convertible into cash), accounts receivable are third (accounts receivable are converted into cash in the short-term in the normal course of business), and inventory appears fourth (with the exception of cash sales, a sale from inventory will become an account receivable prior to translation to cash). In these countries, a similar rationale is applied to the sequencing of liabilities, i.e., those liabilities with the shortest term to payment appear first.

In the UK, however, there has been a convention to reverse this sequencing. This signifies that the first assets presented are long-held assets such as land and buildings (least liquid) and the asset presented last is cash (most liquid). Similarly, in the UK, the first liabilities presented are long-term liabilities such as loans payable, and liabilities that will be paid in the short-term, e.g., amounts owing to suppliers, are listed last.

4) The importance of understanding financial accounting basics

In your working life you are highly likely to meet senior managers who have a poor understanding of the mechanics of financial accounting. In the financial decision making case presented below, we see how an unfamiliarity with the basics of financial accounting can be a recipe for poor decision making.

FINANCIAL DECISION MAKING IN ACTION CASE 2.1

The General Manager's use of balance sheet information

Senior managers are increasingly using the performance of other hotels as a benchmark for appraising their own performance. A widely quoted performance indicator is return on investment (ROI) which is computed by stating a hotel's annual profit as a percentage of the investment in its assets (ROI will be more extensively discussed in Chapter 5). Considerable care needs to be exercised in this type of analysis, however, as balance sheets record assets (i.e., investment) at their historical cost and not their current value.

Imagine hotels A and B are in the same hotel chain and are highly comparable in terms of markets served, size, quality and profits generated. Hotel A was purchased seven years ago at a price that was 30 per cent less than the price paid for Hotel B five years ago. The difference in the amount invested resulted from

---

rapid inflation around the time the two hotels were acquired. If ROI is calculated based on conventional accounting records, it will appear that Hotel A is the better performer. This will be attributable more to the time when it was purchased than good management by the general manager, however. To provide a better basis for benchmarking the relative management performance in the two hotels, current market value rather than historical cost could be used as the basis for valuing the investment in each hotel.

This issue of assets being recorded at their historical cost is also pertinent to insurance decisions taken. Senior managers should ensure that all assets are insured for what it would cost to replace them. Replacement cost can be significantly different from the historical cost recorded in a balance sheet.

5) Summary

In this chapter we have seen how two financial implications arise from every financial transaction undertaken by a business. We have also reviewed the nature and content of the main financial reports: the balance sheet and the income statement. We have seen that the balance sheet comprises assets, liabilities and owners' equity accounts. The income statement comprises revenue and expense accounts.

Having read the chapter you should now know:

- the main account headings in a balance sheet and income statement,
- the layout of a balance sheet and income statement,
- how to classify transactions according to their impact on assets, liabilities and owners' equity accounts,
- how profit is determined in the income statement and flows into the balance sheet via the statement of owners' equity,
- the importance of senior managers having a basic understanding of the balance sheet.

References

Harris, P. (1999) *Profit Planning*, 2nd edition, Oxford: Butterworth Heinemann: Chapter 2.

Jackling, B., Raar, J., Wines, G. and McDowall, T. (2010) *Accounting: A Framework for Decision Making*, 3rd edition, Macquarie Park, NSW, Australia: McGraw-Hill: Chapter 3.

Jagels, M.G. (2007) *Hospitality Management Accounting*, 9th edition, Hoboken, NJ: John Wiley & Sons: Chapter 1.

Schmidgall, R.F. (2011) *Hospitality Industry Managerial Accounting*, 7th edition, East Lansing, MI: American Hotel & Lodging Educational Institute: Chapters 2 and 3.

Weygandt, J., Kieso, D., Kimmel, P. and DeFranco, A. (2009) *Hospitality Financial Accounting*, Hoboken, NJ: John Wiley & Sons: Chapter 2.

Problems

Problem 2.1

Describe what is meant by:
a) an asset
b) a liability
c) owners' equity.

Problem 2.2

Describe what is meant by the term "balance sheet equation".

Problem 2.3

Identified below are a set of transactions for the SerenitySleep Hotel which commenced business in Wellington, New Zealand on 1st June.

June
1 Owner commenced business by depositing $20,000 in a new business bank account.
2 Purchased some basic office furniture for $3,000 cash.
3 Purchased inventory stock for $900 cash.
4 Purchased more inventory stock on credit for $1,400.
5 Purchased an office computer for $6,000, paying $1,500 in cash and obtaining a loan for the balance.
6 Billed clients $1,000 for use of conference facilities.
7 The owner withdrew $800 from the business.
8 Banked the first week's cash revenue $1,300.
9 It was determined that $400 of inventory has been used since the commencement of business.
10 Paid $240 for miscellaneous expenses (telephone, electricity, etc.).

Required:
Using a format similar to that appearing in Exhibit 2.1, demonstrate the impact each transaction will have on the balance sheet equation.

Problem 2.4

Describe the difference between an income statement and a balance sheet.

Problem 2.5

"Both owners' drawings and expenses reduce equity. So owners' drawings are really the same as expenses". Explain whether you agree with this statement.

Problem 2.6

The heading of a balance sheet and the heading of an income statement usually provide a reference to a date. Describe how the balance sheet differs to the income statement with respect to the time that it relates to.

Problem 2.7

Classify each of the following accounts as either an asset, liability, revenue, expense or owners' equity item:

Buildings
Wages
Drawings
Sales
Loan owed
Cash
Accounts payable
Loan interest paid
Inventory used
Inventory on hand
Bank account interest earned.

Problem 2.8

Using a schedule similar to that appearing in Exhibit 2.1, record the following ten transactions that occurred for Jane Long's LusciouslyLong restaurant in the first ten days of May.

May
 1 Purchased inventory stock for $350 on credit.
 2 Restaurant makes sales of $2,000, $1,200 for cash and $800 on account.
 3 Paid staff wages $750.
 4 Received $660 in connection with customers billed in (2) above.
 5 Jane Long withdrew $2,400 from the business.
 6 Paid $330 for miscellaneous expenses (telephone, electricity, etc.).
 7 Paid $350 to trade creditors.
 8 Took up a loan of $4,200 from the bank.
 9 Restaurant makes sales of $2,800, $1,500 for cash and $1,300 on account.
10 Purchased furniture costing $3,160 on credit.

Problem 2.9

The Johnson Hotel is located in Perth, Western Australia. Identified below are the account balances for the Johnson Hotel following its commercial activities through the month of December 20X1.

Accounts payable	$ 10,000
Accounts receivable	12,000
Cash	5,000
Linen	8,000
Uniforms	7,500
Buildings	250,000
Loan payable	100,000
Owners' equity	148,000
Sales revenue	38,000

Inventory stock used	6,500
Miscellaneous expenses	3,000
Owner's drawings	4,000

Required:

a) Prepare the Johnson Hotel's income statement for December 20X1.
b) Prepare Johnson Hotel's statement of owners' equity for December 20X1.
c) Prepare Johnson Hotel's balance sheet as at 31 December 20X1.

Problem 2.10

In April 20X1, Jock MacNoodle opened the MacNoodle Italian Restaurant in Glasgow. Identified below are the restaurant's financial transactions in its first month of business.

Date	Transaction
1 April	Jock MacNoodle deposited £10,000 in a newly opened business bank account.
2 April	Paid £400 cash for non-perishable food items to build up an inventory of food.
4 April	Purchased a photocopier costing £1,000. 10 per cent of the purchase price was paid in cash and a loan was taken to cover the balance.
5 April	Purchased £500 of wine stock on credit.
7 April	Banked the £350 received for cash sales made in first week.
8 April	Paid £450 rent for April.
14 April	Paid a kitchen assistant and waiter wages of £100.
18 April	Paid £300 as part settlement of the wine merchant's account.
27 April	It was noted that half of the stock of wine purchased on 5th April had been sold.
28 April	Banked £460 received from cash sales.
29 April	Paid a kitchen assistant and waiter wages of £280.
30 April	It was noted that £60 of food inventory had been used.
30 April	It was noted that credit sales made in the first month of business were £340.

Required:

Using a format similar to that appearing in Exhibit 2.1, demonstrate the impact each transaction will have on the restaurant's balance sheet equation.

Problem 2.11

In connection with the information provided in the previous problem, prepare the following:

a) The MacNoodle restaurant's income statement for April 20X1.
b) The MacNoodle restaurant's statement of owners' equity for April 20X1.
c) The MacNoodle restaurant's balance sheet as at 30 April 20X1.

Problem 2.12

Paul Eastwell owns a Robina tennis resort complex. The resort has a 30th June financial year-end. The resort's account balances are as follows:

Paul Eastwell tennis resort account balances – 30th June 20X1

Accounts payable	$ 22,000
Wages owing	4,600
Bank overdraft	7,300
Accounts receivable	12,000
Food inventory	3,800
Beverage inventory	2,400
Cleaning supplies	1,100
Tennis equipment	800
Land	230,000
Buildings	125,000
Loan payable	100,000
Furniture	13,000
Tax payable	14,200
Sales revenue	115,000
Food and beverage used	23,000
Wages	41,700
Miscellaneous expenses	4,200
Owner's drawings	6,000
Owners' equity	199,900

Required:

a) Prepare the income statement for Paul Eastwell's tennis resort complex for the year ended 30th June 20X1.
b) Prepare the statement of owners' equity for Paul Eastwell's tennis resort complex for the year ended 30th June 20X1.
c) Prepare the balance sheet for Paul Eastwell's tennis resort complex as at 30th June 20X1.

Chapter 3

Double entry accounting

Learning objectives

After studying this chapter, you should have developed an appreciation of:

1. the mechanics of double entry bookkeeping,
2. how the terms "debit" and "credit" are used in financial accounting,
3. the fact that asset and expense accounts normally have a debit balance,
4. the fact that liability, owners' equity and revenue accounts normally have a credit balance,
5. how to produce a trial balance,
6. the distinction between current assets and fixed assets and also current liabilities and long-term liabilities,
7. how to record transactions in a general journal.

1) Introduction

This chapter focuses on the fundamentals of **double entry accounting** and will reinforce the understanding of the **balance sheet** and **income statement** that you acquired from reading Chapter 2. The chapter introduces the use of "T accounts" to record transactions and also the layout of the general journal.

2) Double entry accounting: some background concepts

In Chapter 2 we saw how a double impact arises from any financial transaction. In light of this, it is not surprising that the financial accounting recording process is based on a system of double entries. In this chapter we will see that the columns in the previous chapter's Exhibit 2.1 represent "accounts" in a real accounting system. In Exhibit 2.1 there were columns pertaining to cash, accounts receivable, inventory, etc. In double entry accounting we have a cash account, an accounts receivable account, an inventory account, etc. Further, we will see that the "+" and "−" symbols that indicated the directional change for each of the accounts in Exhibit 2.1 represent a "debit" or "credit" in double entry accounting. An important word of caution is warranted at this point, however. A "+" does not always represent a debit or credit and a "–" does not always represent a debit or credit. As we will see in Exhibit 3.1 presented below, the relationship between the "+" and "–" used in the last chapter and the debit and credit terms used in double entry accounting depends on the nature of the account in question.

Before exploring the workings of the double entry bookkeeping system, it is helpful to review the nature of the five basic account categories. The five basic account categories in an accounting system comprise: assets, liabilities, owners' equity, revenues and expenses. Asset, liability and the owners' equity accounts relate to a certain point in time (they are sometimes referred to as "snapshot" accounts). Their "snapshot" nature should be apparent from the fact that they all appear in the balance sheet. We noted in Chapter 2 that the balance sheet refers to a particular point in time, and not a period of time. Revenue and expense accounts are "flow" accounts (they only make sense when referring to a period of time). Again, this should be apparent from the fact that expense and revenue accounts appear in the income statement which, unlike the balance sheet, refers to a time period and not a particular point in time. A company's set of accounts is referred to collectively as its "general ledger".

Let us now turn to the fundamentals of double entry accounting. In Box 3.1 there is a summary of key principles that can help when first confronting the debits and credits of double entry accounting.

Box 3.1

Key principles of double entry accounting

- With respect to balance sheet accounts: asset accounts normally have a debit balance, liabilities and owners' equity accounts normally have a credit balance. Although this is a helpful rule, be warned that in some situations it can be broken, e.g., while we normally think of a bank account as an asset (i.e., debit balance), if it becomes overdrawn it will represent a liability (i.e., credit balance).
- With respect to income statement accounts: revenue accounts have a credit balance, expense accounts have a debit balance.
- For every debit entry, there must be an equal credit entry.
- Where there is a cash inflow we debit the cash account. For a cash outflow, we credit the cash account.

The first two principles in Box 3.1 provide a framework that can serve as a highly valuable reference point when learning the double entry accounting process. This framework is also depicted as a matrix in Exhibit 3.1. From this matrix we can see that asset accounts usually have a debit balance (column 1). It follows that a debit entry is made to record an increase in an asset account (column 2), and a credit entry is made to record a decrease in an asset account (column 3). Similarly, it is also evident from Exhibit 3.1 that liability accounts usually have a credit balance (column 1), we credit a liability account to increase it (column 2), and debit a liability account to decrease it (column 3).

Exhibit 3.1

The double entry accounting framework

Type of account	(1) Usual balance	(2) If increasing the account	(3) If decreasing the account
Asset (balance sheet account)	Debit	Debit	Credit
Liability (balance sheet account)	Credit	Credit	Debit
Owners' equity (balance sheet account)	Credit	Credit	Debit
Revenue (income statement)	Credit	Credit	Debit
Expense (income statement)	Debit	Debit	Credit

The fourth principle of double entry accounting referred to in Box 3.1 concerns the workings of the cash account. Gaining a familiarity with the workings of the cash account is a useful first step when attempting to understand the double entry accounting system. This is because many transactions affect cash. Cash is an example of an asset account, and once you have mastered the way this account works, you will have gained an insight into the workings of all asset accounts. As cash is an asset, it is evident from Exhibit 3.1 that a receipt of cash (i.e., an increase in cash) will be recorded by debiting the cash account and a disbursement of cash (i.e., a decrease in cash) will be recorded by crediting the cash account.

The cash account's workings can be illustrated using a "T account", as depicted in Exhibit 3.2. The left-hand side of all T accounts (regardless of whether they are assets, liabilities, etc.) is the debit side (sometimes abbreviated as "Dr") and the right-hand side of all T accounts is the credit side (sometimes abbreviated as "Cr"). Some find it helpful to visualise money flowing through the cash T account from left to right, i.e., money flows into the left-hand side of the account (the arrow on the left in Exhibit 3.2), and flows out of the right-hand side of the account (the arrow on the right in Exhibit 3.2). Consistent with this visualisation, a receipt of money is recorded as a debit to the cash account and an outflow of cash is recorded as a credit to the cash account.

Exhibit 3.2

The Cash "T account"

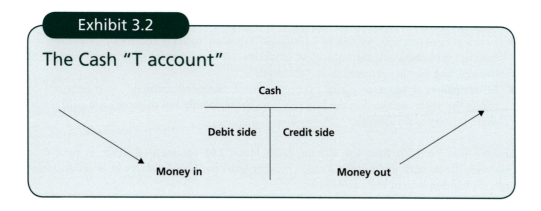

Cash

Debit side | Credit side

Money in | Money out

Double entry accounting

Because of the terminology used by banks, many students of accounting are confused when introduced to the workings of the cash account. They are used to their bank informing them that a deposit of funds in their account represents a credit. This confusion arises because the bank is using terminology from its perspective and not the account holder's perspective. This will be illustrated by the following small example. Imagine that Monica Miser deposits $300 in her savings account held with the Loyalty bank. The double entry that the Loyalty bank will record in its accounting system is as follows:

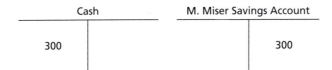

Note that the cash account (which is an asset from the bank's perspective) has been debited. This is consistent with Exhibit 3.2. Note also that the bank's record of Monica Miser's savings account has been credited. This account represents a liability from the perspective of the bank (i.e., it records what the bank owes to M. Miser). As the bank's liability to Monica Miser has increased, the savings account has been credited (check back to column 2 in Exhibit 3.1). When Monica Miser receives a statement from her bank, she will find that the $300 deposit has been recorded as a credit to her savings account. The confusion for the student of accounting stems from the fact that the savings account represents a liability for the bank, but an asset for the account holder.

3) Double entry accounting: a worked example

We are now in a position to explore the nature of double entry accounting through a worked example comprising several transactions. In the following example we will see the double entry recording of a series of transactions and the subsequent preparation of an income statement and balance sheet.

The "Joe Blow Hotel" example worked through in the previous chapter was based on a sole proprietorship. The example that will be worked through in this chapter is based on a company. Differences between sole proprietorships and companies were described at the end of Chapter 1. Key accounting differences between sole proprietorships and companies include:

- In companies, equity is raised from investors by way of issuing shares and this equity funding is referred to as "Share Capital".
- In sole proprietorships, we talk of "drawings" when an owner withdraws capital from the business. In companies, the equivalent payments are viewed more as profit allocations to owners, and they are referred to as "dividends".
- In companies, a separate equity account termed "retained earnings" is maintained to reflect the profits retained in the business (i.e., the accumulation of profits not paid out to share holders as dividends).

Imagine that on 28th June the Winnie Pooh Hotel Ltd commenced business next to a children's theme park in Cardiff, Wales. On 30th June, the only balances in W. Pooh Hotel Ltd's accounting system were as follows:

Cash	£ 8,000
Revenue	£ 300
Share capital	£ 7,700

Identified below are nine transactions that occurred in July, together with the double entry necessary to record each transaction in the accounting system. The circled numbers in the "T-accounts" highlight the entry necessary to record the transaction in question.

Transaction 1:

July 1: From the £8,000 balance in the bank account, beverage stock was purchased for £200 cash.

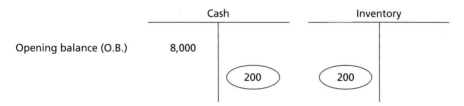

Both cash and inventory are asset accounts. From Exhibit 3.1 it can be determined that the decrease in cash necessitates a credit to the cash account, and the increase of stock necessitates a debit to the inventory account.

n.b. Exhibit 3.1 indicates that we expect to see a debit balance in an asset account (e.g. cash or inventory).

Transaction 2:

July 4: At an American Independence Day banquet function the beverage stock bought on 1st July was sold for £500 cash.

Note: this is a slightly tricky transaction to record as we have to complete two sets of entries. The first set deals with the sales aspect of the transaction, the second set deals with the expense aspect of the transaction.

n.b. Exhibit 3.1 indicates that we expect to see a credit balance in a revenue account.

n.b. Exhibit 3.1 indicates that we expect to see a debit balance in an expense account (e.g. cost of sales). Cost of sales includes the cost of all goods and services consumed in making a sale.

37

Double entry accounting

Transaction 3:
July 5: Purchased inventory stock on credit from Ripoff Ltd for £1,000.

Inventory		Accounts payable	
200			
	200		
(1,000)			(1,000)

n.b. Exhibit 3.1 indicates that we expect to see a credit balance in a liability account (accounts payable is an example).

Transaction 4:
July 10: Sold conferencing services on credit to Ripoff Ltd for £2,000.

Accounts receivable		Revenue	
			300
			500
(2,000)			(2,000)

Transaction 5:
July 11: Purchased ten kitchen ovens on credit for £250,000 from Rusting Ltd.

Kitchen equipment		Accounts payable	
(250,000)			1,000
			(250,000)

Kitchen equipment is an example of a "fixed asset". "Fixed assets" is the term given to all physical assets that will be held by the purchasing company for more than a year. Fixed assets are acquired for use in operations rather than for resale to customers.

Transaction 6:
July 18: Paid Rusting £250,000 to settle the outstanding account.

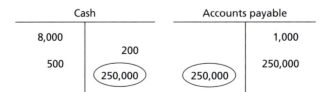

Cash		Accounts payable	
8,000			1,000
	200		
500			250,000
	(250,000)	(250,000)	

Transaction 7:
July 20: Paid £300 for electricity bill.

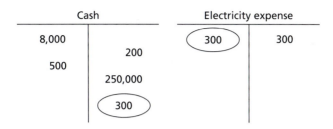

Transaction 8:
July 24: To correct the business bank overdraft, a further £500,000 of share capital is issued.

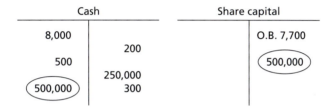

n.b. Exhibit 3.1 indicates that we expect to see a credit balance in the share capital account.

Transaction 9:
July 31: A dividend of £1,500 is declared and paid to shareholders.

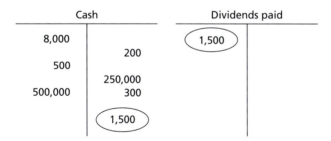

n.b. "Dividends paid" is the one account that does not lend itself to interpretation through the framework outlined in Exhibit 3.1. If attempting to use Exhibit 3.1, it is best to view dividends paid as having a negative impact on owners' equity. If more equity is raised by way of a share issue, we will see a credit made to owners' equity. It follows that a debit to owners' equity refers to a decrease in owners' equity. Instead of debiting an owners' equity account directly, however, when a dividend is declared and paid, we debit the dividends paid account.

As errors can occur in the recording of business transactions, e.g. for transaction 9 we may have erroneously entered a $1,500 credit entry to the "Cash" account and a $150 debit entry to the "Dividends paid" account, it is customary for a **trial balance** to be prepared at the end of an accounting period. The trial balance simply represents a listing of the debit or credit balance on each of the accounts in a business's general ledger. It is called a "trial balance" as it represents a trial to see if the total of the accounts' debit balances equals to the total of the accounts' credit balances. If transaction 9 had resulted in an erroneous $150 debit entry to the dividends paid account, the trial balance would reveal the debit account balances as $1,350 less than the credit account balances. This would signify that a review must be made in order to locate and rectify the accounting error uncovered through the process of producing a trial balance.

The trial balance also assists in the preparation of the year-end financial statements. This is because it lists in one schedule the year-end account balances that will make up the two end of year statements: the income statement and the balance sheet. The trial balance for the Winnie Pooh Hotel Ltd, following the recording of the nine transactions described above, is provided below.

Winnie Pooh Hotel Ltd
Trial Balance
as at 31st July

	Debit	Credit
Cash	£ 256,500	
Accounts receivable	2,000	
Inventory	1,000	
Kitchen Equipment	250,000	
Accounts Payable		£ 1,000
Share Capital		507,700
Dividends Paid	1,500	
Revenue		2,800
Cost of Sales	200	
Electricity Expense	300	
Total	**£ 511,500**	**£ 511,500**

Following the preparation of the trial balance and check that the total of the debit account balances equates to the total of the credit account balances, the income statement for the W. Pooh Hotel can be produced as follows:

Winnie Pooh Hotel Ltd
Income Statement
For the Period ended 31st July

	£	£
Revenue	2,800	
Cost of Sales	200	
Gross Profit		2,600
Electricity Expense		300
Net Profit		2,300

In Chapter 2 we saw that the owners' equity balance can be computed by way of a "statement of owners' equity". In companies it is common practice to segregate owners' equity into two underlying elements: the share capital account and the retained earnings account. The share capital account records direct investments made into a business by shareholders, the retained earnings account records all business profits made and not distributed to the owners. The retained earnings account is increased by the profit made in an accounting period and is reduced by any dividends paid to the owners during the accounting period. For the Winnie Pooh Hotel case, profit for the period ending 31st July is £2,300 and dividends paid are £1,500. The retained earnings account on 31st July can therefore be computed as £800 (£2,300 – £1,500).

In the following balance sheet for the Winnie Pooh Hotel, assets have been segregated between current assets and fixed assets. Current assets include cash and other assets that through the business's operating cycle will be converted into cash, sold or consumed within one year of the balance sheet date. As noted earlier, fixed assets include all physical assets that will not be sold in the next 12 months. Similarly, a distinction can be drawn between current liabilities and longer-term liabilities. Current liabilities include those liabilities that are due for payment in the course of the next 12 months, while long-term liabilities include liabilities that are not due for payment in the next 12 months.

Winnie Pooh Hotel Ltd
Balance Sheet as at 31st July

	£	£		£	£
Current Assets			Current liabilities		
Cash	256,500		Accounts payable		1,000
Accounts receivable	2,000		Owners' equity		
Inventory	1,000		Share capital	507,700	
		259,500	Retained earnings	800	
					508,500
Fixed Assets					
Kitchen equipment		250,000			
		£ 509,500			£ 509,500

For well-established companies, the retained earnings account can be one of the largest accounts appearing in a balance sheet. As highlighted in the financial decision making case 3.1, it is an account that is frequently misunderstood by managers.

FINANCIAL DECISION MAKING IN ACTION CASE 3.1

The General Manager's interpretation of the retained earnings account

The retained earnings account records the accumulated profits earned by a company and retained in the business. There is a common tendency, however, for managers who have had no accounting training to believe that the retained earnings account represents cash held.

It is imperative that senior management do not fall prey to this misconception of the retained earnings account because:

- As will be seen in Chapter 13, careful cash management is fundamental to maintaining business solvency. The immediate factor that causes a bankruptcy is a shortage of cash.
- The retained earnings account is frequently one of the largest accounts appearing in a balance sheet.

Senior managers should not allow the retained earnings balance to influence their thinking in any decision that carries significant cash management implications. To determine how much cash a business holds, look at the cash (or bank) balance that appears as an asset in the balance sheet.

4) Journal entries

The previous section has shown you how a business records transactions as debits and credits in its accounts. We have also seen that these accounts are collectively referred to as the general ledger. Prior to posting transactions to the accounts in a general ledger, they are entered chronologically in a record referred to as a journal. While many businesses maintain a set of journals, with each journal tailored to a particular type of transaction (e.g., cash payments journal, cash receipts journal, etc.), most maintain at least a basic form of journal which is referred to as the "general journal".

Journals are maintained in order to:

1. Provide a chronological record of all transactions. If a business was to experience a problem with its accounting system during a particular time period, the journal could be turned to as a record of transactions occurring during that time period.
2. Provide a complete record of each transaction. Note that in the general ledger, transactions are recorded in more than one place, e.g., a $300 cash sale is recorded in the "cash account" record and the "sales account" record. Recording all information relating to a transaction in a journal helps in the avoidance and detection of errors.

To illustrate the workings of the general journal, imagine two May transactions for a hotel: on 3rd May it bought $4,015 of wine stock on credit, and on 4th May it collected $1,200 of cash owed by a customer. Exhibit 3.3 illustrates how these two transactions would be recorded in the general journal.

The journal shows the date a transaction is recorded, the title of each account affected by the transaction and also the amount to be debited and credited. The name of the account to be credited and also the amount to be credited have traditionally been indented in the journal. The journal also records the account numbers of the accounts affected (accounts in the general ledger are typically numbered to facilitate easy access), referred to as "posting reference" in Exhibit 3.3. A brief description of the transaction recorded is entered below the transaction.

Exhibit 3.3

Illustration of a general journal

Date	Account titles and transaction description	Posting reference	Debit	Credit
20X1				
May 3	Wine stock	144	4,015	
	Accounts payable	201		4,015
	Purchase of wine stock on credit			
4	Cash	101	1,200	
	Accounts Receivable	170		1,200
	Collection of an account receivable			

5) Summary

This chapter has built on Chapter 2's introduction to financial accounting by describing the "debit and credit" system of double entry bookkeeping. A framework was introduced showing you that a debit increases asset and expense accounts and that a credit increases liability, owners' equity and revenue accounts. In connection with a worked example, you were shown an accounting transaction affecting each of these main account groupings.

Having read the chapter you should now know:

- how to increase or decrease asset, liability, owners' equity, revenue and expense accounts,
- how to record transactions in a general journal,
- how to produce a trial balance,
- that profits not paid out to a company's shareholders as dividends are generally credited to an owners' equity account called "retained earnings",
- that current assets include cash and other assets that through the business's operating cycle will be converted into cash, sold or consumed within one year of the balance sheet date,
- that current liabilities include those liabilities that are due for payment in the course of the next 12 months.

References

Jackling, B., Raar, J., Wines, G. and McDowall, T. (2010) *Accounting: A Framework for Decision Making*, 3rd edition, Macquarie Park, NSW, Australia: McGraw-Hill: Chapter 14.

Jagels, M.G. (2007) *Hospitality Management Accounting*, 9th edition, Hoboken, NJ: John Wiley & Sons: Chapter 1.

Schmidgall, R.F. (2011) *Hospitality Industry Managerial Accounting*, 7th edition, East Lansing, MI: American Hotel & Lodging Educational Institute: Chapter 1.

Weygandt, J., Kieso, D., Kimmel, P. and DeFranco, A. (2009) *Hospitality Financial Accounting*, Hoboken, NJ: John Wiley & Sons: Chapter 3.

Problems

Problem 3.1

Describe whether we can say that a debit to an account signifies that something beneficial has happened for the business concerned.

Problem 3.2

Are we able to say that in double entry accounting a debit represents a plus and a credit represents a minus?

Problem 3.3

Dublin's BlarneyStone Pub opened on 1st April and the following six transactions occurred in its first week of business. Record the transactions in appropriately headed T-accounts for the BlarneyStone Pub's manager.

Double entry accounting

a) Owner invested €4,000 in a newly opened bank account for the pub.
b) Purchased €5,000 of "Old Black Creamy" stout on account.
c) Paid cash €450 for a delivery of potato crisps and salted peanuts.
d) Purchased a cash register for €1,000 on credit.
e) Banked the first week's bar takings of €350.
f) Determined that the cost of "Old Black Creamy" sold in the first week was €150.

Problem 3.4

What is the difference between fixed assets and current assets?

Problem 3.5

In terms of debit and credit record keeping, explain why a manager may think there is an error when he notes the direction of the current bank balance in the accounts of their business and compares it with the direction of the balance on the business's most recent bank statement.

Problem 3.6

Business transactions are recorded in a general ledger. A general journal is also used to record business transactions. So doesn't maintenance of a general journal therefore signify significant duplication in record keeping?

Required:
Provide two reasons why many businesses maintain a general journal in addition to a general ledger.

Problem 3.7

Develop your own balance sheet by listing your assets and liabilities. From this listing determine your "net worth" which corresponds to "owners' equity" in a business reporting context.

Problem 3.8

Fill in each of the blank boxes in the matrix appearing below with either the word "debit" or "credit".

Type of account	Usual balance	To increase the account	To decrease the account . . . .
Asset			
Liability			
Owners' equity			
Revenue			
Expense			

Problem 3.9

From the following listing of Jackie Cridland's CreatureComforts hotel accounts, distinguish between the debit and credit balances.

	$
Buildings	120,000
Wages payable	1,300
Bank overdraft	2,240
Trade Creditors	3,300
Soft drink inventory	880
Office supplies	540
Drawings	3,600
Owners equity	78,450
Bank loan	18,420
Accounts receivable	4,500
Sales	24,600
Bank interest revenue	1,210

Problem 3.10

Record a hotel's following five transactions in appropriately headed T-accounts.

a) Hotel receives $500 for room sales.
b) Hotel pays staff $400 in wages.
c) Hotel makes $600 of restaurant sales all on credit.
d) Hotel owner withdraws $1,000 from the business.
e) Hotel buys $700 of inventory stock on account.

Problem 3.11

(a) Using "T-accounts", record debit and credit entries for each of the following transactions that all occurred in January 20X1 for a San Francisco restaurant. The T-accounts you will need are: Cash, Food Inventory, Beverage Inventory, Accounts Receivable, Furniture and Equipment, Accounts Payable, Bank Loan, Owners' Equity, Revenue, Food Purchase Expense, Beverage Purchase Expense, Wage Expense, Supplies Expense, Rent Expense, Interest Expense.

a. Mr T. Francis commenced business by investing $30,000 cash in the restaurant.
b. Purchased on credit food stock for $4,000 and beverage stock for $6,000.
c. Purchased furniture and equipment for $20,000, paying $12,000 cash and owing the balance.
d. The bank extended a loan of $20,000 to the business.
e. Made sales of $40,000 during the month – 75 per cent of this was cash sales, the remainder was on credit.
f. Purchased $9,000 of perishable food items (food purchase expense) on credit and paid $2,000 cash for beverages (beverage purchase expense). The business has established that both these purchases should be immediately expensed.
g. Paid $12,000 to trade creditors.
h. Repaid $2,000 of the bank loan plus interest of $100.

    i. Paid $10,800 of wages.

    j. Paid $4,000 for miscellaneous supply items. The business has a policy of expensing these items on purchase.

    k. On the last day of the month, paid $1,500 rent for January.

(b) Once the T-account entries have been recorded, prepare an income statement for January 20X1 and a balance sheet as at 31st January 20X1.

Problem 3.12

The following transactions occurred during the first month of operations for "Oz Hinterland Ltd", a new hotel business located in the Australian Kimberleys:

a. $80,000 of share capital was raised.

b. In order to provide further capital, a bank extended a loan of $40,000 to the business.

c. Paid cash for land and buildings $99,500.

d. Purchased kitchen equipment for $20,000. $8,000 of this was paid for in cash, with the balance owing.

e. Purchased on credit a stock of linen and uniforms for $5,800.

f. During month received revenue of $12,000 for room sales and restaurant revenue.

g. Paid $1,500 for first month's wages.

h. Paid $300 covering one month's interest on the bank loan.

i. Paid $1,200 insurance premium covering the first year of operations.

j. Paid $6,000 of the balance owing for kitchen equipment.

k. Purchased beverage stock of $1,500 for cash. By the end of the first month it was determined that one-third of this stock had been sold in the restaurant.

l. Determined that during the month the kitchen had purchased $1,800 of perishable food supplies for cash. No balance of food stock remained at the end of the month.

m. Oz Hinterland declared and paid a total dividend of $2,000.

Required:

(a) Enter these transactions on T-accounts.

(b) Prepare an income statement for the first month and a balance sheet as at the month end.

Chapter 4

Adjusting and closing entries

Learning objectives

After studying this chapter, you should have developed an appreciation of:

1. what is meant by "closing entries",
2. what is meant by "adjusting entries",
3. the distinction between periodic and perpetual inventory accounting systems,
4. how the accountant accounts for bad debts,
5. how the accountant accounts for depreciation.

1) Introduction

This chapter focuses on adjusting entries and closing entries. "**Adjusting entries**" is the term used to describe the set of bookkeeping entries that need to be made in order to **update** some accounts prior to the preparation of the accounting year-end income statement and balance sheet. "**Closing entries**" is the term used to describe the set of year-end accounting entries that are made in order that all accounts relating to a period of time (i.e., revenue, expense and the drawings or dividends account) **begin the new accounting year with a zero balance**. It is only once all adjusting entries have been completed that closing entries can be made. This is because closing entries result in the transference of account balances to the income account.

As the mechanics of adjusting entries are more challenging than the mechanics of closing entries, the chapter is structured around the different types of adjusting entries that can be encountered. In the course of considering a range of adjusting entries, the mechanics of making closing entries will also be demonstrated.

2) Why do we need closing entries?

Immediately prior to entering the new accounting year, all accounts that relate to a period of time (i.e., those accounts that do not flow directly to the balance sheet) need to be wound back to zero. If these accounts were not wound back to a zero balance on an annual basis, their balances would not reflect the current year's sales revenue (for a revenue account) or the current year's expenses (for an expense account). In effect, failure to close these accounts would result in the revenue account and also all expense accounts showing balances that reflect sales achieved and expenses incurred since the inception of the business. The term "closing entry" is used to describe the year-end transference of balances in these accounts to the income statement (the income statement can be thought of as an account in which revenues are credits and expenses are debits).

In Chapter 2, we saw that the balance on the income statement (i.e., net profit) is transferred to the owners' equity section of the balance sheet by way of the statement of owners' equity. This highlights the fact that all accounts flow eventually into the balance sheet. This flow is direct for those accounts that are sometimes described as "permanent" (i.e., asset, liability and owners' equity accounts) and indirect via the income statement for other accounts that are sometimes referred to as "temporary" (e.g., revenue and expense accounts).

3) Why do we need adjusting entries?

In many cases the need for adjusting entries arises because the timing of cash flows (either receipts or disbursements) does not coincide with the period in which it is appropriate to recognise the related revenue or expense. This distinction between the timing of a cash flow and the timing of the recognition of a revenue or an expense item stems from the accrual concept of accounting. The nature of this concept, as well as some examples of year-end adjusting entries, are presented in Box 4.1.

Box 4.1

Adjusting entries and the nature of the accrual concept

Most year-end adjusting entries arise because of the accrual concept of accounting which holds that:

- revenue is recognised when it is earned and certain, rather than simply when cash is received,
- an expense is recognised in the period when the benefit derived from the associated expenditure arises (e.g., wages for work conducted during the current period are treated as an expense of the current period, regardless of whether or not they have been paid for during the current period).

Examples of year-end adjusting entries include:

- recording wages accrued (at the year-end there are wages owing for employee work conducted but not yet paid for),
- allocating the cost of a fixed asset to those accounting periods in which the benefit of owning the fixed asset occurs (this is "depreciation"),
- allocating a pro-rated portion of prepaid insurance to the most recent accounting period,
- adjusting accounts receivable (debtors) to recognise that some of the balance appearing in the accounts receivable ledger may prove to be uncollectible.

The examples of year-end adjusting entries provided in Box 4.1 will be more fully explained in the next section which provides worked examples of year-end adjusting entries.

4) Worked examples highlighting types of adjusting entry

In this section, the following four basic types of adjusting entry will be explained by way of worked examples:

● Costs paid for but not yet incurred (i.e., expenses pre-paid),
● Costs incurred but not yet paid for (e.g., money owing for wages),
● Unearned revenue (i.e., cash received prior to delivery of a good or service),
● Revenue earned but no cash received (e.g., interest on an investment account that is earned but not yet received).

In addition, three further commonly confronted situations that give rise to adjusting entries are explored:

● Supplies used,
● Bad debts (uncollectible account receivables),
● Depreciation.

Adjusting entry type 1: Costs paid for but not yet incurred

This situation arises for insurance and rent (in rental and insurance situations the payee typically pays prior to the period in which the rental or insurance benefit is received).

Imagine that on 1st January 20X1 Winnipeg's TrudeauInn took advantage of a special insurance offer and purchased 18 months' insurance coverage for $3,000. On 30th June 20X2 this policy was renewed for a further 12 months at a cost of $2,400. TrudeauInn's accounting year-end is on the 31st December.

To compute the insurance expense to be charged to the income statement, prorate the amounts paid to the periods of time in which the insurance coverage expired, i.e.:

20X1 Insurance expense = Two-thirds of $3,000 = $2,000.
20X2 Insurance expense = One-third of $3,000 + half of $2,400 = $2,200.

Accounting treatment:

1 January 20X1:

n.b. The insurance cover is paid for in advance of the period of time that it pertains to. This signifies that immediately following the payment of the insurance premium, we have an asset (i.e., insurance coverage) that runs for the life of the insurance contract. This asset is referred to as "insurance prepaid".

Adjusting and closing entries

31 December 20X1 (adjusting entry):

Insurance expense		Insurance prepaid	
(2,000)		3,000	
			(2,000)

n.b. The need to make this year-end entry can be viewed from an asset depletion perspective or an expense incurred perspective. With respect to the asset depletion perspective, two-thirds of the insurance coverage paid for at the beginning of the year has now expired due to the passage of time. This signifies that the $3,000 asset (i.e., prepaid insurance) has diminished by $2,000. With respect to the expense perspective, 12 months of insurance cover was "consumed" in 20X1. From the prorated calculation above, we found that the 20X1 insurance cover effectively cost $2,000.

31 December 20X1 (closing entry):

Insurance expense		Income statement	
2,000		(2,000)	
	(2,000)		

n.b. Prior to entering the new accounting year, all revenue, expense and drawing accounts (i.e., "period related" or "temporary" accounts) need to be wound back to zero in order that their balance at any time reflects the revenue, expense or drawings for the current accounting year. This process is generally referred to as making closing entries. These accounts are closed by transferring their balances to the income statement, which results in the compilation of a profit or loss for the year.

30 June 20X2:

Insurance prepaid		Cash	
3,000			(2,400)
	2,000		
(2,400)			

This 30 June 20X2 entry is to record the $2,400 insurance premium paid.

31 December 20X2 (adjusting entry)

Insurance expense		Insurance prepaid	
		3,000	
(2,200)			2,000
		2,400	
			(2,200)

n.b. Again, we can take an asset depletion or an expense incurred perspective on this adjusting entry. With respect to the asset depletion perspective, in the first six months of 20X2, $1,000 of the $3,000 prepayment expired. In the second six months of 20X2, $1,200 of the $2,400 prepayment expired. From the expense perspective, this signifies that insurance coverage costing a total of $2,200 is attributable to 20X2. Note also that a rationale can be offered for the $1,200 year-end debit balance remaining on the insurance prepaid account. This represents the cost of acquiring insurance cover for the first six months of 20X3, i.e., the cost of insurance cover that is prepaid as at 31/12/X2.

31 December 20X2 (closing entry)

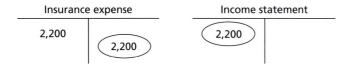

Finally, on 31st December 20X2, all revenue and expense accounts are closed off to the income statement.

In this example, it has been presumed that on payment of the premium, "insurance prepaid" is debited. In some accounting systems this amount may be charged immediately to "insurance expense". This approach is referred to as "expensing on purchase". If this alternative approach is taken, the year-end adjusting entry will have to set up the prepaid amount. For example, in the case described above, if the company had immediately expensed the $3,000 insurance cover purchased on 1st January 20X1, the year-end adjusting entry would be as follows:

31 December 20X1 (adjusting entry)

n.b. Note how regardless of the initial method taken to record the insurance cover purchased, once the year-end adjusting entries have been made, the insurance expense account has a debit balance of $2,000 and the insurance prepaid account has a debit balance of $1,000. Some find it helpful to approach adjusting entries by first considering what year-end balance is needed in the prepaid account and the expense account. If you can determine what year-end balance needs to be reflected in these accounts you can work out what adjusting entry needs to be made in order to get to the year-end balance that you seek.

Adjusting entry type 2: Expenses incurred but not paid for (accrued expenses)

Costs incurred but not yet paid are frequently referred to as "accrued expenses". One of the main examples of accrued expenses arises in connection with wages and salaries. If, at the end of the accounting period, employee work costing $1,000 has been performed but has not yet been paid for, accrued wages are recorded as follows (the wages accrued account is a liability account that reflects wages owing):

Like all expense accounts, at the year-end the debit balance of the wage expense account will be closed off to the income statement. In the new accounting year, if the first wage bill paid amounts to $5,000, the following entry will have to be made:

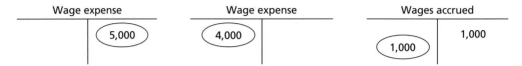

n.b. This first entry in the new accounting year is slightly complicated as it involves three accounts. The cash account credit entry of $5,000 is straightforward as $5,000 has been paid out. The wage expense account starts the new year with a zero balance as a result of the closing entry made at the end of the previous year. Of the $5,000 wage payment, $1,000 relates to the previous year (this is evident from the $1,000 credit balance in the wages accrued account). $4,000 of the $5,000 wage payment must therefore relate to work conducted this year. As the wage expense account is supposed to reflect the cost of work completed this year, it is appropriate that it be debited with $4,000. Finally, prior to the wage payment, the wages accrued account reflects a liability of $1,000. Immediately following the payment of wages the liability to employees is removed, therefore it is appropriate that a zero balance be reflected, i.e., a $1,000 debit entry is warranted. The intricacies of this particular set of accounting entries only arise around the year-end, as in most accounting systems this is the only time that entries are made to the wages accrued account.

Adjusting entry type 3: Unearned revenue

Imagine that on 1st December the Captain Cook Hotel in Whitby, Yorkshire received £50,000 as an advance payment from a conference organiser, covering the cost of a five-day conference that the hotel will host commencing on 30th December. At the close of business on 31st December (the hotel's accounting year-end), 40 per cent of the conference service can be seen to have been provided (i.e., the hotel has completed the hosting of two days of the five-day conference).

The accounting entries that would be made in the hotel's books are as follows:

1st December accounting entry:

n.b. Unearned revenue is the name of the account that is credited when cash is received in advance of the provision of goods or services associated with a sale. This is a liability account. In the above example, in the period following the £50,000 receipt but prior to hosting the convention, the £50,000 can be seen to represent a liability. Under a typical conference contract, if a contingency arises preventing the hotel from hosting the convention, it will have to refund the conference organiser.

31st December accounting entry (adjusting entry):

n.b. As 40 per cent of the work contracted for (i.e., hosting the conference) has been completed by the year-end, 40 per cent of the original unearned revenue amount can be viewed as earned by 31st December. We therefore make a credit entry of £20,000 (40 per cent of £50,000) to the revenue account and reduce the balance on the unearned revenue account by making a debit entry of £20,000.

Adjusting entry type 4: Revenue earned but not received

The issue of accounting for revenue that has been earned but not received frequently arises when a reporting entity has an investment in an interest bearing account. Imagine Aberdeen's Scrooge Hotel has an investment of £24,000 yielding 10 per cent annual interest with cash interest paid semi-annually. The last time the Scrooge Hotel updated its records with respect to this investment occurred on 30th September which is when it last received an interest payment of £1,200 earned for the six months commencing 1st April. If the Scrooge Hotel has a 31st December year-end, the year-end adjusting entry required to record the interest that it is owed as a result of holding the investment through October, November and December is as follows:

31st December accounting entry (adjusting entry):

n.b. The Scrooge Hotel's investment is earning interest at the rate of £200 per month. At the year-end, it has not recorded the interest earned in the final three months of the year. A £600 credit entry to the interest revenue account updates the hotel's record of interest earned in the year. The £600 debit entry to the interest receivable account highlights that the hotel has an asset in the form of interest that it is owed at the year-end.

Adjusting entry type 5: Accounting for supplies

Supplies such as office stationery generally represent a relatively small investment for most hotels. As a result, many hotels adopt the relatively simple accounting procedure of periodically determining the supplies balance by conducting a stock-take (this approach is generally referred to as a periodic inventory accounting system). Under a periodic inventory system, the purchases of supplies are simply recorded by debiting a "supplies purchases" account. Operation of a periodic inventory system and the adjusting entry that it gives rise to are demonstrated through the worked example in Exhibit 4.1.

> ## Exhibit 4.1
>
> ## Determining stock used in a periodic inventory system
>
> Suzy Defoe is the office manager of Manchester's Old Trafford Hotel. The hotel operates a periodic inventory system with respect to office supplies. At the year-end, the hotel accountant asked Suzy to oversee a year-end stock-take of supplies, in order that the cost of supplies used during the year could be determined. The year-end stock-take revealed that £2,000 of office supplies were held on 31st December 20X1. Suzy then consulted the supplies inventory account, which had last been updated 12 months previously (i.e., following the previous year-end's stock-take), and noted a debit balance of £2,800. Throughout the year she debited the "supplies purchases" account whenever purchasing supplies. She notes that prior to making any adjusting entries, this account had a year-end debit balance of £14,000.
>
> The cost of supplies used in the year can be determined by solving for? in the schedule below.
>
> | | £ |
> |---|---|
> | Opening balance | 2,800 |
> | *Add*: Supplies purchased | 14,000 |
> | Supplies made available | 16,800 |
> | *Less*: Supplies used | ? |
> | Closing balance | £2,000 |
>
> As we have determined that the cost of supplies made available is £16,800, and we know that at the end of the year the stock of supplies available cost £2,000, we can conclude that £14,800 of supplies must have been used during the year.

The year-end adjusting entries that would have to be made in the scenario described in Exhibit 4.1 can be managed in two stages. Firstly, the purchases account balance can be transferred to the supplies inventory account. Consistent with the philosophy of closing entries, this results in the purchases account starting the new accounting year with a balance of zero.

Supplies purchases		Supplies inventory	
14,000		2,800	
	14,000	14,000	

Secondly, the supplies expense account can be debited with the £14,800 cost of supplies used that was calculated above. The corresponding credit entry should then be made to the supplies inventory account. These entries result in the recognition of an expense (the supplies expense account will be closed to the income statement). They also result in a £2,000 debit balance in the supplies inventory account, which reflects the result of the year-end stock-take. This inventory account balance will comprise part of the total assets recorded in the year-end balance sheet.

Supplies expense		Supplies inventory	
(14,800)		2,800	
		14,000	
			(14,800)

Using a periodic inventory control system signifies that a degree of control is lost with respect to inventory. Between stock-takes the manager responsible for ordering supplies will have no administrative record of the supplies held in stock. If this is believed to represent a significant problem, the manager could consider using a perpetual inventory system. The relative merits of perpetual and periodic inventory systems are outlined in Financial decision making in action case 4.1.

FINANCIAL DECISION MAKING IN ACTION CASE 4.1

The F&B manager's choice of inventory control procedures

Rather than depending on a periodic stock-take to determine what amount of stock is held, a perpetual inventory system can be operated. A perpetual inventory accounting system involves debiting the inventory account every time inventory is purchased and crediting it every time a sale or issue of stock is made. Deciding between a periodic and perpetual inventory approach can be a significant issue for an F&B manager due to the many low-cost food items that can be held.

Perpetual accounting systems are generally more expensive to operate due to the number of individual inventory records that have to be maintained. Despite this, an F&B manager would consider adopting a perpetual inventory accounting approach for particular food and drink items if one or all of the following issues is believed to be significant:

1. Significant stock shrinkage is occurring due to theft.
2. A significant loss of customer goodwill would result if certain menu items were to become unavailable.
3. Observing whether the stock item in question needs to be reordered is awkward and time consuming.

Adjusting entry type 6: Bad and doubtful accounts

An initial word of warning is warranted here. Without wanting to sound alarmist, accounting for bad debts gives rise to what is probably the most complicated set of accounting entries described in this book. Proceed at a gentle pace through this section!

At the end of the accounting period, an adjusting entry needs to be made to reflect the fact that some of the balance in "accounts receivable" may prove to be uncollectible. If some of the accounts receivable balance does prove to be uncollectible, the revenue account will be overstated as it will include "bad sale" entries, i.e., sales for which we will obtain no receipt of funds.

The following three steps outline a widely adopted approach to accounting for bad and doubtful debts.

Step 1: The provision

Periodically (say, every month end during the accounting year) update records to reflect and provide for the problem of potentially non-collectible accounts. If every month we make $100,000 of credit sales and we believe that on average 2 per cent will prove to be uncollectible, having already debited "accounts receivable" $100,000 and credited "revenue" $100,000, we can make the following month end "adjusting entry".

Bad debts expense		Allowance for doubtful accounts	
2,000			2,000

The "bad debts expense" account can be described as a "contra" account, as it flows through to the income statement where it will off-set the revenue account's credit balance. The "allowance for doubtful accounts" account can also be described as a contra account as its credit balance will be recorded in the balance sheet in a manner that off-sets the account receivables' debit balance.

Step 2: An account turns bad

Imagine that half way through the accounting year one of our clients, Untrustworthy Ltd, went bankrupt while owing us $3,500. It is determined that we are unlikely to collect any of the amount outstanding. The "step 1" month-end entry is designed to **provide** for this type of eventuality. Now the eventuality has been **realised** and we need to update the books as follows:

a) remove the $3,500 from "accounts receivable" (if we don't do this, the account will contain a growing amount of entries for amounts that will never be collected),

b) remove the $3,500 from "allowance for doubtful accounts", as, following removal of the amount from "accounts receivable" we no longer have a need to allow for it, i.e., no need for an off-setting contra entry.

Allowance for doubtful accounts		Accounts receivable	
3,500			3,500

Step 3: Year-end adjusting entry

Following an appraisal of the $150,000 year-end accounts receivable balance, it is estimated that $3,200 may well prove to be uncollectible. An investigation of the books reveals that the "allowance for doubtful accounts" has a balance of $3,000. Therefore, prior to making a year-end adjusting entry, "net" accounts receivable is recorded at $147,000 ($150,000 – $3,000). As we expect to be able to collect $146,800 ($150,000 – $3,200), net accounts receivable is overstated by $200 and we need to make a $200 adjusting entry.

The debit and credit entries made here are the same as the "step 1" entries. The need for the year-end adjusting entry has arisen because the "step 1" entries during the year had not been sufficient to create the requisite year-end balance on the "allowance for doubtful accounts". If at the year-end it is found that there is an over-provision in "allowance for doubtful accounts", we would need to reverse the above entry by crediting "bad debts expense" and debiting "allowance for doubtful accounts".

Adjusting entry type 7: Depreciation

Depreciation refers to the process of allocating the cost of a fixed asset (i.e., an asset with a useful life greater t han one year) across the years in which the asset's owner can be expected to derive benefit from owning the asset. If depreciation accounting entries were not made, the type of scenario outlined in Box 4.2 could arise.

Box 4.2

A scenario highlighting the need for depreciation

The following hypothetical discussion between a user of accounting information prepared by SouthPark, a hotel with an untrained accountant, and one of SouthPark's managers highlights the need for depreciation.

Accounting information user (e.g., a prospective shareholder):

"How come the SouthPark Hotel had a healthy profit for the last five years except for 20X1, when you reported a huge loss?"

SouthPark manager:

"Oh, 20X1 just so happened to be the year in which we bought our most expensive fixed asset. We received delivery of it on 28th December and in fact didn't get around to using it until 20X2. We had expected the delivery to be made a week later, in which case you would have seen 20X2 as having the big loss".

> **Accounting information user:**
> "So what you're saying is that the profit figure reported for 20X1 is misleading. It doesn't really reflect SouthPark's underlying performance relative to other years. You know this means that your profit for 20X1 is understated and your profit in the other years is really overstated. While 20X1 took a big hit, it's as if the subsequent years have had use of the asset for free".

Main depreciation methods

There are several distinct approaches to determining the timing of the fixed asset cost write off. In the following description of three methods, it will be assumed that a fixed asset has been purchased for $1,200,000, and that it has been estimated that the asset can be salvaged in five years' time for $200,000.

a) Straight line method: This widely used method involves apportioning the net cost of the fixed asset (purchase price – salvage value) equally across the life of the asset.

$$\text{Annual depreciation charge} = \frac{\text{Purchase price} - \text{salvage value}}{\text{Estimated number of years asset will be owned}}$$

$$= \frac{\$1,200,000 - \$200,000}{5} = \$200,000$$

b) Reducing balance method: Under this method, each year a fixed percentage of the asset's net book value (the net book value is the cost of the asset minus the accumulated depreciation charged on the asset since its purchase) is expensed as depreciation. This will result in a reducing depreciation charge as the net book value (NBV) will be reducing. In the following example, suppose 40 per cent has been identified as the annual percentage rate.

	$
Opening net book value – year 1	1,200,000
1st year dep'n charge (NBV × 40%)	480,000
Opening net book value – year 2	720,000
2nd year dep'n charge (NBV × 40%)	288,000
Opening net book value – year 3	432,000
3rd year dep'n charge (NBV × 40%)	172,800

c) Usage based method: This is not a widely used method. To demonstrate how it can be applied, imagine that the asset purchased is a small airplane and that it has been estimated that the plane will fly 1 million kilometres in its life with the company.

If 200,000 kilometres were flown in 20X1, 20X1 depreciation charge =

$(200,000 \div 1,000,000) \times \$1,000,000 = \$200,000$

If 300,000 kilometres were flown in 20X2, 20X2 depreciation charge =

$(300,000 \div 1,000,000) \times \$1,000,000 = \$300,000$

Recording depreciation

Similar to the contra account set up for doubtful accounts, when depreciating, we set up an "accumulated depreciation" account, which acts as a contra account off-setting the balance in the fixed asset account.

For the 20X2 depreciation charge of $300,000 in the airplane example above, the 20X2 year-end depreciation entry would be as follows:

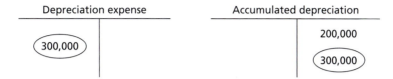

Depreciation expense	Accumulated depreciation
300,000	200,000
	300,000

As the depreciation expense account and the accumulated depreciation account have somewhat similar names, it is vital that their very different roles are clearly understood. The depreciation expense account is closed off to the income statement at the year-end. The fact that it is closed off in this manner should be evident from the word "expense" appearing in its title.

The accumulated depreciation account is reported in the balance sheet as a contra account that off-sets the fixed asset account. The fact that it is an account that accumulates across accounting periods suggests that it is a balance sheet account. Note how, by the end of 20X2, the accumulated depreciation account has accumulated from the $200,000 depreciation expensed in 20X1 to $500,000, as a result of the $300,000 expensed in 20X2. The fixed asset section of the company's balance sheet at the end of 20X2 would appear in a format such as that presented below:

	$	$
Fixed assets at cost	1,200,000	
Less accumulated depreciation	500,000	
Net book value of fixed asset		700,000

5) Summary

Through the use of worked examples, this chapter has outlined the nature of closing and adjusting entries. At the end of each financial year, closing entries are made to all accounts relating to a period of time, i.e., revenue, expense and dividend accounts. If these accounts are not closed at the end of a year, they would not have a zero balance at the start of the new financial year. Adjusting entries need to be made in advance of preparing the year-end statements in order to update some accounts. For example, as depreciation is a function of time, periodically an adjusting entry has to be made to update all depreciation accounts.

Having read the chapter you should now know:

- all revenue, expense and dividend accounts have to be closed at the end of the financial year,
- costs paid for but not yet incurred represent prepaid expenses and are treated as assets,
- expenses incurred but not yet paid for represent accruals and are treated as liabilities,
- if a customer pays for a service in advance of receiving the service, the receipt is referred to as unearned revenue and is treated as a liability,
- the difference between perpetual and periodic inventory accounting procedures,

- how to account for bad debts,
- how to account for depreciation.

References

Jackling, B., Raar, J., Wines, G. and McDowall, T. (2010) *Accounting: A Framework for Decision Making*, 3rd edition, Macquarie Park, NSW, Australia: McGraw-Hill: Chapter 16.

Jagels, M.G. (2007) *Hospitality Management Accounting*, 9th edition, Hoboken, NJ: John Wiley & Sons: Chapter 1.

Schmidgall, R.F. (2011) *Hospitality Industry Managerial Accounting*, 7th edition, East Lansing, MI: American Hotel & Lodging Educational Institute: Chapter 1.

Weygandt, J., Kieso, D., Kimmel, P. and DeFranco, A. (2009) *Hospitality Financial Accounting*, Hoboken, NJ: John Wiley & Sons: Chapter 4.

Problems

Problem 4.1

Describe the difference between adjusting entries and closing entries.

Problem 4.2

Given the following information for Dunedin's CityCentre Hotel, post relevant adjusting entries to CityCentre's general ledger. Assume 30th June is the year-end.

a) The telephone account of $500 for June is unpaid and unrecorded.
b) Rent of $3,600 for the six month period ending 31st August is due to be paid in arrears in October.
c) It was estimated at the time of purchasing a car two years ago for $6,000 that the car would be salvaged five years later for $1,000. The company uses straight line depreciation for all fixed assets. This year's depreciation entry for the car is still to be made.
d) The next fortnightly pay date for the company's employees is 7th July. The fortnightly payroll is $140,000.
e) On 2nd March received $1,600 cash from a client. This was an advance payment for services to be rendered. At the time of receipt, $1,600 was recorded as a credit to unearned revenue. On 30th June, 75 per cent of this service had been provided.
f) On 1st May received six months' rent revenue in advance totalling $600. At the time of the receipt, this was recorded as a credit to rental revenue.

Problem 4.3

On 30th November, account balances relating to the accounts receivable management function of Minnesota's CitySlickers Hotel were as follows:

Accounts receivable	$141,500	Debit balance
Allowance for doubtful accounts	$2,400	Credit balance
Revenue	$1,320,000	Credit balance
Bad debts expense	$12,400	Debit balance

The following transactions occurred in December:

1. Cash collected from credit sale customers was $92,000.
2. Credit sales were $101,000.

On a monthly basis, the manager of accounts receivable has made an allowance of 1.25 per cent of sales to cover the contingency of trade debts turning bad. At the hotel's year-end, on 31st December, a review of accounts receivable has revealed the following:

Year-end estimate of doubtful accounts		
Age of account	Account receivable amount	% Estimated as uncollectible
0–30 days	$ 84,000	0.75
31–60 days	44,000	1.25
61–180 days	18,000	5
Over 180 days	4,500	100
	$150,500	

The company accountant has decided that all accounts with an age of 180 days or more should be written off from the accounts receivable ledger. In addition, the doubtful accounts balance should be revised to reflect the remaining estimated doubtful accounts following the year-end review of the accounts receivable ledger.

Required:

(a) Record December's credit sales and cash collected transactions in appropriately titled "T-accounts".
(b) Record all necessary year-end adjusting entries in appropriately titled "T-accounts".

Problem 4.4

Classify each of the following accounts as either an asset, liability, revenue, expense or owners' equity item (you can also use the term "negative asset", if you feel it is more appropriate for any of the accounts):

Interest revenue
Wages accrued
Depreciation expense
Insurance prepaid
Unearned revenue
Bad debts expense
Supplies inventory
Allowance for doubtful accounts
Accumulated depreciation

Problem 4.5

The general ledger of the Cardigan Arms Pub includes the following accounts:

Sales revenue
Inventory
Interest revenue
Wages accrued
Prepaid insurance
Insurance expense
Accumulated depreciation
Depreciation expense
Rent expense
Prepaid rent
Allowance for doubtful accounts

Required:

(a) Indicate for which of these accounts, a year-end closing entry will need to be made.
(b) For each of the accounts requiring a year-end closing entry, indicate what account will need to be debited and what account will need to be credited.

Problem 4.6

Marlow's WatersEdge Hotel operates a periodic inventory system with respect to its cleaning supplies. A year-end stock-take has identified a balance of £4,200 cleaning supplies held on 31st December 20X1. The cleaning supplies stock account, which has not been adjusted since the previous year-end stock-take, reflects a debit balance of £3,400. Throughout the year, all cleaning supplies purchased have been debited to the "cleaning supplies purchases" account, which has a closing debit balance of £36,000. In addition, any returns to suppliers have been credited to a "cleaning supplies returns" account, which has a year-end closing balance of £1,020.

Required:
Using appropriately titled "T-accounts", make all required adjusting and closing entries.

Problem 4.7

The accounting manager at Antwerp's TranquilStay Hotel has prepared the following income statement that pertains to the most recent accounting year.

TranquilStay Hotel
Income Statement
for the year-ended 30 June 20X1

	€	€
Sales revenue		420,000
Less: Cost of sales		80,000
Gross profit		340,000
Add: Interest revenue		11,000
		351,000

Less: Expenses
Salaries and wages expense	145,000	
Depreciation expense	82,000	
Car park rental expense	3,000	
Insurance expense	18,000	
Sundry expense	14,000	
		262,000
		€ 89,000

The accounting manager is uncertain how to handle year-end adjusting entries and has sought your advice. Following a review of the business, you determine the following:

1. A €2,500 advance payment received in connection with a conference to be held in late July has been included in the sales revenue figure.
2. Employees have not been paid €4,000 in wages and salaries earned in the last four days of June.
3. Depreciation of €10,000 on a new car purchased this year has not been recorded.
4. The hotel rents a small adjoining property which it uses for patrons' car parking whenever the hotel's underground car park is full. The last rental fee paid was €900. This payment was made on 1st May and covered a three-month period. The account manager recorded this as prepaid rent and no entry has been made to adjust this account at the year-end.
5. The hotel holds an investment that earns €1,000 interest per month. June's interest, which will be received in July, has not been recorded in the accounts.
6. Annual property insurance of €24,000 is paid semi-annually in advance. The last €12,000 payment, which was made on 1st April 20X1 was debited to prepaid insurance. No adjusting entry to the prepaid insurance account has been made.

Required:

a) Prepare the necessary adjusting entries for the TranquilStay Hotel.
b) Following completion of the adjusting entries, prepare TranquilStay's revised income statement for the year-ending 30th June 20X1.

Problem 4.8

Given the following information for Ottawa's Capital Hotel, prepare relevant adjusting entries. Assume that 30th June is the year-end.

a) On 1st June the hotel received $4,000 in advance for services to be rendered. This transaction was recorded on 1st June by debiting bank and crediting unearned service revenue. It was determined that by 30th June, 25 per cent of the service paid for had been provided.
b) On 1st May six months' insurance premium was purchased for $1,800. When the payment was made, the hotel debited prepaid insurance and credited bank.
c) The hotel has an investment that is earning a return of $2,400 interest per annum. The last interest payment was received on 30th April. The accounting records need to be adjusted to reflect the last two months of interest accrued.
d) In the current financial year, the hotel's supplies account had an opening balance of $600. $7,000 of supplies have been purchased during the year and debited to the supplies account. A year-end stock-take has revealed $400 of supplies in stock. During the year no accounting entries reflective of supplies usage have been made.

Problem 4.9

Given the following year-end account balances for Boston's Johnson Hotel, prepare:

a) an income statement for the period ended 30/6/20X1,
b) a balance sheet as at 30/6/20X1.

Johnson Hotel
Account Balances
as at 30th June 20X1

	Debit	Credit
Cash at bank	2,200	
Dividends paid	2,000	
Accounts receivable	1,500	
Closing inventory	400	
Depreciation expense	250	
Plant and machinery	11,000	
Accumulated depreciation		1,020
Sales revenue		26,500
Cost of sales	16,000	
Wage expense	4,500	
General operating expenses	140	
Accrued wages		100
Accounts payable		2,200
Unearned revenue		200
Share capital		4,800
Retained profits		3,170
	$37,990	$37,990

Problem 4.10

Match each of the following eight year-end adjustments with the appropriate year-end adjusting journal entry.

Year end adjustments

1. An expense has been incurred but not yet paid.
2. A $5,000 deposit for a conference to commence in two weeks' time has been received. At the time the deposit was received, cash was debited and revenue was credited.
3. A bus insurance payment was expensed during the year, but at the end of the year there is still a period of insurance cover that has not been used up.
4. A car insurance payment was recorded by debiting insurance prepaid during the year, but at the end of the year there is still a period of insurance cover that has not been used up.
5. Some revenue appears to be unearned at the year end.
6. A new fixed asset purchased at the beginning of the year was accounted for by debiting the fixed asset accounting and crediting the cash account.
7. A portion of rent for a large land parcel was paid in advance three weeks before the year end, but has not been used up at the year end. When the rent was paid by the hotel, the accountant debited rent expense and credited cash.

8. Rent for a smaller land parcel has not been paid by the hotel and is owing at the year-end.

Year-end journal entries

    a. Debit revenue, credit unearned revenue.
    b. Debit depreciation expense, credit accumulated depreciation.
    c. Debit rent expense, credit rent payable.
    d. Debit expense, credit expense payable.
    e. Debit prepaid insurance, credit insurance expense.
    f. Debit prepaid rent, credit rent expense.
    g. Debit revenue, credit unearned revenue.
    h. Debit insurance expense, credit insurance prepaid.

Problem 4.11

Prior to making year-end adjusting entries, the accountant at Hong Kong's KowloonKingdom hotel has produced the following abbreviated income statement for the most recent financial year.

KowloonKingdom Hotel Income statement for the year ending 31st December 20X1	
Revenue	$346,000
Less: Operating expenses	102,000
Net profit	244,000

Information for adjusting entries:

1. Depreciation of $42,000 has yet to be charged.
2. Accrued wages at the year-end are $3,200.
3. The hotel hosted an engineers' conference that concluded three days before the year-end. At the year-end, the hotel had still to invoice the conference organiser for the final $13,000 conference instalment payment.
4. The hotel will be holding an accountants' conference commencing two weeks after the year-end. At the year-end, the hotel had received a deposit of $5,000 from the conference organiser and recorded it as revenue.
5. The hotel's annual property insurance policy was renewed on 1st April 20X1 with a premium payment of $4,000. This payment was recorded by debiting insurance prepaid.
6. The kitchen cleaning supplies account is maintained on a periodic inventory basis. At the beginning of the year, the supplies account had a $1,100 debit balance. During the year, $5,400 of cleaning supplies were purchased and a year-end stock-take determined a cleaning supplies balance of $800.

Required:

a) Prepare a schedule showing the impact on revenue and operating expenses resulting from preparation of the required year-end adjusting entries.
b) Prepare a revised abbreviated income statement, as it would appear following the completion of the adjusting entries.

Problem 4.12

Prior to making adjusting entries, the Tewkesbury Kings Arms pub and guest house manager has provided you with the following financial year-end information:

1. Wages owing at the year end are £340.
2. Rent of £580, covering a two-month period was paid one month before the year-end. When the rent was paid the rent expense account was debited £580.
3. £212 of interest revenue owed to the pub has not been received or recorded.
4. The £880 prepaid insurance account balance includes $340 of insurance premium paid to provide insurance cover for the first four months of the next financial year.

Required:

a) Prepare the year end adjusting entries for the Kings Arms pub and guest house.
b) If the adjusting entries were not made, demonstrate whether the Kings Arms pub and guest house profit would be understated or overstated.
c) If the adjusting entries were not made, indicate the effect on the assets, liabilities and owners' equity sections of the Kings Arms pub and guest house's balance sheet.

Chapter 5

Financial statement analysis

Learning objectives

After studying this chapter, you should have developed an appreciation of:

1. how insights can be gained from dissecting ROI (return on investment) into its two underlying elements: profit margin and asset turnover,
2. how a systematic analysis of a hotel's profit performance can be conducted through the use of ratios,
3. how an analysis of a hotel's short-term and long-term financial stability can be achieved through ratio analysis,
4. how operational ratios can be used as an aid to monitoring the operating performance of hotels,
5. how an aged schedule of accounts receivable can assist the management of receivables,
6. how it is important that an analyst develops the ability to tailor ratios with due regard to the nature of the hotel under investigation.

1) Introduction

This chapter moves us closer to management accounting and financial management as it focuses on techniques that can be used to analyse the financial performance and stability of organisations. Much of the analysis can be conducted through the use of ratios, e.g., return on investment (ROI tells us the **ratio** of return to investment), and, as a consequence, we frequently refer to "**ratio analysis**" in a manner synonymous to financial statement analysis.

The results of a ratio analysis convey limited information unless they are put into some context, however. Ratio analyses are most usually conducted in the context of a comparison to one or more of the following four benchmarks:

- a hotel's ratios from prior years (a trend analysis);
- ratios that have been set as goals (i.e., ratios underlying a hotel's budget);
- ratios achieved by other hotels (or divisions) in the same company;
- industry average ratios compiled by companies such as *Dun and Bradstreet* and the large accounting firms (this type of benchmarking is sometimes referred to as a cross-sectional analysis).

In this chapter's description of a systematic approach to conducting a financial analysis of the year-end accounts, two distinct perspectives will be taken:

● Firstly, we will see how the **profit performance** of a company can be appraised.
● Secondly, we will see how to appraise the **financial stability** of a company.

We will conduct these analyses by drawing on the year-end financial statements of Melbourne's Celestial Hotel Ltd. These statements are presented in Exhibits 5.1 and 5.2.

Following this overview of a financially oriented analysis, the chapter will review the main ratios used to analyse a hotel's operational performance. Operational ratios focus more on day-to-day operating issues, e.g., room occupancy levels, restaurant covers served per employee hour worked, etc. Although many operational ratios do not involve financial measures, they represent important performance indicators as a strong operating performance is a precursor to a strong financial performance.

2) Profit performance

If you were to ask an investor how their investment portfolio performed in a particular year, they would likely answer by referring to their overall return on investment (ROI). This casual observation is important as it highlights the degree to which ROI represents a fundamental indicator of performance. If limited to one ratio in an appraisal of a company's performance, a financial analyst would most likely use ROI.

Exhibit 5.1

Celestial Hotel Ltd
Income statement for the year ending 31/12/20X1

	$'000	$'000
Revenue (60% of sales on credit)		100
less Cost of Sales		40
Gross Profit		60
less Expenses		
Selling	15	
General Administration	5	
		20
Earnings (profit) before interest and tax (EBIT)		40
less Interest		10
Taxable profit		30
less Taxation		15
Net Income after Tax		$ 15

Exhibit 5.2

Celestial Hotel Ltd
Balance sheet as at 31/12/20X1

Assets	$'000	$'000
Current Assets		
Cash	5	
Accounts receivable	7	
Inventory	8	
		20
Fixed Assets		
Equipment	10	
Buildings	20	
		30
Total Assets		$ 50
	$'000	$'000
Liabilities		
Current liabilities		
Accrued wages	1	
Accounts payable	4	
		5
Long-term liabilities		
Loans		15
Total Liabilities		20
Owners' Equity		
Paid up capital (100,000 shares)	20	
Retained profits[1]	10	
		30
Total Liabilities and Owners' Equity		$ 50

1 The company must have started 20X1 with an accumulated loss of $5,000 (i.e., a negative retained profit account). This is apparent from the fact that the income statement for 20X1 indicates profit earned and retained during 20X1 to be $15,000, yet the retained profit at the end of the year is only $10,000 (from the information provided, it appears no dividends were declared for 20X1). Much can be gleaned from a careful review of the accounts!

In the analysis of profit performance that follows, we will take a systematic approach by first computing ROI and then dissecting it into its underlying components. The perspective of appraising a hotel management's performance in generating a return (profit) from the assets available will be taken. This signifies that EBIT (earnings before interest and tax) is the appropriate profit level to focus on. This is because EBIT captures the operating performance of a hotel, as interest expense (the first item appearing after EBIT in the income statement) relates to a financing decision which is frequently outside the influence of the hotel general manager. Accordingly, we will calculate ROI in the following way:

$$\textit{Return on investment (ROI)} = EBIT \div Total\ assets$$

Celestial's 20X1 ROI = 40 ÷ 50 = 0.8 (or 80%)

This 80 per cent ROI can be broken into two elements (a profit margin and a turnover component) as illustrated in Exhibit 5.3.

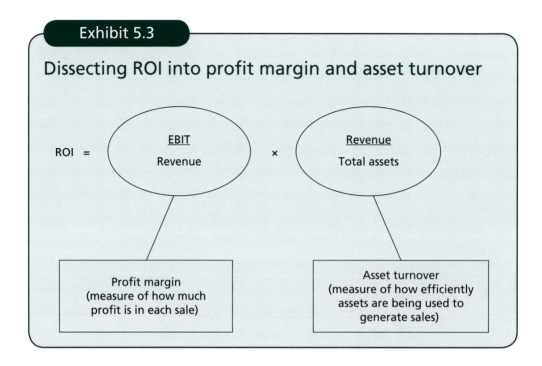

Exhibit 5.3

Dissecting ROI into profit margin and asset turnover

$$\text{ROI} = \frac{\text{EBIT}}{\text{Revenue}} \times \frac{\text{Revenue}}{\text{Total assets}}$$

Profit margin (measure of how much profit is in each sale)

Asset turnover (measure of how efficiently assets are being used to generate sales)

The equation in Exhibit 5.3 can be verified very simply by cancelling "revenue" in the left-hand circle (or profit margin component) with "revenue" in the right-hand circle (or asset turnover component) to leave us with the basic ROI formula (EBIT ÷ Total assets).

This dissection of ROI into the two underlying ratios is widely referred to as the "Dupont formula" (the formula was first observed in use in the Dupont company in the USA). The Dupont formula is highly significant as it provides the basis for a systematic analysis of ROI under two headings:

a) profit margin
b) asset turnover.

a) Profit margin

Following our first step in the ratio analysis, we found Celestial's ROI to be 80 per cent. While this may appear to represent a healthy return, imagine it is down from last year's figure of 85 per cent. Management would want to know what lies behind this decline. By using the Dupont formula, we can determine whether the decline stems from a decrease in the company's profit margin or its asset turnover (or a combination of both). If the profit margin is down from last year, we can work systematically through the income statement, picking up all profit figures provided and comparing them to revenue. In the Celestial example, the first profit figure in the income statement is gross profit. Paralleling the approach taken to compute profit margin in Exhibit 5.3, we compute gross profit margin (GPM) as follows:

$$Gross\ profit\ margin\ (GPM) = Gross\ profit \div Revenue$$

$$Celestial's\ 20X1\ GPM = 60 \div 100 = 0.6\ (or\ 60\%)$$

If this 60 per cent GPM is similar to last year's GPM, we would be able to conclude that the lower overall margin has not resulted from a change in the ratio of selling price to cost of sales. It would be apparent that the decline in the ratio of EBIT to revenue must have resulted from a relative increase in selling and general administration costs, as these represent the two expense categories appearing after gross profit, but before EBIT, in the income statement. By taking this approach of progressively moving down the income statement, comparing every level of reported profit to revenue, we are able to isolate the category of expense that has caused a change in the overall profit margin. If we had originally used net profit margin (net profit after tax ÷ revenue) in the ROI computed above, we could have computed more profit margins in the course of systematically progressing through the income statement. Published accounts of large companies generally provide data sufficient to allow the calculation of several profit margins.

b) Asset turnover

Returning to the Dupont formula in Exhibit 5.3, now imagine that we have noted that a decline in the total asset turnover ratio has occurred and that this decline lies behind the lower ROI. This observation would lead the analyst to look into those ratios that feed in to the total asset turnover ratio.

Similar to the approach of working systematically through the income statement when exploring for factors resulting in a changed profit margin, we can work through the balance sheet looking for that group of assets that lie behind a changed asset turnover ratio.

Whenever the term "turnover" is used, it signifies we are comparing an asset to revenue (or, in the case of inventory, cost of sales). Consistent with the total asset turnover ratio computed above as part of the Dupont formula, for each turnover ratio we divide revenue (or, in the case of inventory, cost of sales) by the particular asset grouping under investigation.

Each "turnover" ratio tells us how "hard" the particular asset has "worked" to generate revenue. For this reason, the turnover ratios are frequently referred to as "efficiency" ratios. Widely computed "turnover" ratios include:

- accounts receivable turnover
- inventory turnover
- fixed asset turnover.

Accounts receivable turnover

$$Accounts\ receivable\ turnover = Credit\ sales \div Accounts\ receivable$$

$$Celestial's\ 20X1\ A.R.\ turnover = (100 \times 0.6) \div 7 = 8.57$$

Many managers find it difficult to conceptualise the meaning of the 8.57 computed above. For this reason the information is commonly converted into "number of days" by dividing the number of days in a year by the turnover.

$$\frac{Average\ number\ of\ days\ to}{collect\ accounts\ receivable} = \frac{365}{A.R.\ turnover}$$

$$\text{Celestial's average number of days to collect accounts receivable} = \frac{365}{8.57} = 42.6 \text{ days}$$

If the accounts receivable turnover ratio is decreasing, the average number of days to collect accounts receivable will be increasing.

Inventory turnover

Calculation of inventory turnover and also the "number of days inventory held" parallel the approach just taken for accounts receivable. There is one key difference, however. Unlike all the other "turnover" ratios, we divide inventory into cost of sales and not revenue. The reason for this difference is that inventory is recorded at cost price and not selling price. If we were to compare inventory to revenue and during the year selling prices doubled, we would see the inventory turnover ratio computed also double. The doubling of the ratio would be the result of a changed selling price and not a changed stocking policy, however. The potential for this misinterpretation is avoided if we compute inventory turnover using a consistent valuation basis, i.e., cost for the denominator (inventory) and cost for the numerator (cost of sales).

Inventory turnover = Cost of sales ÷ Inventory

Celestial's 20X1 inventory turnover = 40 ÷ 8 = 5

Similar to accounts receivable turnover, inventory turnover can be converted into a measure of the average number of days that inventory is held by dividing 365 by the inventory turnover.

$$\text{Celestial's average number of days inventory held} = \frac{365}{5} = 73 \text{ days}$$

When analysing a hotel's inventory turnover performance, it is desirable that beverage inventory be treated separately from the inventory of food supplies. This is because there might be differing stocking policies in the two areas. Drawing this distinction is particularly important where different personnel exercise stock making decisions in the two areas. Failure to distinguish between the two types of inventory might mask the existence of a low turnover in one area if there is a high turnover in the other area.

Fixed asset turnover

Fixed asset turnover = Revenue ÷ Fixed assets

Celestial's 20X1 fixed asset turnover = 100 ÷ 30 = 3.33

Fixed asset account balances do not tend to be as volatile as accounts receivable and inventory account balances. Nevertheless, due to the large relative size of fixed assets in hotels, a small percentage movement can have a significant impact on total asset turnover. The large investment in fixed assets can warrant the calculation of a turnover figure for every fixed asset sub-category identified, if such further information is available, i.e., in the Celestial example we could have computed a turnover figure for equipment as well as buildings.

General comments on turnover ratios

Except for cash, we have now computed the turnover ratio for each asset in Celestial's balance sheet. If we had noted a decline in total asset turnover, and had subsequently discovered that none of the turnovers computed above had declined, then there must have been a decrease in the ratio of revenue to cash. Consistent with the other ratios, we could compute a "cash turnover ratio" by dividing "revenue" by "cash". Due to the relatively small nature of the cash account, however, this ratio is seldom calculated. If we found that the problem lay in a declining cash turnover ratio, we would know that relative to revenue, the business is now holding more cash. We would then need to turn to question whether this development is desirable.

While it might appear from Exhibit 5.3 that we would like to see increasing turnover ratios (a higher asset turnover will increase ROI), the downside implication of turnover ratios becoming too high should also be appreciated. If inventory turnover becomes very high, we might experience stock-outs, which could result in lost sales and loss of customer goodwill. If the accounts receivable turnover increases, we are on average extending less credit to our customers. If other hotels are extending longer periods of credit, this could result in the loss of some sales.

In the worked example presented above, we took year-end balances of the asset accounts when computing the turnover ratios. A preferred approach, however, would be to take the average balance of the asset account throughout the year. It could be that the year-end inventory balance is at an all-time temporary low and that Celestial normally holds twice this amount of inventory. If this is the case, the turnover computed will be a poor reflection of reality, i.e., the inventory holding period computed will be half the year's average holding time for inventory. If the asset in question is subject to high seasonal volatility, the average asset balance throughout the year should be sought. This could be done by calculating the average of the 12-month end balances for the year. While using an average asset balance provides a better picture of the asset's average turnover over the whole year, a new inventory manager who has been in place for only three months would be justified in arguing that her inventory turnover performance should be assessed by appraising average inventory balances since she took up her position, and not inventory balances recorded in advance of her job commencement. The same rationale would apply to a recently recruited credit manager.

The problem of defining ROI

It can be confusing trying to "tie down" ROI. It is a generic term that is tailored to many different situations, e.g., it could be used in the sense of the interest rate you earn on a bank account, or the net after tax return made on a portfolio of shares. Its exact calculation depends on the perspective being taken in an analysis. The following is an inexhaustive list of types of ROI that can be used to assess a company's performance:

- return on assets employed
- return on assets available
- return on long-term funds
- return on equity.

"Assets employed", "assets available", "long-term funds" and "equity" are all types of investment. If we wish to judge the performance of a manager who has been placed in charge of a group of assets that include some assets which, for some reason, he cannot currently employ (maybe rooms undergoing refurbishment), we might like to compare EBIT to assets employed and not assets available. If we take a shareholder's perspective, we might like to compare net profit after tax to shareholder's equity. It can thus be seen that **the definition of return and the definition of investment is dependent on the context in which the analysis is being made.**

A review of how profit margin ratios and asset turnover ratios both feed into the ROI ratio is provided in Financial decision making in action case 5.1.

FINANCIAL DECISION MAKING IN ACTION CASE 5.1

The Financial Controller and analysing ROI

The General Manager of the BeauChandelier restaurant chain is preparing for next month's year-end meeting with senior staff. He wishes to commend the staff on a great year as the hotel's ROI (EBIT ÷ Assets × 100) has increased by 38 per cent over the year from 39 per cent in the previous financial year to 64 per cent in the current year. The General Manager has a background in marketing and has never felt particularly comfortable interpreting financial data. Not wishing to appear ill-informed at the meeting he asked the Financial Controller to quickly prepare a more detailed financial analysis that will point to what aspects of the business's operations lie behind the increased ROI.

The following day the Financial Controller sent the following email to the General Manager:

Hi Sam
I've completed the following financial analysis of our ROI performance over the last two years. The key data are as follows:

	This year	*Last year*
ROI (EBIT ÷ Assets × 100)	64%	39%
Gross profit margin (Gross profit ÷ Sales × 100)	55%	40%
Operating profit margin (EBIT ÷ Sales × 100)	35%	23%
Accounts receivable turnover (Credit Sales ÷ Average Accounts Receivable)	12.5	14.3
Inventory turnover (Cost of sales ÷ Average inventory)	6.5	4
Fixed Asset turnover (Sales ÷ Fixed assets)	2.95	3.22

To understand ROI you need to know that two key things feed into it: profit margin (which is the ratio of profit to revenue) and asset turnover (computed by dividing revenue by assets).

Based on our data for the year, I can see that both profit margin and asset turnover have improved. Both improvements have had a positive impact on our ROI.

Firstly, with respect to profit margin, the key result is our 37.5 per cent increased gross profit margin. As this ratio compares gross profit to sales, we are really looking at the relationship between the cost of goods sold and revenue, as gross profit equals revenue minus the cost of goods sold. I've done some further digging around and can confirm that last year our cost of goods sold consumed 60 per cent of our revenue and this year it has consumed only 45 per cent of revenue. Most of the change in the operating profit margin that you see (23 per cent to 35 per cent) is down to the improved gross profit margin, so don't get too drawn into the change in that ratio. The change in the gross profit margin shows that the discounted deal that you struck with our new main food supplier at the end of last year was clearly a master stroke. It's pushed up the profit to sales element that feeds into ROI.

Secondly, with respect to asset turnover, the big change to note is the increase in our inventory turnover. We've gone from holding inventory for an average of 91.25 days (365 ÷ 4) to holding it for 56.15 days (365 ÷ 6.5), which represents a 38.5 per cent improvement. The quicker and more reliable shipments from that new supplier has helped us get by with less inventory. This has pushed up the revenue to assets element that feeds into ROI.

The other sales to assets ratio changes that you can see (12.6 per cent decline in accounts receivable turnover and an 8.4 per cent decline in fixed asset turnover) are pretty small relative to our improved inventory turnover performance.
Cheers
Ray

3) Financial stability

Analysis of financial stability (sometimes referred to as solvency, i.e., the ability to repay liabilities as they fall due) can be broken into short-term and long-term perspectives.

a) Short-term

Appraisal of a company's short-term financial stability is sometimes referred to as a "liquidity analysis". Analysis of liquidity concerns assets that in the normal course of business will be converted to cash, sold or consumed within a year (current assets) and also liabilities that are due for payment within a year (current liabilities). One indicator of liquidity is "working capital" (current assets – current liabilities), however, this indicator does not provide a sound basis for comparison across companies of varying sizes. More widely advocated measures of liquidity are the current asset ratio and the quick asset ratio (sometimes called the "acid test ratio"). The current asset ratio is calculated as follows:

$$\textit{Current asset ratio} = \textit{Current assets} \div \textit{Current Liabilities}$$

Celestial's current asset ratio as at 31/12/X1 = 20 ÷ 5 = 4

This signifies that Celestial's "close to cash" assets cover its liabilities that will fall due for payment in the next 12 months by 4 times. This suggests a highly liquid situation.

If inventory is held for some time in the business prior to conversion to cash, a case can be made for its exclusion from current assets. This approach is taken in the acid test ratio, a liquidity measure which also excludes prepaid expenses from current assets. Prepaid expenses are excluded because in the normal course of business they will not be converted to cash. The acid test ratio is calculated as follows:

$$\frac{\textit{Acid test}}{\textit{ratio}} = \frac{\textit{Current assets} - \textit{Inventory} - \textit{Prepaids}}{\textit{Current liabilities}}$$

Celestial's acid test ratio as at 31/12/X1 = 12 ÷ 5 = 2.4

In the hotel sector, due to the relatively "liquid" nature of most inventory, it is usual to base an appraisal of short-term liquidity on the current ratio rather than the acid test ratio. If a hotel had a large inventory of slow-moving wine, however, it would be appropriate to calculate a tailored liquidity ratio by deducting the wine inventory from current assets. Tailoring ratios in this manner can be justified if they result in a more accurate insight into the particular aspect of the company that is under investigation.

While we would certainly be concerned to see the current ratio or the acid test ratio fall below "1", it is difficult to provide an optimal current or acid test ratio. Much will depend on hotel-specific factors. A lender to the hotel would like to see high liquidity ratios as this would indicate a high ability to pay short-term debts. In fact, some lenders seek to protect themselves by requiring the borrower to maintain liquidity indicators, such as the current ratio, above a certain level. A loan provision can be drafted to this effect, and if the borrower's current ratio falls below what is stipulated in the loan provision, the lender can require the borrower to immediately repay the loan. If a business experiences liquidity problems, a variety of rectification options can be considered. For instance:

- Some fixed assets could be sold, maybe under a sale and lease-back agreement (increase to cash, no effect on current liabilities).
- A long-term loan could be sought (increase to cash, no effect on current liabilities).
- Further equity could be sought (increase to cash, no effect on current liabilities).

Caution needs to be exercised in liquidity management, however, as high liquidity ratios do not signify astute management. High liquidity ratios signify sub-optimal use of funds, as funds invested in short-term assets do not provide a high rate of return to owners. If funds can be freed up from current assets, greater investment can be made in long-term assets which can be seen to represent the engine room from which owners derive profits. Further discussion of working capital management issues is provided in Chapter 13.

b) Long-term

Over the long term we are concerned with a firm's ability to pay all its debts, not merely short-term debt.

c) Contribution pricing

Contribution pricing is a particular type of cost plus pricing where a mark up is attached to a service or product's variable cost. While contribution pricing can be applied in the rooms, restaurant and bar areas, it will be explored here in the context of conference and banqueting operations. Applying contribution pricing in this area is particularly appropriate due to the fact that it is relatively easy to identify the variable costs associated with hosting conferences and banquets (i.e., the cost of additional refreshments and covers served). In addition, contribution management can provide a useful perspective on conference and banquet price decision making during periods of excess capacity (i.e., during a period of low demand for conferences).

Contribution pricing allows the conference manager to determine what is the lowest price that can be charged while ensuring a positive contribution towards profit results from hosting the conference. Such an aggressive pricing policy might be particularly pertinent during a period of excess capacity if any of the following applies:

a) Competitors are very aggressively pricing their conference facilities,
b) Hosting a conference results in the hotel increasing profits earned in other areas, e.g., the rooms and F&B departments,
c) hosting a particular conference carries the potential of stimulating further conference sales in the future.

Box 12.4

Applying contribution pricing

Imagine a European conference organiser has approached a Munich hotel in connection with a proposed conference to be attended by approximately 200 delegates (the organiser estimates an attendance of not less than 150 and not more than 250 delegates). If a price quotation is being sought where the organiser has confirmed an attendance of exactly 200 attendees, the variable cost can be calculated at the level of the total conference as follows:

Variable cost for hosting conference with 200 attendees

	€
Morning refreshments (€1 per person × 200 attendees)	200
Lunch (€5 per person × 200 attendees)	1,000
Afternoon tea (€1 per person × 200 attendees)	200
Cost of 2 additional casual staff	300
Total variable cost for conference	**€1,700**

If, however, the conference organiser is seeking a quotation on a "per attendee" basis, the variable cost analysis would have to be modified, as the cost of additional casual staff does not vary according to the number of attendees (it is assumed that the two additional casual staff would be required regardless of whether there are 150 or 250 attendees). The cost of two casual staff therefore represents an incremental cost of the conference, but a fixed cost in terms of the number of attendees.

Variable cost per attendee attending proposed conference

	€
Morning refreshments (€1 per person × 200 attendees)	1
Lunch (€5 per person × 200 attendees)	5
Afternoon tea (€1 per person × 200 attendees)	1
Total variable cost per attendee	**€7**

In variable costing, it is generally claimed that so long as a price is charged that exceeds variable cost, a positive contribution towards profit results. In this case, the variable cost analysis conducted at the "per attendee" level has resulted in the exclusion of casual labour. As the two additional casual staff represent an incremental cost of holding the conference, if pricing is based on the above "per attendee" analysis, an additional mark up would have to be included to cover the incremental cost of casual staff.

From the example in Box 12.4, it is apparent that the unit of analysis affects the way that we look at variable cost (i.e., in this example we have conducted the analysis at the level of the whole conference as well as the individual attendee level). While this aggressive approach to pricing can be justified in the short term (in order to utilise capacity that would otherwise be idle), or on the basis of one or more of the three factors outlined above, it should be noted that it should not be viewed as a long-term pricing strategy. Over the long term, fixed as well as variable costs have to be covered if a profit is to result. Despite this, a justification could be made for running conferences at a price that results in a loss to the conference department, if increased conference activity has a positive impact on the hotel's overall profitability due to increased F&B and room sales.

4) Summary

Due to the subject matter of this book, the pricing approaches outlined in this chapter have a financial orientation. As noted in the introduction, the provision of accurate financial information is imperative in a price sensitive industry such as the hospitality industry. This price sensitivity has doubtlessly resulted in some managers, uninformed by an appropriate financial analysis, setting prices below cost. The significance of cost information for pricing becomes particularly apparent when we recognise that setting prices below variable cost means that the more we sell, the more we lose. We should nevertheless remind ourselves that provision of costing information is only part of the management information required for well-informed pricing setting. Marketing factors, which can include issues such as competitor pricing, image sought, the possibility of loss-leader pricing etc., also need to be considered when formulating a pricing strategy.

In this chapter we have reviewed how factors such as perishability affect pricing policy. We have also seen how "cost plus" pricing approaches can be used in the context of F&B. Due to the high fixed cost structure associated with the provision of accommodation, room pricing is slightly more complicated. Several approaches to setting room rates, including basing prices on room size and a required rate of return, were reviewed. In addition, the importance of revenue management was described in the context of a hotel's sales and marketing function.

Having read the chapter you should now know:

- the meaning of the price elasticity of demand and the significance of product and service perishability when approaching pricing decisions,
- how a "cost-plus" approach can be used in F&B pricing,
- how to apply the "rule of a thousand" when setting room rates,
- how to apply the "relative room size" approach to setting room rates,
- how to apply the required rate of return approach to setting room rates,
- what is meant by revenue management,
- the importance of maintaining a positive contribution margin (i.e., covering variable cost) when discounting prices.

References

Adams, D. (2006) *Management Accounting for the Hospitality, Tourism and Leisure Industries: A Strategic Approach*, 2nd edition, London: Thomson: Chapter 5.

Harris, P. (1999) *Profit Planning*, 2nd edition, Oxford: Butterworth Heinemann: Chapter 6.

Jagels, M.G. (2007) *Hospitality Management Accounting*, 9th edition, Hoboken, NJ: John Wiley & Sons: Chapter 6.

Kotas, R. (1999) *Management Accounting for Hospitality and Tourism*, 3rd edition, International Thomson Publishing: Chapter 8.

Schmidgall, R.F. (2011) *Hospitality Industry Managerial Accounting*, 7th edition, East Lansing, MI: American Hotel & Lodging Educational Institute: Chapter 8.

Problems

Problem 12.1

Describe the difference between a contribution pricing philosophy and a revenue management pricing philosophy.

Problem 12.2

a) Using an example, explain what is meant by perishability when talking about a product or service.
b) Why is perishability a key concept when approaching price making decisions?

Problem 12.3

Aberdeen's Thrifty hotel has 40 rooms and has historically achieved an average occupancy of 55 per cent. The hotel's assets have a book value of £450,000 and the owners believe the assets should generate a 15 per cent return after tax. Assume tax is charged at the rate of 50 per cent.

The hotel has several fixed costs, these include 9 per cent interest charged on a £250,000 bank loan, £40,000 of equipment and fittings depreciation and other fixed costs of £65,000 per year.

The hotel's manager believes that the 55 per cent occupancy level will again be achieved next year, and estimates that this level of activity will result in £85,000 of operating expenses.

Required:
Assuming the hotel is open 365 days per year, calculate the room rate that should be charged in order to provide the owners with their target profit level.

Problem 12.4

The rooms manager of a new 90-room hotel in Texas has approached you seeking advice on what room rates should be charged. The hotel, which will be open for 365 days of the year, has the following three types of room:

Number of rooms	Type	Size
30	Economy	60 sq. meters
30	Double	80 sq. meters
30	Deluxe	110 sq. meters

The hotel's balance sheet indicates that $18,000,000 has been invested in the building. Thirty per cent of the building is dedicated to non-accommodation activities such as F&B.

Required:

a) According to the "rule of a thousand" approach ($1 charge for each $1 invested), what should be the average room rate charged.
b) Assume the rooms manager projects that each room type will achieve a 70 per cent occupancy level. If the hotel is seeking to achieve a total revenue of $3,066,000 from rooms next year and wishes to set room rates based on size, what rate should the hotel charge for each of its rooms?

Problem 12.5

The following information relates to a family-owned Adelaide restaurant:

Manager's salary:	$55,000 p.a.
Interest:	Loan of $100,000 is outstanding; 8 per cent annual interest rate.
Depreciation:	Equipment and furniture with book value of $120,000 is being depreciated at 25 per cent of book value.
Licence:	$5,000 p.a.
Insurance:	$6,000 p.a.
Maintenance:	$4,000 p.a.
Other salaries:	$28,000 p.a.
Variable costs:	75 per cent of revenue
Before tax operating profit target:	50 per cent of owners' investment of $120,000

Required:

a) What sales revenue does the restaurant have to achieve in order to make its before tax operating profit target?

b) The restaurant is closed for three weeks each year. In the remainder of the year (assume 49 weeks) it opens every day except Mondays. The restaurant has 50 seats, and averages a seat turnover of 2 times per day in the week and 3 times per day on Saturdays and Sundays. What must the average cover price be in order to achieve the target profit level?

Problem 12.6

The manager responsible for pricing merchandise in a souvenir shop located in the foyer of a hotel is discussing pricing strategy with a shop assistant. The two have agreed on a policy of aggressively pricing a specific set of items. When discussing pricing, the shop assistant is used to talking of marking up cost by a specific percentage. The manager, however, is more familiar with referring to "gross profit margin", a term which tends to be used at management meetings in the hotel. The assistant has indicated that based on her experience in other merchandising situations, the minimum acceptable cost mark up is 25 per cent. Following discussions at the most recent monthly management meeting, the manager feels that a gross profit margin of 20 per cent is acceptable for loss leader items. The manager realises, however, that h   different terminology to that used by the assistant. As a result of this he has decid   lifference between "per cent cost mark

Requ
Thro   iether a 25 per cent cost mark up
result   .

Prol

Ham   over of 5 while charging $40 per
cove   The chef is considering increasing
the   this will reduce the Sunday seat
turne

Requ
For   ll you can eat" Sunday special is
price

Pro

Bris   an aid to determining what prices
to c   ngs of a recent analysis of the cost
of t   . The restaurant has a policy of
mar

Ingredient	£ Cost
Beef	1.68
Potatoes	0.24
Carrots	0.16
Peas	0.14
Sprouts	0.20
Yorkshire pudding	0.10
Total	£2.52

Required:

a) What price should the restaurant charge for the roast beef dinner if it wishes to achieve a mark up multiple of 8.

b) The restaurant is considering taking a simpler approach to its mark up calculations of menu items. Under this simplified approach, only the main ingredient of each meal will be costed and price will be determined by using a revised cost mark up multiple. If the restaurant wishes to earn the same level of profitability from its roast beef dinner, what mark up multiple should it attach to the cost of the main ingredient?

Problem 12.9

Quebec's BonVivant hotel has 200 rooms. It sets its room rates according to a policy of charging $120 per night to business clients and $90 per night for group bookings. It has found that most guests stay for three nights. A manager is attempting to determine whether a four week advance reservation should be made for a group of 40 seeking accommodation on the nights of 20th, 21st and 22nd June. 80 rooms for these three nights have already been booked by business clients and past purchasing patterns suggest that, subject to availability, 90 per cent of the remaining 120 rooms will also be sold to business clients.

Required:
Determine whether it is in the hotel's interest to accept the group booking for the party of 40.

Problem 12.10

The 140-room PyramidsPlaza has just been constructed adjacent to the site of a forthcoming world Expo in Cairo. A significant return on investment is expected to be earned by the hotel once the Expo opens, however the General Manager is seeking to make a profit in the intervening years. The General Manager has estimated the following operating costs in the next year:

Variable operating costs	£6 per room sold
Fixed costs:	
Salaries and wages	£350,000
Maintenance	74,000
Other costs	280,000
Total fixed costs	£704,000

The General Manager believes that if rooms are priced in the range of £42 to £48, 32,000 room nights will be sold next year. All rooms are to be priced at the same rate. Capital invested in the hotel is £1,920,000 and the General Manager's target return on investment is 30 per cent.

Required:

a) In order to achieve the 30 per cent target ROI, what price should be charged per room?
b) If the room rate was to be set at £50 per night, how many nights accommodation would have to be sold in order to breakeven?

Problem 12.11

The 200-room Hotel PoshPlace is soon to open in Perth, Australia. It is projected that the hotel will be financed with a loan of $6,000,000 at 12 per cent annual interest, and the owners will invest $2,000,000. The owners will be seeking a 15 per cent annual return on their investment. The hotel will be open 365 days per year and it is expected that it will achieve a 70 per cent average occupancy. Hotel profits will be taxed at the rate of 40 per cent.

Hotel fixed costs are expected to be:

Insurance	$180,000
Depreciation	200,000
Administration	150,000
Information systems	100,000
Human resources	50,000
Marketing expenses	140,000
Property maintenance	200,000
	$1,020,000

It is estimated that the hotel's food and beverage department will generate an annual profit of $150,000 and that variable room cleaning costs will be $12 per room night sold.

Required:
Calculate the minimum average room rate that PoshPlace will need to charge in order to provide the hotel's owners with the 15 per cent return on their investment that they are seeking.

Problem 12.12

Explain what is meant by the "price elasticity of demand" and describe whether you would expect price elasticity to change during the year for a hotel that is subject to highly seasonal demand.

Chapter 13

Working capital management

Learning objectives

After studying this chapter, you should have developed an appreciation of:

1. the manner in which cash budgeting represents an important tool in cash management,
2. the reasons profit is not the same as cash,
3. factors that need to be considered when extending credit to a customer,
4. the role of an accounts receivable aging schedule in credit management,
5. how the economic order quantity (EOQ) can inform purchasing decisions,
6. when to take advantage of a supplier's offer of a discount for early payment,
7. the risk/return trade-off apparent in short- vs. long-term financing of current assets.

1) Introduction

Working capital was defined in Chapter 5 as current assets minus current liabilities. In this chapter we explore financial management issues relating to the main elements comprising current assets and current liabilities, i.e., cash, accounts receivable, inventory and accounts payable.

Initially, we will highlight the distinction between cash flow and profit. A clear understanding of this distinction is important. The immediate cause of bankruptcy is not a business's failure to make profit. Bankruptcy occurs when a firm does not have enough cash to honour liabilities that are due for payment. We will highlight this distinction between cash flow and profit by working through the mechanics of preparing a **cash budget**. The cash budget is particularly important as it predicts the timing of cash surpluses and deficits. Knowing when there will be a cash surplus allows investment plans to be formulated. Knowing the timing of a projected cash deficit allows short term borrowing arrangements to be made in advance of the cash shortfall occurring. Failure to predict the timing of cash shortfalls can result in costly borrowing arrangements, or, much worse, bankruptcy.

In connection with **accounts receivable management**, we will consider factors that need to be examined when deciding whether to extend credit to a customer. In addition, the nature and use of an accounts receivable aging schedule will be introduced. Following this, the economic order quantity (EOQ) which is a tool that can shed light on the optimal purchase order size for **inventory**, will be described.

In connection with **accounts payable management,** a technique enabling you to determine whether to accept a supplier's offer of a discount for early payment will be introduced. This technique is not only useful in accounts payable management, it also represents a fundamentally important analytical tool for any manager considering offering corporate customers a discount for early payment.

Finally, issues surrounding different approaches to financing a hotel's investment in current assets will be explored. We will see that a risk/return trade-off underlies the question of how much short-term, relative to long-term, borrowing should be undertaken. If a hotel uses a relatively high degree of short-term financing, it will be reducing its costs (i.e., increasing its return) but decreasing its net working capital (i.e., increasing its risk), and vice versa.

2) Cash management

It is important to understand that net cash flow is not the same as profit earned in a period. It is an alarming reality that many business managers have a negligible appreciation of this fundamental aspect of accounting. As a result, business failures can frequently be attributed to managers' failure to recognise a looming liquidity crisis (liquidity refers to the ability to honour short-term financial obligations when they are due). Part of the problem stems from management's tendency to give insufficient attention to cash management, due to an overly blinkered focus on profit. This management tendency is understandable when we recognise the widespread use of profit as a key business performance indicator.

By requiring regular and careful preparation of cash budgets, we can counter this tendency for "profit myopia". This is because cash budgets:

1. Identify periods in which a cash deficit is anticipated. Failure to predict such periods is not only potentially costly, it can represent commercial suicide. If a hotel unexpectedly runs out of cash and no lender can be found at short notice, it will have to either liquidate some assets, quickly arrange some long-term finance, or default on liabilities due. An attempt to hastily pursue either of the first two options is likely to result in a costly outcome. By predicting cash deficit periods, however, early negotiations can be conducted with a lending institution (e.g., a bank), and a crisis avoided by establishing a short-term borrowing facility. By taking these steps in a timely manner, not only will a hotel greatly enhance its chances of negotiating favourable loan terms, in extreme cases financial collapse will be averted.
2. Identify periods in which a cash surplus is anticipated. By predicting cash surpluses, plans concerning the optimal investment of the surplus can be developed.

The need for cash budgeting is especially apparent in the hotel industry due to the degree of seasonality experienced in many properties (see discussion in Chapter 1). As careful cash budgeting is a key element of effective cash management, in this section we closely review a cash budget's preparation. By working through the example, your understanding of how cash differs to profit will be consolidated. Although it is an important management tool, you should not be intimidated by the idea of a cash budget. In many ways it is very similar to your bank statement, i.e., it identifies an opening cash balance, lists cash inflows and outflows, and shows the closing cash balance. To minimise any sense of intimidation, prior to working through the example, why not take a quick sneak preview of the cash budget presented in Exhibit 13.5.

For the cash budgeting example, imagine the BackWoods Retreat, a hotel located in Banff, Canada. The hotel offers accommodation, dining, bar and also seminar facilities. Sue George,

BackWoods' General Manager, wishes to refocus the marketing of the hotel's seminar facilities by pursuing the small corporate convention and retreat market. Consistent with this, plans have been finalised to refurbish the hotel's two seminar rooms and equip them with state of the art presentation technology.

Following two meetings with the hotel accountant, the projected income statements presented in Exhibit 13.1 have been developed for January, February and March next year. In compiling this budgeted statement, it has been assumed that the hotel's seminar facilities will be refurbished during December this year and that the first conventions will be sold in January next year. No convention, restaurant or bar sales will be made in December while the refurbishment work is underway. Consistent with the higher prices that will be charged upon completion of the refurbishment, the projections indicate higher profit margins than those earned in the past by the hotel. Sue George is particularly encouraged by the projected profit and would like to draw up plans to invest cash earned during this period. It is in connection with this that she has asked you to prepare a cash budget for the January–March period.

Exhibit 13.1

BackWoods Retreat budgeted income statements for January, February and March

	January		February		March	
Revenue						
Conventions	$ 34,000		$ 36,000		$ 40,000	
Restaurant & Bar	16,000		17,000		20,000	
		$ 50,000		$ 53,000		$ 60,000
Expenses						
Food & drink	8,000		9,000		10,000	
Wages & salaries	7,000		7,400		7,800	
Supplies	1,000		1,100		1,200	
Electricity	400		400		400	
Insurance	500		500		500	
Advertising	2,000		2,000		2,000	
Depreciation	3,000		3,000		3,000	
		21,900		23,400		24,900
Profit		$ 28,100		$ 29,600		$ 35,100

In addition to the budgeted income statements, the information detailed in Exhibit 13.2 has been gathered to facilitate your preparation of BackWoods' cash budget.

Exhibit 13.2

Information relating to BackWoods' projection of cash flows

(i) **Receipts**: It is anticipated that favourable credit terms will have to be extended to the corporate clients targeted when marketing the hotel's new convention facilities. It is projected that 5 per cent of convention revenue will be received in the month prior to the convention as a deposit. Forty per cent of convention revenue will be received at the time the seminar is held, and the remaining 55 per cent will be received in the month following the convention. $42,000 in convention sales are predicted for April. In the past, 40 per cent of restaurant and bar sales have been for cash and 60 per cent have been charged and collected in the month following the sale. This cash to credit ratio for restaurant and bar sales is expected to continue.

(ii) **Food & drink purchases**: Food and drink stocks are replenished frequently. This signifies that food and drink purchases in a month are approximately equal to food and drink expenses for the month. One month's credit is taken for all food and drink purchases.

(iii) **Wages, salaries and supplies payments**: Wages, salaries and supplies are paid in the month they are incurred as an expense.

(iv) **Electricity payments**: Electricity is paid quarterly. The cost per quarter has been estimated at $1,200 and the first annual payment is made in March.

(v) **Insurance payments**: The annual insurance premium of $6,000 is paid in February.

(vi) **Advertising payments**: In order to promote the hotel's new seminar facilities, a major advertising campaign costing $5,000 per month will be undertaken during the first four months of the year. In May, following the initial period of intensive promotion, advertising will revert to the hotel's traditional level of $500 per month. This signifies that $24,000 will be spent on advertising over the course of the year ([4 × $5,000] + [8 × $500]). The hotel's accountant felt that for income statement purposes, it is reasonable to pro rata this $24,000 equally across the year at the rate of $2,000 per month. He defended this approach on the grounds that sales for the whole year would benefit from the additional market exposure achieved during the initial intensive advertising campaign. All advertising is paid for in the month the service is provided.

(vii) **Fixed asset payments**: Following an appraisal period in which tests will be conducted to ensure that the new presentation equipment is meeting the vendor's specifications, a final instalment payment of $150,000 for the seminar room equipment will be made in February. The expense associated with this refurbishment has been included in the depreciation figure in BackWoods' budgeted income statement for January–March.

(viii) **Opening bank balance**: It is projected that BackWoods will be holding a bank balance of $6,000 at the beginning of January.

The income statements presented in Exhibit 13.1, together with the projected cash receipts and payments details presented in Exhibit 13.2 provide you with sufficient information to prepare BackWoods' cash budget for next January, February and March. The easiest way to compile a cash budget involves breaking the exercise into the following three steps:

1. Prepare a schedule of projected receipts by month,
2. Prepare a schedule of projected cash disbursements (payments) by month,
3. Prepare the monthly cash budget by consolidating the monthly receipts and payments schedules and also the estimated cash balance at the beginning of the budget period.

We will now work through each of these steps, in turn, for the BackWoods Retreat.

BackWoods' schedule of projected cash receipts

Preparing the schedule of cash receipts can be tricky when there is a significant variation in the period of credit taken by customers. In the BackWoods Retreat case, we have convention receipts occurring in three instalments (5 per cent in the month prior to the sale, 40 per cent in the month of the sale and 55 per cent in the month following the sale). In addition, we have 40 per cent of restaurant and bar receipts coinciding with the month of sale (i.e., cash sales) and 60 per cent of receipts occurring one month after the sale.

The best way to deal with this slightly awkward pattern of collections is to develop a table with months as columns and types of receipt as rows. The types of receipt are classified according to the period of credit taken (e.g., month prior to sale, month of sale, one month's credit, etc.). BackWoods' schedule of projected cash receipts is presented in Exhibit 13.3. Most people find it easier to prepare this schedule by moving along the rows (i.e., consider each type of receipt in turn), rather than moving down the columns. The total monthly receipts is found by adding the convention monthly receipts to the restaurant and bar monthly receipts. The total presented as the final column is not strictly needed; however, it does provide a useful check that the sum of the rows equals the sum of the columns.

Exhibit 13.3

Schedule of projected cash receipts for BackWoods Retreat

	Jan.	Feb.	Mar.	Total
Convention sales	$ 34,000	$ 36,000	$ 40,000	
Deposit (5% of next month's sales)	$ 1,800	$ 2,000	$ 2,100[a]	$ 5,900
40% received in month of sale	13,600	14,400	16,000	44,000
55% received in month following sale	0	18,700	19,800	38,500
Total convention receipts	$ 15,400	$ 35,100	$ 37,900	$ 88,400
Restaurant & bar sales	$ 16,000	$ 17,000	$ 20,000	
40% cash sales	$ 6,400	$ 6,800	$ 8,000	$ 21,200
60% received in month following sale	0	9,600	10,200	19,800
Total restaurant & bar receipts	6,400	16,400	18,200	41,000
Total all receipts	$ 21,800	$ 51,500	$ 56,100	$ 129,400

a: Point (*i*) in Exhibit 13.2 indicates that $42,000 is predicted for April's convention sales.

BackWoods' schedule of projected cash disbursements

Consistent with the projected cash receipts schedule, the schedule of cash disbursements can be compiled by placing months in columns and cash flow type in rows. BackWoods' schedule of projected disbursements is presented in Exhibit 13.4. The key to accurately projecting cash receipts and also cash disbursements lies in using well laid out schedules such as those presented in Exhibits 13.3 and 13.4. If your schedule is well designed, compiling the data required becomes a relatively straightforward exercise. Now work carefully through Exhibit 13.4 to ensure you can see how each disbursement item has been determined. Again, you will find it easiest to approach the table on a "row by row", rather than "column by column" basis. The disbursement items are presented in Exhibit 13.4 in the same sequence that they are described in Exhibit 13.2.

Exhibit 13.4

Schedule of projected cash disbursements for BackWoods Retreat

Disbursements	January	February	March	Total
Food and drink (paid in month following purchase).	$ 0	$ 8,000	$ 9,000	$ 17,000
Wages and salaries (paid in month expense is incurred).	7,000	7,400	7,800	22,200
Supplies (paid in month expense is incurred).	1,000	1,100	1,200	3,300
Electricity (paid quarterly).			1,200	1,200
Insurance (paid annually).		6,000		6,000
Advertising (paid in month advertising is conducted).	5,000	5,000	5,000	15,000
Final instalment payment for presentation equipment.		150,000		150,000
Total disbursements	$ 13,000	$ 177,500	$ 24,200	$ 214,700

BackWoods' cash budget

Once the projected cash receipts and cash disbursements schedules have been prepared, preparation of the cash budget becomes a relatively straightforward exercise. In the cash budget we determine each month's net cash flow by subtracting the month's total disbursements from the month's total receipts. We then add the opening cash balance to determine the projected cash balance at each month end. This is the approach that has been taken in preparing BackWoods' cash budget presented in Exhibit 13.5.

Exhibit 13.5

A cash budget for BackWoods Retreat

	January	February	March	Total
Total cash receipts[a]	$ 21,800	$ 51,500	$ 56,100	$ 129,400
Less Total cash disbursements[b]	13,000	177,500	24,200	214,700
Net cash flow	8,800	(126,000)	31,900	(85,300)
Add Opening cash balance[c]	6,000	14,800	(111,200)	6,000
Ending cash balance (negative balance in brackets)	$ 14,800	$ (111,200)	$ (79,300)	$ (79,300)

a: From Exhibit 13.3.
b: From Exhibit 13.4.
c: January's opening balance provided in Exhibit 13.2 (point viii).

Cash versus profit

It is very important to note that while BackWoods is profitable throughout the quarter (see Exhibit 13.1), it is projected that over the same period its cash balance will decline. Having seen the budgeted monthly income statements, BackWoods' General Manager had anticipated a growing cash balance for the quarter. It is surprising how often in business you will encounter the misconception that cash equates to profit. This example, however, should give you a strong sense of why **cash flow is not the same as profit**. If you have any continuing uncertainty over this issue, you should review Box 13.1 which provides an overview of some of the main reasons why profit is not the same as cash.

Box 13.1

Why is profit not the same as cash?

Revenue vs receipts	We recognise revenue at the time a service is provided, not when cash is received. When a sale is made on account, an account receivable is created and the receipt will lag behind revenue. For BackWoods, as 55 per cent of convention sales and 60 per cent of restaurant and bar sales are on credit, receipts will tend to lag behind revenue.
Purchases vs payments	To facilitate trade, many suppliers extend credit. BackWoods' supplier of food and drink items extend one month credit. This signifies that payments lag behind purchases.

Wages and salaries	Employees are paid following the completion of work or a working period. While most waged employees are paid weekly, the payment nevertheless lags behind the time when work is performed, which is the time wage expense is recognised. This is more marked for salaried employees, especially in those countries where monthly salary payments are common.
Electricity	In many countries, electricity accounts are settled on a quarterly basis. This signifies at least a three month discrepancy between some of the electricity expense incurred and payment for electricity.
Insurance	Insurance and rent are paid in advance of charging the associated expense to the income statement. In the case of insurance, payment is made a year in advance of a portion of the expense.
Fixed asset accounting (i.e., depreciation)	One of the most significant reasons causing a discrepancy between cash and profit arises in connection with depreciation accounting. There are two reasons for this: 1) Fixed assets can be very expensive items; 2) The time lag can be considerable. If a fixed asset is being depreciated over 10 years, a portion of the asset's expense lags 10 years behind the actual payment for the asset.
Long-term financing	When a company arranges a loan or increases its share capital there is an immediate large positive impact on cash flow. The only income statement impact concerns the loan's annual interest expense, however.

Appreciating that profit is not the same as cash is important for two reasons:

1. It highlights why we need to prepare budgeted cash flow statements in addition to budgeted income statements.
2. It highlights the potential of profitable firms becoming bankrupt. Many new profitable ventures expand very quickly. This period of expansion can be a very dangerous stage in the life of an organisation, as expansion signifies an outflow of funds on assets such as accounts receivable, inventory and fixed assets. The cash flow associated with this expansion can result in a liquidity crisis, i.e., the expanding firm can run out of cash. Just look at the highly profitable BackWoods Retreat example. The hotel's investment in assets resulted in it having a negative cash balance in February. If BackWoods management did not take care to produce a cash budget and arrange a loan to cover its projected cash deficit period, its inability to pay creditors could put it out of business. This clearly shows how profitable firms can go bankrupt. **If you ensure maintenance of sufficient cash, you will ensure maintenance of a business.**

3) Accounts receivable management

One of the closest to cash assets is accounts receivable. This is because in the normal course of business an account receivable will become cash in the short term. There are two costs associated with extending credit to customers:

1) The cost of the selling company not being able to deposit the monetary value of a completed sale in its bank, i.e., as a result of not collecting cash at the time of a sale, the vendor will forgo some bank account interest (or if the vendor has a bank overdraft, it will incur additional interest expense).
2) The cost associated with lost revenue due to some accounts receivable proving to be uncollectible.

These costs might cause you to question why companies extend credit. The answer is because credit facilitates trade. Considerable sales would be lost if credit was not extended. It is hard to contemplate a 5-star hotel not allowing customers to use a credit card to settle their accounts. This shows how much we are conditioned to expect the granting of credit whenever we purchase a service from a hotel. In addition to credit card sales, many large hotels have corporate clients that purchase on account.

The cost associated with extending trade credit signifies that hotels have to perform a credit balancing act, i.e., they have to ensure the credit period extended is neither too much nor too little. In addition, a hotel has to ensure that credit is only granted to creditworthy customers. The widely acknowledged five C's of credit management provides a useful checklist of factors to consider when deciding whether to grant credit to a particular customer. The five C's comprise character, capacity, capital, conditions and collateral, and are described in Box 13.2.

Box 13.2

The five C's of credit management

The following issues should be appraised when considering whether to extend trade credit to a customer:

1. *Character*: does the customer have a predisposition towards timely payment of accounts?
2. *Capacity*: does the customer have the capacity to run a successful business?
3. *Capital*: does the customer have sufficient working and long-term capital to honour the account when it is due for payment?
4. *Conditions*: are there any particular economic conditions that might affect the potential customer's ability to pay? In addition, there might be particular circumstances such as low occupancy in the off season that might cause a hotel to consider extending credit to less creditworthy customers.
5. *Collateral*: does the customer have assets that could be liquidated relatively easily in the event of a liquidity crisis that threatened timely reimbursement of the account due?

When appraising a hotel's accounts receivable strategy and performance, it can be useful to determine the average number of days' credit that it extends to customers. We saw in Chapter 5 that we can gauge the accounts receivable turnover and average number of days' credit advanced by a company if we can determine its level of credit sales and average accounts receivable balance. For example, imagine that London's HighTowers hotel made £2,835,000 in credit sales during the most recent calendar year and that its year-end accounts receivable balance was £270,000. By dividing credit sales by the accounts receivable balance, we can determine HighTowers' accounts receivable turnover, as follows:

$$\frac{Credit\ sales}{Accounts\ receivable\ balance} \quad i.e., \quad \frac{£\ 2,835,000}{£\ 270,000} \quad = \quad 10.5$$

By dividing 365 days (i.e., the days in a year) by the accounts receivable turnover, we can determine the average number of days that credit is extended, as follows:

$$\frac{Days\ in\ a\ year}{Accounts\ receivable\ turnover} \quad i.e., \quad \frac{365}{10.5} \quad = \quad 34.8\ days$$

For those working within a company, a more detailed analysis of the accounts receivable balance can be conducted by preparing an "Accounts Receivable Aging" schedule. An example of such a schedule is presented in Exhibit 13.6. This schedule provides a breakdown of HighTowers' total accounts receivable balance according to the number of days that each amount owing is overdue. When reviewing the schedule, assume that we are currently standing at the end of December and that HighTowers has a policy of extending 30 day credit terms. This signifies that credit arising from sales made during December can be described as current, i.e., it is not yet overdue.

Exhibit 13.6

Accounts receivable aging schedule

		Days overdue				
	Current	0–30	31–60	61–90	Over 90	
Sale period	December	November	October	September	August	Total
Accounts receivable	£4,900	£490	£1,400	£140	£70	£7,000
Percentage of total	70%	7%	20%	2%	1%	100%

With the exception of the 31–60 days overdue accounts, the schedule reveals a fairly typical time distribution of the accounts receivable balance. To have 20 per cent of the accounts receivable balance falling within the 31–60 days overdue category is cause for some concern, however. Immediate management action addressing this issue may be warranted. It may be that one large account is in dispute, or one or more debtors are experiencing liquidity problems. If further detail is sought, an accounts receivable aging schedule that separately analyses the age of each individual debtor's account can be prepared. Most computerised accounting systems have the capacity to provide accounts receivable aging schedules in such a format.

Once problem accounts have been identified, a series of steps designed to collect outstanding debts can be initiated. These steps are summarised in Box 13.3. If an account is particularly large, several initial steps can inform what collection strategy would be most appropriate. These include:

1) Determine why the customer has withheld payment.
2) Determine the payment history of the customer.
3) Determine whether the customer is a large client that might take their business elsewhere if a significant dispute over credit develops.
4) Determine whether we have personnel who might be able to expedite payment through their contacts in the debtor firm.

Box 13.3

Accounts receivable collection techniques

The following account collection methods are listed in the order with which they are generally used in connection with a particular account:

1. *Letters*: once an account has been overdue for a number of days, a polite reminder can be mailed. Following a designated period, if payment is not forthcoming, a second more strongly worded letter can be sent.
2. *Telephone calls*: in addition to letters, one or more telephone calls to the accounts payable officer concerned can be made. This technique can be particularly effective if the credit manager possesses good negotiating skills and has extensive business contacts.
3. *Site visits*: visiting the debtor can be an effective counter to the "cheque is in the mail" syndrome, as payment can be made on the spot. It is only feasible, however, when the debtor is located in the vicinity of the company seeking reimbursement.
4. *Collection agency*: there are an increasing number of factoring companies that specialise in credit management and debt collection. As this can represent an expensive way to collect accounts receivable, it should only be used if none of the techniques referred to above have been successful.
5. *Legal action*: this can be regarded as the most radical step in a collection strategy. It is expensive and can trigger the debtor company's bankruptcy. Even if successful, legal action can be expected to sour relations with the debtor firm and signify the end of a trading relationship.

4) Inventory management

Paralleling the balancing act that has to be performed when determining the credit period to be extended to customers, care has to be taken in inventory management to ensure that neither too little nor too much inventory is held. A hotel that holds low inventory balances runs the risk of experiencing stock-outs. This can result in the immediate loss of sales and, perhaps more significantly, it can also significantly damage customer goodwill (e.g., a restaurant customer becoming disgruntled when several menu items are unavailable). If too much inventory is held, the hotel will experience high inventory carrying costs that include:

1. The opportunity cost of money tied up in inventory, i.e., money invested in inventory can be viewed as money that could be earning interest if it was invested in a bank account.
2. The cost of pilferage.
3. Cost of deterioration of perishable items.
4. Cost of inventory insurance.
5. Handling costs, i.e., if large amounts of inventory are held, additional costs may result from problems associated with storing, locating and moving inventory.
6. The cost of maintaining and financing storage space.

The correct amount of inventory to be held is largely a matter of judgement. One way to inform such a judgement is to monitor inventory turnover. As noted in Chapter 5, this can be computed by dividing the cost of sales by the average inventory balance. If a hotel is part of a hotel chain, it can be a useful exercise to benchmark inventory turnover rates in order to identify those members of the chain holding relatively high or low levels of inventory.

A second aspect of inventory management that lends itself to analysis is the question of how much inventory should be ordered when making a purchase order. The EOQ model is a technique enabling us to estimate the optimal order size for purchase orders. While theoretically correct, the model does require fairly restrictive assumptions. Despite this, the model can be applied in many hotel situations and it does highlight how purchasing officers should attempt to balance the trade-off between minimising inventory holding costs and the costs of processing orders and shipments. The model is outlined in Box 13.4.

Box 13.4

Using the EOQ model to determine optimal order size

The EOQ model assumes:

- rate of demand for inventory item in question is relatively predictable
- administrative order costs do not vary with size of order processed.

The EOQ can be calculated by applying the following formula:

$$EOQ = \sqrt{(2 \times U \times O \div C)}$$

---

where:

U = Usage per period of time (same period of time as used for carrying cost).
O = Cost of ordering and receiving an order.
C = Carrying cost per unit of inventory per period of time (same period of time as used for usage).

Example:

Imagine that New York's Elite Restaurant offers an extensive menu of fine wines. The average case of wine costs Elite $360. Past experience indicates 750 cases of wine are sold per year by the restaurant. Following discussions with Elite's purchasing and store managers, Elite's accountant has estimated that the cost of ordering and receiving a shipment of wine is $30. As the restaurant holds any excess working capital as marketable securities that earn 5 per cent per annum, the accountant estimates the cost of holding a case of wine for a year to be $18 (i.e., $360 × 5 per cent).

The EOQ for Elite's wine inventory can be calculated as follows:

$$\sqrt{(2 \times 750 \times \$30 \div \$18)} =$$
$$\sqrt{(2,500)} = 50 \text{ cases per order.}$$

By applying the EOQ, we have determined that if Elite orders its wine in shipment sizes of 50 cases, the sum of its annual carrying and ordering costs will be minimised.

5) Accounts payable management

Accounts payable management can be seen as the flip side of accounts receivable management. For an account receivable, bank interest that could be earned is lost due to money that relates to a sale being held by a customer. For an account payable, we can gain bank interest from holding money that relates to a purchase already made. Care should be taken not to abuse credit terms extended by suppliers, however. Good supplier relations can be a key source of competitive advantage. Characteristics of a good supplier include a willingness to:

1. meet rush orders,
2. tailor shipments to specific requests,
3. maintain high quality in goods and services supplied,
4. provide flexible credit terms.

One particular issue that can arise in connection with accounts payable management is a discount offered by a supplier for early payment of an account. This type of trade discount is typically stated using abbreviated terms such as "1/10 *net* 30". This means that the purchaser can deduct a 1 per cent discount off the invoiced amount if payment is made ten days after the start of the credit period (typically the invoice date), and if the discount is not taken, the invoiced amount is due for payment 30 days after the start of the credit period. A method enabling you to appraise whether the discount should be taken is described in the financial decision making in action case 13.1.

FINANCIAL DECISION MAKING IN ACTION CASE 13.1

The Financial Controller determining whether to take a trade discount

In most organisations, accounts payable management falls within the financial controller's jurisdiction. An issue that needs to be managed in accounts payable management is the question of whether to take the early payment discount offered by some suppliers. This issue can be analysed by viewing an early payment as an advance of funds that earns a return. We can determine the effective annual rate of return on this advance relatively easily in the following way.

Imagine British Airways has received a £1,000 invoice and credit terms of 2/10 net 45 from one of its contract food suppliers. This means BA can either pay £980 in 10 days' time, or £1,000 in 45 days' time. By advancing £980 35 days earlier than necessary, BA will get a return of £20 (i.e., the £20 saved on the invoice payment). To find what this represents in terms of an annual rate of return, we have to gross up the £20 return on the £980 advance to translate it from a 35-day period to 365 days, i.e.:

$$\frac{£20}{£980} \times \frac{365}{35} = 0.213 \ (\text{or } 21.3\%)$$

This calculation used the actual monetary amounts involved. Alternatively, the following generic formula can be used:

$$\frac{\% \text{ discount offered}}{100 - \% \text{ discount offered}} \times \frac{\text{Days in a year}}{\text{Days difference in final due date and discount date}}$$

This generic formula can be applied to the above example as follows:

$$\frac{2}{98} \times \frac{365}{(45-10)} = 0.213 \ (\text{or } 21.3\%)$$

For this example, the financial controller would conclude that if BA has enough cash to enable early payment, and if it is earning less than 21.3 per cent per annum interest on any cash balances held, then it should take the discount and gain the benefit of an effective 21.3 per cent annual rate of return. If BA does not have sufficient cash and must borrow to take the discount, then as long as the cost of borrowing is less than 21.3 per cent, it is in its interest to borrow £980 and take advantage of the trade discount offered.

6) Working capital management

As noted in the chapter's introduction, net working capital is defined as current assets – current liabilities. So far we have considered management issues arising in connection with the main elements of working capital, i.e., cash, accounts receivable, inventory and accounts payable. We now turn to consider a more holistic dimension of working capital management. Working capital management can be a particularly important dimension of financial management in hotels, as high seasonality translates into high working capital volatility. During the busy season, a hotel will have a relatively high level of current assets. This is because:

● higher levels of cash will be needed to support the above average levels of daily purchase payments,
● higher accounts receivable will result from the above average levels of sales,
● higher inventory levels will be needed to support the above average levels of activity.

Figure 13.1 depicts investment in fixed and current assets for a resort hotel that experiences a busy mid-summer and mid-winter season. Note how the hotel's fixed assets remain constant throughout the year. Its current assets, however, exhibit considerable volatility, rising to highs during busy seasons and lows during quiet seasons. It is this volatility in current assets that results in the volatility of the hotel's total asset base.

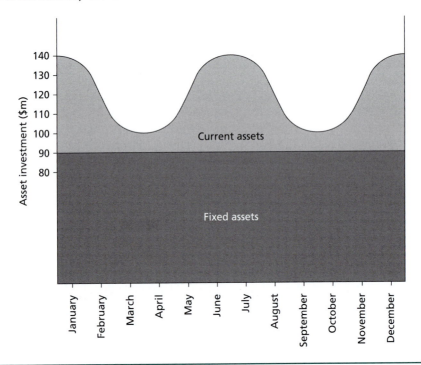

Figure 13.1 The impact of seasonality on asset investment

A key working capital management issue that arises in connection with Figure 13.1 concerns the mix of current liabilities and long-term capital that should be used to finance a hotel's fluctuating asset base. It is widely acknowledged in the finance literature that long-term assets (i.e., fixed assets) should be financed through long-term capital. Therefore, for the hotel depicted in Figure 13.1, the minimum amount of long-term financing that should be raised is $90m. It is also apparent from Figure 13.1 that the permanent amount of funds required during the year is $100m (total assets never drop below $100m), and a case could be made for financing all of this permanent portion of total assets with long-term capital.

The issue of what proportion of the moving current asset base should be financed through current liabilities boils down to a profit vs risk trade-off decision. This is because, as is explained in Box 13.5, a relatively high ratio of current liabilities to long-term capital signifies a high profit/high risk strategy, and a relatively low ratio of current liabilities to long-term capital signifies a low profit/low risk strategy. While all managers like to see increased profit levels, it is obvious that care must be taken not to jeopardise an organisation's solvency by becoming too dependent on current liability financing.

Box 13.5

The profit/risk trade-off in current liability financing

The profit aspect: Current liabilities are cheaper to finance than long-term capital. Accounts payable and wages accrued generally have no cost associated with them. In addition, except for times when there is a widespread expectation that interest rates will decline in the future, it is normal for short-term lending rates to be below long-term lending rates.

The risk aspect: If a hotel increases its current liabilities relative to long-term capital its net working capital will decline. Net working capital is a key indicator of a firm's ability to pay its debts over the short term. A decrease in net working capital signifies increased risk due to the lower short-term asset coverage of short-term liabilities.

Effects of high current liability financing: Synthesizing the profit and risk aspects of current liability financing, we can conclude that a relatively high short- to long-term financing ratio has a positive impact on profit and risk.

Effects of low current liability financing: It also follows that a relatively low short- to long-term financing ratio has a negative impact on profit and risk.

When considering this short- versus long-term financing issue, if an aggressive financing approach is taken, it should be noted that not all incremental investments in current assets have to be financed by short-term loans. This is because part of the extra current asset investment occurring during busy seasons will be financed spontaneously by higher current liabilities that also arise during busy seasons. This spontaneous financing occurs because higher business activity levels will stimulate higher accounts payable balances and higher average wage accrued balances due to increased levels of purchasing and casual staff employment.

7) Summary

In this chapter we have looked at management issues associated with the main accounts that comprise working capital, i.e., cash, accounts receivable, inventory and accounts payable. A particularly important aspect of the chapter concerned an illustration of how cash flow is not the same as profit.

Having read the chapter you should now know:

- how cash budgeting represents an important aspect of cash management,
- how cash differs to profit,
- what issues need to be considered when deciding whether to extend credit to a new customer,
- how an accounts receivable aging schedule can aid the identification of customer accounts warranting particular attention,
- how application of the EOQ model can aid the reduction of costs associated with inventory management,
- how to analyse whether to accept a supplier's offer of a discount for early payment of an account payable,
- how a risk/return trade-off exists when deciding what proportion of short- versus long-term capital should be used to finance current asset investments.

References

Adams, D. (2006) *Management Accounting for the Hospitality, Tourism and Leisure Industries: A Strategic Approach*, 2nd edition, London: Thomson: Chapter 7.

Gitman, L.J., Juchau, R. and Flanagan, J. (2011) *Principles of Managerial Finance*, 6th edition, Frenchs Forest, NSW: Pearson Education Australia: Chapter 14.

Jagels, M.G. (2007) *Hospitality Management Accounting*, 9th edition, Hoboken, NJ: John Wiley & Sons: Chapter 11.

Kotas, R. (1999) *Management Accounting for Hospitality and Tourism*, 3rd edition, London: International Thomson Publishing: Chapter 18.

Langfield-Smith, K., Thorne, H. and Hilton, R. (2012) *Management Accounting: Information for Creating and Managing Value*, 6th edition, Macquarie Park, NSW, Australia: McGraw-Hill: Chapter 9.

Problems

Problem 13.1

Explain why cash flow for a particular period of time can be different to profit for the same period of time.

Problem 13.2

Identify five factors that should be appraised when considering whether to extend trade credit to a new customer.

Problem 13.3

The marketing department of Singapore's CrownJewel Hotel has projected the following sales in the last half of the current financial year.

CrownJewel projected sales (in $ thousands)

	July	August	September	October	November	December
Rooms	630	660	600	540	500	600
Restaurant & Bar	90	100	80	70	60	80

Most of CrownJewel's room sales are made to corporate clients. Past experience indicates that 10 per cent of room sales are for cash, 50 per cent is collected in the month following the sale, 35 per cent is collected two months following the sale and 5 per cent of sales are to a large company that takes three months to settle accounts.

In the past, 30 per cent of restaurant and bar sales have been for cash and 70 per cent have been charged and collected in the month following the sale.

Required:
Prepare a schedule showing CrownJewel's projected cash receipts in October, November and December.

Problem 13.4

In connection with the CrownJewel sales estimates provided in the previous Problem, past experience has shown that room variable costs are 20 per cent of room revenue. 60 per cent of these variable costs are paid for in the month the expense is incurred and the remainder is paid for in the following month.

Restaurant and bar variable costs comprise wages, food and drink. Wages are 10 per cent of restaurant and bar revenue and are paid for in the month incurred. The cost of food and drink is 15 per cent of restaurant and bar revenue. Due to the CrownJewel's inventory stocking policy, 40 per cent of food and drink is purchased one month before it is sold. The remainder is purchased in the month of sale. All food and drink is purchased from the same company which extends one month trade credit.

The hotel has fixed costs of $15,000 per month which are paid for in the month incurred. In addition, the hotel estimates it will make a quarterly electricity payment of $3,000 in November and its annual insurance premium of $7,500 is due for payment in December.

Required:
Prepare a schedule showing CrownJewel's projected cash disbursements for October, November and December.

Problem 13.5

Draw on your solutions provided to the previous two Problems to prepare CrownJewel's cash budget for October, November and December. It has been estimated that the hotel will have a positive cash balance of $12,000 on 30th September.

Problem 13.6

The ShireLodge provides a residential convention service in England's Yorkshire Dales. The lodge's general manager is concerned about cash flow in the next few months particularly as insurance will soon be due for payment.

The following revenue and expense estimates have been developed for the first four months of 20X2:

	January	February	March	April
Convention sales revenue	£10,000	£12,000	£13,000	£14,000
Fixed costs:				
Salaries	£4,000	£4,000	£4,000	£4,000
Ground maintenance	£500	£500	£500	£500
Insurance	£420	£420	£420	£420

It has been estimated that sales in December 20X1 will be £8,000. Previous cash collections indicate that 10 per cent of all sales are collected in the month prior to the sale as a deposit. 50 per cent of all sales are collected in the month of the sale, and 40 per cent of sales are collected in the month following the sale.

Variable costs are 15 per cent of revenue. Ninety per cent of variable costs are paid in the month of the sale to which they relate, and the remainder are paid in the month prior to the sale (purchase of some food and other items in preparation for conventions). Salary and ground maintenance fixed costs are paid for as they are incurred. Insurance is paid for twice a year, in January and July. It is estimated that on 1st January 20X2 the lodge will have £4,200 in its bank account.

Required:
Prepare a cash budget showing receipts, disbursements and opening and closing cash balances for each of the first three months of 20X2.

Problem 13.7

A review of the accounts receivable records of Auckland's CreatureComforts Hotel reveals the following year-end information.

CreatureComforts Hotel –
Analysis of age of accounts receivable as at 31/12/X1

Month of sale	Accounts receivable	%
July	$ 2,594	1
August	13,448	5
September	2,782	1
October	7,890	3
November	26,300	10
December	210,000	80
Total year-end balance	$263,014	100

The credit manager believes that the report accurately shows the proportion of the year-end accounts receivable balance that can be traced to months in which credit sales were made. Forty per cent of the hotel's $6,000,000 annual sales are on credit. The hotel extends 30-day credit terms.

Required:

a) Using the year-end account balance, evaluate the effectiveness of the hotel's accounts receivable collection system.
b) If the hotel's peak season runs from November through to January, how does this additional information affect your answer to a).
c) Prepare an aging of accounts receivable schedule in order to obtain additional insight into the status of the hotel's accounts receivable balance. What further observations can be made from the aging schedule.

Problem 13.8

The laundry department of the Edinburgh hotel, TartanDays, orders concentrated laundry detergent in 10 kilogram boxes. Each box costs £32. It costs £20 to place, process and receive a laundry detergent order and TartanDays has estimated that it would cost £2 to hold a box of detergent in inventory for a year. The hotel uses 25 boxes of detergent per month.

Required:
What is the TartanDays' EOQ for laundry detergent?

Problem 13.9

Toronto's Roma Pizzeria sells a variety of pizzas. The largest inventory item held by Roma is cheese. The owner has approached you for advice in connection with the size of orders that should be placed when ordering cheese. You have ascertained the following:

- Cheese is ordered in blocks at $20 per block.
- Roma currently places an order with its cheese supplier every two weeks and the average order size is 500 blocks. Roma has a policy of timing its cheese reordering so that its inventory of cheese has declined to 40 blocks when the new shipment arrives.
- Money not invested in inventory could be invested in a bank account to earn Roma 5 per cent per annum.
- The cheese is shipped in refrigerated transport and the cost of ordering, shipping and receiving a shipment is $30.

Required:

a) What is the Roma's EOQ for cheese? Assume 52 weeks in a year.
b) What is the sum of Roma's current cheese carrying and ordering costs? Assume 52 weeks in a year.
c) What would Roma save in total carrying and ordering costs if it changed its order size to the most economic order quantity (EOQ).

Problem 13.10

Johannesburg's "MouthWatering" Restaurant has approached you for assistance in determining whether it should take the 1/10 net 30 trade discount terms offered by its main food supplier. The restaurant currently has invested excess liquidity in marketable securities earning an 8 per cent average annual rate of return.

Required:
Conduct an analysis to demonstrate whether the MouthWatering Restaurant should take the trade discount offered.

Problem 13.11

Feast'N'Run provides a contract catering service to several university and college campuses. One of its main suppliers has offered trade discount terms of 1/10 net 40. In the past, Feast'N'Run has taken an average of 50 days credit when settling its trade accounts. The chief accountant feels that this policy has not damaged relations with any of its suppliers and proposes to continue with it, except when making an early payment to secure a discount. Feast'N'Run finances its investment in working capital by short-term borrowing that carries an annual interest rate of 9.5 per cent.

Required:
Conduct an analysis to demonstrate whether Feast'N'Run should take the trade discount offered.

Problem 13.12

Le SlopeVerticale is a French skiing hotel complex offering accommodation, restaurant, bar, ski shop and equipment hire facilities. The complex has estimated it will have the following assets for the forthcoming year:

Month	Current assets	Fixed assets	Total assets
January	€ 60,000	€ 1,000,000	€ 1,060,000
February	60,000	1,000,000	1,060,000
March	60,000	1,000,000	1,060,000
April	40,000	1,000,000	1,040,000
May	6,000	1,000,000	1,006,000
June	2,000	1,000,000	1,002,000
July	2,000	1,000,000	1,002,000
August	2,000	1,000,000	1,002,000
September	2,000	1,000,000	1,002,000
October	6,000	1,000,000	1,006,000
November	40,000	1,000,000	1,040,000
December	60,000	1,000,000	1,060,000

With respect to the cost of financing these assets, no interest is paid on the balance of trade accounts payable or accrued wages, which fluctuate through the year. At any time, the aggregate of these two accounts is generally 60 per cent of current assets. The remainder of SlopeVerticale's investment in assets is financed by:

- Long-term financing costing an average of 10 per cent per annum.
- A floating short-term bank loan carrying an interest rate of 6 per cent per annum (used to cover any financing shortfall).

Required:

a) If SlopeVerticale's long-term financing is €1,000,000:

1. Based on the asset projections provided, determine the floating short-term bank loan required in each month of the year.
2. Determine SlopeVerticale's total financing cost for the year.

b) If SlopeVerticale's long-term financing is €1,020,000:

1. Determine the floating short-term bank loan required in each month of the year.
2. Determine SlopeVerticale's total financing cost for the year.

c) What are the profit/risk trade-offs associated with the different financing options identified in a) and b).

Chapter 14

Investment decision making

Learning objectives

After studying this chapter, you should have developed an appreciation of:

1. how the accounting rate of return, payback, net present value and internal rate of return investment appraisal techniques can be applied,
2. the relative merits of these investment appraisal techniques,
3. what is meant by the "time value of money",
4. how the present value of a cash flow occurring in the future can be determined using discounting tables.

1) Introduction

This chapter focuses on analytical methods that can be used to assess the merit of long-term investment proposals. The process of rationing funds to long-term investment proposals is often referred to as "capital budgeting". In the context of financial management, the term "capital" is used when referring to long-term funds (we talk of a company "raising capital" when it issues more equity finance or borrows long-term debt). In the earlier chapter concerned with budgeting, it was noted that the "budget" relates to plans for the forthcoming year. It follows that "capital budgeting" relates to longer-term budgeting, i.e., decision making concerned with investing in fixed assets such as laundry or kitchen equipment, or the decision to refurbish rooms. As a large proportion of a hotel's assets are fixed assets, it is evident that **capital budgeting is an important decision making area for hotel managers**.

The chapter is structured around the following four investment appraisal techniques:

- accounting rate of return,
- payback,
- net present value,
- internal rate of return.

2) Accounting rate of return

A worked example that highlights the calculation of the accounting rate of return is presented in Box 14.1.

Box 14.1

Finding an investment proposal's accounting rate of return

The accounting rate of return (ARR) can be found by applying the following formula:

$$ARR = \frac{\textit{Average annual profit generated by the investment}}{\textit{Average investment}}$$

Usually, ARR is stated as a percentage, therefore multiply the above formula by 100.

Imagine Auckland's KiwiStay Hotel is appraising a 1st January 20X0 investment of $8,000 in a drinks vending machine that will increase accounting profits by $1,000 in 20X0, $2,000 in 20X1 and $3,000 in 20X2. At the end of 20X2, it is estimated the vending machine will be sold for $2,000.

Calculating the average annual profit generated by the investment is relatively straightforward. We find it is $2,000 by taking the average of the profit generated in years 20X0, 20X1 and 20X2 ([$1,000 + $2,000 + $3,000] ÷ 3).

The average investment is a slightly more challenging concept to grasp, however. Try thinking of it as "The average amount of money invested in the asset during its life". At the beginning of 20X0, it is evident that $8,000 is invested in the asset (i.e., the initial investment). At the end of the life of the asset, it is evident that $2,000 is effectively invested, as this is the amount that could be liquidated if the asset is sold. As the asset is worth $8,000 at the beginning of its life and $2,000 at the end of its life, its average value over the duration of its life is $5,000. This is the midpoint between $8,000 and $2,000, and can be computed as follows: ([$8,000 + $2,000] ÷ 2).

As the average annual profit is $2,000 and the average investment in the asset is $5,000, the ARR can be computed as follows:

$$ARR = \frac{\$2,000}{\$5,000} \times 100 = 40\%$$

At first glance the ARR might appear conceptually appealing. It has major shortcomings, however. These shortcomings include:

1. The ARR fails to consider the period of the investment. Suppose a hotel is deciding whether to take the 40 per cent ARR investment option with a 3 year life described in Box 14.1, or a second $8,000 investment option that has a 10 year life and an ARR of 38 per cent. Both returns appear very high. Consequently, we are left to question, would you like to make an investment that provides a very high return for 3 years, or an investment that provides a very high return for 10 years? Let's assume that the hotel in question generally makes an average return of 12 per cent on its assets. By investing in the 10 year asset that provides a 38 per cent ARR, it will be able to increase its average return on assets for seven years longer than if it invests in the 3 year asset that provides a 40 per cent ARR. In this case, it appears that the 10 year 38 per cent ARR investment option is preferable to the 3 year 40 per cent ARR option.
2. The ARR is based on accounting profits. These figures involve some apportioning of cash flows to different accounting periods (e.g., depreciation). As a result, profits are not "real" in a tangible sense. They represent nothing more than the accountant's "account" of performance. Cash flows, however, are real, and it is the commercial reality of the timing of money entering and exiting the organisation, and not the accountant's account, that we need to incorporate in the decision model.

3) Payback

Surveys of capital budgeting practice highlight the popularity of the payback investment appraisal technique amongst hotel managers (e.g., Guilding and Lamminmaki 2007). Payback's popularity may result from it being an intuitively appealing approach that is relatively simple to understand. In addition, payback can be used as an initial screening mechanism prior to the use of more sophisticated investment appraisal techniques. Application of the payback approach to appraising an investment proposal is outlined in Box 14.2.

Box 14.2

Finding an investment proposal's payback

Payback can be calculated as follows:

> *Payback = The time taken to recoup the cash invested in an asset.*

Payback example 1:
Imagine an initial investment of $20,000 will increase operating cash inflows by $5,000 in each of the 8 years of an asset's life.

> Payback = 4 years
> *(It takes 4 years to get the $20,000 back).*

Payback example 2:
A 1st January 20X0 investment of $10,000 will increase operating cash inflows by $3,000 in 20X0, $4,000 in 20X1 and $6,000 in 20X2.

Payback = 2.5 years

(After two years, $7,000 of the $10,000 investment will have been recouped. As the operating cash inflow in the third year is $6,000, it is assumed that the final $3,000 needed will have been recouped half way through 20X2).

Like accounting rate of return, the payback technique has several shortcomings. Two major shortcomings of the payback approach are:

1. It fails to consider any cash flows occurring after the payback period. The second of the two examples presented in Box 14.2 has the faster payback; however, the first example generates the most lifetime cash inflows. In the first payback example, note that if the projected operating cash inflows had been $100,000 in each of the last four years of the investment's life, the payback would still be four years.
2. It fails to recognise the time value of money, i.e., $1 today does not have the same value as $1 in a year's time. Payback treats cash flows occurring in different time periods as if they have the same value.

4) Net present value (NPV)

NPV is based on the concept that $1 in one time period is not worth the same as $1 in another time period ($1 today is worth more than $1 in a year's time). If $1 could be invested in a bank account to earn 10 per cent, then we would be indifferent between having $1 now or $1.1 in a year's time. Therefore, if we expect an interest rate of 10 per cent for the foreseeable future, $1 today has the same value as $1.1 in one year's time.

The view that $1 today does not have the same value as $1 in a year's time is not recognised in the accounting rate of return nor the payback method. Note that in the examples above, no attempt was made to adjust the value of future profits (in the ARR example), or future cash flows (in the payback example) in order to bring them into line with cash flows occurring at the beginning of the project's life.

The NPV investment appraisal technique involves finding today's value of future cash flows associated with an investment proposal. When today's value of a project's inflows are greater than today's value of the project's outflows, the project is described as having a positive "net present value". A positive net present value signifies that a project is acceptable; a negative net present value (i.e., the present value of a project's outflows are greater than the present value of its inflows) signifies that a project should be rejected.

Today's value of a future cash flow can be found by multiplying the future cash flow by the appropriate factor appearing in Table 14.1 or Table 14.2. These tables are widely referred to as "discounting tables". Table 14.1 presents the present value factors to be used when finding the present value of a single cash flow. Table 14.2 presents the present value factors to be used when finding the present value of a series of equal cash flows (a series of equal cash flows is

Table 14.1 Present value factors for a single cash flow (PV)

Year	1%	2%	3%	4%	5%	6%	7%	8%	9%	10%	11%	12%	13%	14%	15%	16%	17%	18%	19%	20%
1	0.990	0.980	0.971	0.962	0.952	0.943	0.935	0.926	0.917	0.909	0.901	0.893	0.885	0.877	0.870	0.862	0.855	0.847	0.840	0.833
2	0.980	0.961	0.943	0.925	0.907	0.890	0.873	0.857	0.842	0.826	0.812	0.797	0.783	0.769	0.756	0.743	0.731	0.718	0.706	0.694
3	0.971	0.942	0.915	0.889	0.864	0.840	0.816	0.794	0.772	0.751	0.731	0.712	0.693	0.675	0.658	0.641	0.624	0.609	0.593	0.579
4	0.961	0.924	0.888	0.855	0.823	0.792	0.763	0.735	0.708	0.683	0.659	0.636	0.613	0.592	0.572	0.552	0.534	0.516	0.499	0.482
5	0.951	0.906	0.863	0.822	0.784	0.747	0.713	0.681	0.650	0.621	0.593	0.567	0.543	0.519	0.497	0.476	0.456	0.437	0.419	0.402
6	0.942	0.888	0.837	0.790	0.746	0.705	0.666	0.630	0.596	0.564	0.535	0.507	0.480	0.456	0.432	0.410	0.390	0.370	0.352	0.335
7	0.933	0.871	0.813	0.760	0.711	0.665	0.623	0.583	0.547	0.513	0.482	0.452	0.425	0.400	0.376	0.354	0.333	0.314	0.296	0.279
8	0.923	0.853	0.789	0.731	0.677	0.627	0.582	0.540	0.502	0.467	0.434	0.404	0.376	0.351	0.327	0.305	0.285	0.266	0.249	0.233
9	0.914	0.837	0.766	0.703	0.645	0.592	0.544	0.500	0.460	0.424	0.391	0.361	0.333	0.308	0.284	0.263	0.243	0.225	0.209	0.194
10	0.905	0.820	0.744	0.676	0.614	0.558	0.508	0.463	0.422	0.386	0.352	0.322	0.295	0.270	0.247	0.227	0.208	0.191	0.176	0.162
11	0.896	0.804	0.722	0.650	0.585	0.527	0.475	0.429	0.388	0.350	0.317	0.287	0.261	0.237	0.215	0.195	0.178	0.162	0.148	0.135
12	0.887	0.788	0.701	0.625	0.557	0.497	0.444	0.397	0.356	0.319	0.286	0.257	0.231	0.208	0.187	0.168	0.152	0.137	0.124	0.112
13	0.879	0.773	0.681	0.601	0.530	0.469	0.415	0.368	0.326	0.290	0.258	0.229	0.204	0.182	0.163	0.145	0.130	0.116	0.104	0.093
14	0.870	0.758	0.661	0.577	0.505	0.442	0.388	0.340	0.299	0.263	0.232	0.205	0.181	0.160	0.141	0.125	0.111	0.099	0.088	0.078
15	0.861	0.743	0.642	0.555	0.481	0.417	0.362	0.315	0.275	0.239	0.209	0.183	0.160	0.140	0.123	0.108	0.095	0.084	0.074	0.065
16	0.853	0.728	0.623	0.534	0.458	0.394	0.339	0.292	0.252	0.218	0.188	0.163	0.141	0.123	0.107	0.093	0.081	0.071	0.062	0.054
17	0.844	0.714	0.605	0.513	0.436	0.371	0.317	0.270	0.231	0.198	0.170	0.146	0.125	0.108	0.093	0.080	0.069	0.060	0.052	0.045
18	0.836	0.700	0.587	0.494	0.416	0.350	0.296	0.250	0.212	0.180	0.153	0.130	0.111	0.095	0.081	0.069	0.059	0.051	0.044	0.038
19	0.828	0.686	0.570	0.475	0.396	0.331	0.277	0.232	0.194	0.164	0.138	0.116	0.098	0.083	0.070	0.060	0.051	0.043	0.037	0.031
20	0.820	0.673	0.554	0.456	0.377	0.312	0.258	0.215	0.178	0.149	0.124	0.104	0.087	0.073	0.061	0.051	0.043	0.037	0.031	0.026

Table 14.2 Present Value Factors for an annuity (PVA) [assumes first cash flow occurs at end of first year]

Year	1%	2%	3%	4%	5%	6%	7%	8%	9%	10%	11%	12%	13%	14%	15%	16%	17%	18%	19%	20%
1	0.990	0.980	0.971	0.962	0.952	0.943	0.935	0.926	0.917	0.909	0.901	0.893	0.885	0.877	0.870	0.862	0.855	0.847	0.840	0.833
2	1.970	1.942	1.913	1.886	1.859	1.833	1.808	1.783	1.759	1.736	1.713	1.690	1.668	1.647	1.626	1.605	1.585	1.566	1.547	1.528
3	2.941	2.884	2.829	2.775	2.723	2.673	2.624	2.577	2.531	2.487	2.444	2.402	2.361	2.322	2.283	2.246	2.210	2.174	2.140	2.106
4	3.902	3.808	3.717	3.630	3.546	3.465	3.387	3.312	3.240	3.170	3.102	3.037	2.974	2.914	2.855	2.798	2.743	2.690	2.639	2.589
5	4.853	4.713	4.580	4.452	4.329	4.212	4.100	3.993	3.890	3.791	3.696	3.605	3.517	3.433	3.352	3.274	3.199	3.127	3.058	2.991
6	5.795	5.601	5.417	5.242	5.076	4.917	4.767	4.623	4.486	4.355	4.231	4.111	3.998	3.889	3.784	3.685	3.589	3.498	3.410	3.326
7	6.728	6.472	6.230	6.002	5.786	5.582	5.389	5.206	5.033	4.868	4.712	4.564	4.423	4.288	4.160	4.039	3.922	3.812	3.706	3.605
8	7.652	7.325	7.020	6.733	6.463	6.210	5.971	5.747	5.535	5.335	5.146	4.968	4.799	4.639	4.487	4.344	4.207	4.078	3.954	3.837
9	8.566	8.162	7.786	7.435	7.108	6.802	6.515	6.247	5.995	5.759	5.537	5.328	5.132	4.946	4.772	4.607	4.451	4.303	4.163	4.031
10	9.471	8.983	8.530	8.111	7.722	7.360	7.024	6.710	6.418	6.145	5.889	5.650	5.426	5.216	5.019	4.833	4.659	4.494	4.339	4.192
11	10.368	9.787	9.253	8.760	8.306	7.887	7.499	7.139	6.805	6.495	6.207	5.938	5.687	5.453	5.234	5.029	4.836	4.656	4.486	4.327
12	11.255	10.575	9.954	9.385	8.863	8.384	7.943	7.536	7.161	6.814	6.492	6.194	5.918	5.660	5.421	5.197	4.988	4.793	4.611	4.439
13	12.134	11.348	10.635	9.986	9.394	8.853	8.358	7.904	7.487	7.103	6.750	6.424	6.122	5.842	5.583	5.342	5.118	4.910	4.715	4.533
14	13.004	12.106	11.296	10.563	9.899	9.295	8.745	8.244	7.786	7.367	6.982	6.628	6.302	6.002	5.724	5.468	5.229	5.008	4.802	4.611
15	13.865	12.849	11.938	11.118	10.380	9.712	9.108	8.559	8.061	7.606	7.191	6.811	6.462	6.142	5.847	5.575	5.324	5.092	4.876	4.675
16	14.718	13.578	12.561	11.652	10.838	10.106	9.447	8.851	8.313	7.824	7.379	6.974	6.604	6.265	5.954	5.668	5.405	5.162	4.938	4.730
17	15.562	14.292	13.166	12.166	11.274	10.477	9.763	9.122	8.544	8.022	7.549	7.120	6.729	6.373	6.047	5.749	5.475	5.222	4.990	4.775
18	16.398	14.992	13.754	12.659	11.690	10.828	10.059	9.372	8.756	8.201	7.702	7.250	6.840	6.467	6.128	5.818	5.534	5.273	5.033	4.812
19	17.226	15.678	14.324	13.134	12.085	11.158	10.336	9.604	8.950	8.365	7.839	7.366	6.938	6.550	6.198	5.877	5.584	5.316	5.070	4.843
20	18.046	16.351	14.877	13.590	12.462	11.470	10.594	9.818	9.129	8.514	7.963	7.469	7.025	6.623	6.259	5.929	5.628	5.353	5.101	4.870

referred to as an "annuity"). Box 14.3 presents two small examples that illustrate how the tables can be used to find the present value of a future cash flow.

Box 14.3

Using discounting tables to find the present value of future cash flows

Discounting example 1

Assuming an interest rate of 10 per cent, what is today's value of a $300 cash inflow occurring in 4 years' time?

Answer: Firstly, note that we are dealing with a single cash flow, therefore we turn to Table 14.1 (Present value factors for a single cash flow). In this Table, move along the columns until you come to the column headed 10%. Then move down the rows in this column until you come to the 4 year row. The factor you will find is 0.683. This signifies that if we multiply $300 by 0.683, we will have found today's value (or the present value) of a $300 cash flow occurring in 4 years' time.

In the calculation presented below, the term "PV" is an abbreviation of "Present Value" and is used to highlight the fact that the factor used has been drawn from the "present value of a single cash flow" table. The first number following the "PV" term refers to the relevant interest rate and the second number following the term refers to the relevant number of years. We find the present value of $300 in four years' time to be $204.90.

$$\text{Present value} = \$300 \ (PV_{10\%, \ 4yr}) = \$300 \times 0.683 = \$204.90$$

Discounting example 2

Assuming an interest rate of 12 per cent, what is today's value of receiving an annual payment of $400 in each of the next 5 years? Assume the first payment is in 1 year's time.

Answer: Firstly, note that in this second example we are dealing with a series of equal cash flows, therefore we turn to Table 14.2 (Present values factors for an annuity). This table has been compiled on the basis that the first cash flow of the stream of equal cash flows will occur one year from today. In the same manner to that used in the first discounting example, move along the columns until you come to the column headed 12 per cent. Then move down the rows in this column until you come to the 5 year row. The factor you will find is 3.605. In the calculation presented below, the term "PVA" is an abbreviation of "Present Value of an Annuity" and is used to highlight the fact that the factor used has been drawn from the "present value factors for an annuity" table.

$$\text{Present value} = \$400 \ (PVA_{12\%, \ 5yr}) = \$400 \times 3.605 = \$1,442$$

Having seen how the discounting tables can be used, we can now turn to calculating the NPV of an investment proposal. To do so, we need to isolate all incremental cash flows resulting from a decision to invest (including changed taxation cash flows), then bring these cash flows to present value. Remember, if a proposed investment has a positive NPV, it is acceptable. If it has a negative NPV, it should be rejected. If we are choosing between two mutually exclusive projects, select the one with the higher NPV. Two examples that illustrate the determination of an investment proposal's NPV are provided in Box 14.4.

Box 14.4

Finding an investment proposal's net present value

A project's NPV is determined by deducting its initial investment from the present value of the cash inflows that the project will generate.

NPV example 1: A proposed investment of $20,000 will increase net cash inflows by $5,000 in each of the following 8 years. The company considering the investment has determined that it requires a 12 per cent return for this proposal to be acceptable.

$$NPV = -\$20,000 + \$5,000 \ (PVA_{12\%, \ 8yr}) =$$
$$-\$20,000 + \$5,000 \ (4.968) =$$
$$-\$20,000 + \$24,840 = \$4,840$$
NPV is positive, therefore proposal is acceptable.

NPV example 2: A 1st January 20X0 investment of $10,000 will increase cash inflows by $3,000 in 20X0, $4,000 in 20X1 and $6,000 in 20X2. The company considering the investment requires a 12 per cent return on investments.

$$NPV = -\$10,000 + \$3,000 \ (PV_{12\%, 1yr}) + \$4,000 \ (PV_{12\%, 2yr}) + \$6,000 \ (PV_{12\%, 3yr}) =$$
$$-\$10,000 + \$3,000 \ (.893) + \$4,000 \ (.797) + \$6,000 \ (.712) =$$
$$-10,000 + 2,679 + 3,188 + 4,272 = \$139$$
NPV is positive, therefore proposal is acceptable.

The discount rate to be used when calculating NPV

It is widely suggested that the discount rate that should be used when calculating a project's net present value is the risk adjusted cost of capital. Much finance research and discussion has focused on this issue. Stated simply, the cost of capital is the average cost (stated as a percentage) of the capital funds raised by a company. Its calculation is illustrated in Box 14.5.

> ### Box 14.5
>
> ## Calculating the cost of capital
>
> The cost of capital can be defined as a firm's average cost of long-term financing. It is widely used by companies as the discount rate to be used when calculating NPV.
>
> Imagine the UK-based Trafalgar Hotel group has raised £1,000,000 in capital. £400,000 comprises long-term debt with an annual interest of 8 per cent. £600,000 has been raised in equity. Equity holders expect an annual return of 12 per cent on their investment.
>
> From the table below it can be seen that calculating Trafalgar's cost of capital involves using weights that reflect the relative size of each of Trafalgar's long-term sources of finance (i.e., equity is 60 per cent of capital, debt is 40 per cent of capital). Multiplying the cost of each source of finance by its weighting, and summing the products, we find the Trafalgar group's weighted average cost of capital to be 10.4 per cent.
>
> | | Cost | Relative size of capital source (weighting) | Cost × Weighting |
> |---|---|---|---|
> | Equity (£0.6m) | 12 per cent | 0.6 | 7.2 per cent |
> | Debt (£0.4m) | 8 per cent | 0.4 | 3.2 per cent |
> | Cost of Capital | | | 10.4 per cent |

The 10.4 per cent cost of capital computed for the Trafalgar group in Box 14.5 would be an appropriate discount rate to use when appraising one of the company's average risk investment proposals. If appraising a higher risk investment, a risk premium reflecting the higher risk should be added to the cost of capital. This is because investors are risk averse and they would want to be compensated via a higher return if the hotel group were to assume a more risky profile. Likewise, if a below average risk investment is under consideration, net present value should be calculated using a rate below the 10.4 per cent cost of capital. Readers seeking more information on the cost of capital will find extensive discussion devoted to the topic in most introductory corporate finance texts.

Concluding comments on NPV

In the interest of simplification, we have treated future cash flows as if they occur at the end of the year rather than during the year. This approach is widely taken and signifies that if the investment proposal under consideration fits the typical cash flow pattern of a large initial outlay followed by incremental net inflows, the net present value of the project will be slightly understated.

In theory, NPV is the preferred investment appraisal technique. If a company commits itself to a project with an NPV of $5m, and the share market is working efficiently, the company's value should increase by $5m. This is because today's value of all the company's future cash flows has been increased by $5m.

5) Internal rate of return

Like the NPV, the internal rate of return (IRR) investment appraisal technique is also based on discounting cash flows that occur in the future. Calculation of the IRR is illustrated through a worked example in Box 14.6.

Box 14.6

Finding an investment proposal's internal rate of return

Internal Rate of Return (IRR) = the discount rate that causes the present value of a project's inflows to equal the present value of its outflows, i.e., the discount rate that causes a project's NPV to equal zero.

If a proposed project's IRR is greater than the company's risk adjusted cost of capital, the project is acceptable.

An IRR example:
Imagine a proposed investment of $20,000 will increase cash inflows by $5,000 in each of the following 8 years. The company considering the investment has determined that it requires a 12 per cent return for this proposal to be acceptable.

The method taken to find the IRR of a proposed investment that generates future equal annual inflows (an annuity) involves setting the "NPV equation" equal to zero. We then determine what discount rate yields the zero NPV.

IRR calculation:
$$0 = -\$20,000 + \$5,000 \, (PVA_{IRR, \, 8yr}),$$
$$\$20,000 \div \$5,000 = (PVA_{IRR, \, 8yr}),$$
$$4 = (PVA_{IRR, \, 8yr}),$$

In PVA table, looking along the 8 year row, we find 4 corresponds to between 18 per cent and 19 per cent.

IRR = is between 18 per cent and 19 per cent
Project is acceptable as IRR > 12 per cent

This example represents a relatively easy IRR computation, as the cash inflows are in the form of an annuity. Where the inflows are not an annuity, a trial and error approach has to be adopted. This involves trying different discount rates until one is found that results in an NPV of zero. If you have an advanced pocket calculator, it might be able to compute the IRR, otherwise it can be a lengthy exercise!

The IRR approach to investment appraisal has the following shortcomings:

1. In some cases, where a project's cash flows include future cash outflows, two different discount rates can result in an NPV of zero (i.e., two IRRs for one project).
2. In a single project, accept or reject situation, NPV and IRR will give the same indication (i.e., if IRR > required rate of return, NPV will be > 0). When ranking projects, however, NPV and IRR can give conflicting signals, i.e., the highest NPV project will not necessarily be the highest IRR project. If this situation arises, preference should be given to the NPV indication as it is the theoretically preferred technique.

Despite IRR's shortcomings (which are not as great as those apparent for ARR and payback), it is widely used in practice. This may be because managers can conceive of a proposed investment's projected rate of return more easily than its projected net present value.

6) Integrating the four investment appraisal techniques

In capital budgeting decision making, many hotels use more than one of the four investment appraisal techniques described in the previous section. Guilding and Lamminmaki (2007) surveyed Australian hotels and found that 21 per cent used two methods, 11 per cent used three methods and 13 per cent used all four methods described in this chapter.

Financial decision making in action case 14.1 is designed to underline the fact that most organisations use more than one investment appraisal technique. In addition, it highlights that investment appraisal techniques can be used when considering a cost saving investment.

FINANCIAL DECISION MAKING IN ACTION CASE 14.1

The Chief Engineer and investment appraisal

Imagine the Bermuda Beach Hotel's chief engineer is deliberating whether to upgrade the hotel's old air conditioning system. Investment in the new system would be $250,000 and it has been estimated that it will save the hotel $75,000 in electricity and maintenance expenses in each of the next five years. The investment would be depreciated at the rate of $50,000 per annum and have no salvage value at the end of its five year life. The hotel has a 10 per cent cost of capital and operates in a tax haven (i.e., no tax applies).

If the chief engineer knows that the hotel's finance department uses a breadth of investment appraisal techniques, he could review the financial viability of the proposed investment by computing its ARR, payback, NPV and IRR in the following manner:

Accounting Rate of Return (Annual profit generated ÷ Average investment × 100)
ARR = ($75,000 − $50,000) ÷ $125,000 × 100 = 20 per cent

Payback (time taken to recoup the cash invested in an asset)
Payback = $250,000 ÷ $75,000 = 3.33 (i.e., 3 years and 4 months).

Net Present Value

$$NPV = -\$250,000 + \$75,000 \, (PVA_{10\%, \, 5yr})$$
$$= -\$250,000 + \$75,000 \, (3.791)$$
$$= -\$250,000 + \$284,325 = \$34,325.$$

Internal Rate of Return

$$0 = -\$250,000 + \$75,000 \, (PVA_{IRR, \, 5yr}),$$
$$\$250,000 \div \$75,000 = (PVA_{IRR, \, 5yr}),$$
$$3.33 = (PVA_{IRR, \, 5yr}),$$

In PVA table, in the 5 year row, we find 3.33 corresponds to between 15 per cent and 16 per cent.
IRR is therefore between 15 per cent and 16 per cent

From the above analysis, the chief engineer would have established that the air conditioning upgrade is financially justifiable as its projected NPV is positive and its IRR is greater than the cost of capital. Capital budgeting is not always conducted in a completely rational way, however.

It may be that the Bermuda Beach Hotel has a risk-averse general manager who is unwilling to authorise any capital expenditure that does not meet a predicted payback of less than three years. It may also be that the proposal is rejected as its submission coincides with a year of several other worthy investment projects. While the proposal may be financially justifiable, the chief engineer will soon realise that it cannot be approved if the hotel has insufficient capital funds available.

7) Summary

In this chapter we have looked at the main financial techniques that can be used to appraise investment proposals. You should now know:

- how to compute a proposed investment's accounting rate of return, payback period, net present value and internal rate of return,
- the relative merits of these four investment appraisal techniques,
- what is meant by the "time value of money",
- how present values can be determined using discounting tables.

References

Eyster, Jr., J.J. and Geller, A.N. (1981) "The Capital-Investment Decision: Techniques Used in the Hospitality Industry", *The Cornell Hotel and Restaurant Administration Quarterly*, May, 69–73.

Guilding, C. and Lamminmaki, D. (2007) "Benchmarking hotel capital budgeting practices to practices applied in non-hotel companies", *Journal of Hospitality & Tourism Research*, Volume 31, No. 4, 486–503.

Harris, P. (1999) *Profit Planning*, 2nd edition, Oxford: Butterworth Heinemann: Chapter 12.

Jagels, M.G. (2007) *Hospitality Management Accounting*, 9th edition, Hoboken, NJ: John Wiley & Sons: Chapter 12.

Langfield-Smith, K., Thorne, H. and Hilton, R. (2012) *Management Accounting: Information for Creating and Managing Value*, 6th edition, Macquarie Park, NSW, Australia: McGraw-Hill: Chapter 21.

Schmidgall, R.F. (2011) *Hospitality Industry Managerial Accounting*, 7th edition, East Lansing, MI: American Hotel & Lodging Educational Institute: Chapter 13.

Problems

Problem 14.1

Describe the strengths and weakness of using the payback method in capital budgeting.

Problem 14.2

a) Four investment appraisal techniques have been described in this chapter: 1) Accounting Rate of Return, 2) Payback, 3) Net Present Value, and 4) Internal Rate of Return. Which is the theoretically preferred investment appraisal technique?

b) With respect to your answer to a), describe why the technique you have identified is the theoretically preferred investment appraisal technique?

Problem 14.3

Michael Johnson has been given the opportunity of investing in a financial security that will pay him $600 in five years' time. Assuming similar risk investments earn an annual return of 8 per cent, what value should Michael put on this investment opportunity today?

Problem 14.4

a) What is the value today of a stream of cash flows paying $500 at the end of each of the next 8 years. Assume an interest rate of 10 per cent.

b) What is the value today of a stream of annual cash flows paying $500 at the beginning of each of the next 8 years (i.e., the first cash flow will occur today). Assume an interest rate of 10 per cent. (Helpful hint: remember that the PVA table is compiled on the basis that the first cash flow occurs in one year's time.)

Problem 14.5

Given the following two sets of cash flows, determine whether A or B has the higher present value. Assume an interest rate of 12 per cent. (Helpful hint: remember that the PVA table is compiled on the basis that the first cash flow occurs in one year's time.)

Year[a]	Cash stream A	Cash stream B
1	$3,000	$3,500
2	$3,000	$3,500
3		$3,500
4	$3,000	$3,500
5	$3,000	
6	$3,000	
7	$3,000	$3,500
8	$3,000	$3,500

[a] Assume that year 1 refers to a cash flow occurring in 1 year's time, year 2 refers to a cash flow occurring in 2 years' time, etc.

Problem 14.6

As part of its annual capital budgeting cycle, the Welsh Westmede hotel is deciding whether investment proposal A or investment proposal B is more financially justifiable. Investment proposal A requires an initial outlay of £36,000. It is estimated that £3,000 of this initial investment will be salvaged at the end of the investment's five year life. Investment B also requires an initial investment of £36,000. It is estimated that this asset will be salvaged for £7,000 in five years' time.

The schedule below presents the timing of estimated increases to Westmede's operating cash flows and also operating profit that would result if either investment were to be made.

| Year | Investment A | | Investment B | |
	Net cash operating inflows	Increased operating profit*	Net cash operating inflows	Increased operating profit*
1	£14,000	£6,400	£5,000	£0
2	£12,000	£4,900	£7,000	£800
3	£10,000	£3,400	£15,000	£8,400
4	£8,000	£1,900	£18,000	£10,400
5	£8,000	£2,400	£13,000	£5,400

* Annual depreciation charges associated with the new investment will cause operating profits to be less than operating cash flows.

Required:

a) Calculate the accounting rate of return for the two investment proposals.

b) Calculate the payback for the two investment proposals.
c) Calculate the net present value for the two investment proposals assuming that the company has a required rate of return of 12 per cent. Assume that no tax implication will arise as a result of salvaging either of the proposed investments at the end of their useful lives.
d) Which is the preferred investment opportunity?

Problem 14.7

Edmonton's Green Park Hotel is considering purchasing some new laundry equipment for $200,000. Currently the hotel is outsourcing its laundry activities. The hotel's financial controller has estimated that if the laundry equipment is purchased, annual cash flows of $50,000 will be saved in each of the next five years, at which time the laundry equipment will have a zero salvage value. The hotel has a 10 per cent cost of capital.

Required:

a) What is the laundry equipment's approximate internal rate of return.
b) In light of your answer to a), would you recommend that the hotel invests in the laundry equipment?

Problem 14.8

a) Imagine you are trying to find the IRR of an investment project that has increasing estimated future cash inflows in each of the next eight years. You have tried a discount rate of 12 per cent and have discovered that this results in a positive NPV for the investment project. Explain whether the project's IRR is more or less than 12 per cent.
b) Your hotel is considering two options with respect to a major overhaul of an existing restaurant. The restaurant will either be themed as an Italian restaurant, which will require the installation of a wood-fired pizza oven, or it will be themed as a British pub, which will require the installation of extensive bar facilities. It has been estimated that the Italian restaurant option will provide an IRR of 16 per cent and an NPV of $420,000. It has also been projected that the British pub option will provide an IRR of 17 per cent and an NPV of $350,000. From a financial perspective, explain which of the two options is preferable.

Problem 14.9

Viking Hotels, a large international hotel chain is structured according to seven geographically based divisions worldwide. Shortly after he joined the company, the Chief Executive of the European division informed General Managers in Viking's European hotels that he wanted an improved profit performance. This head of the European division believes in a decentralised policy and likes to give Hotel General Managers considerable autonomy in running their hotels as they see fit.

Eighteen months after the European division's Chief Executive took up his position, the performance of the group's Birmingham and Manchester hotels caught his eye. Both hotels had managed to increase their return on capital employed, following some expansion in the Birmingham hotel's assets and some contraction in the Manchester hotel's assets. The schedule below summarises the performance of the two hotels.

	Birmingham hotel		Manchester hotel	
	20X2	20X1	20X2	20X1
Net operating profit	£144,000	£60,000	£228,000	£288,000
Capital employed	£2,400,000	£1,500,000	£1,200,000	£1,600,000
Return on capital employed	6 per cent	4 per cent	19 per cent	18 per cent

In addition to providing a financial summary of their hotel's performance, each Hotel General Manager is expected to provide the division's Chief Executive with a written commentary that provides background to the financial performance. The following represents extracts taken from the commentaries provided by the General Managers in the Birmingham and Manchester hotels.

The Birmingham hotel General Manager commented:

> We've managed to expand operations this year following the completion of the hotel's east wing extension. This expansion is already proving to be highly successful with operating profit more than doubling and return on capital employed increasing from 4 per cent to 6 per cent. I, together with the hotel's senior management, am confident that continued expansion is possible and that next year we will again be able to increase return on capital employed by a further percentage point to 7 per cent.

The General Manager of the Manchester hotel commented:

> 20X2 has been a year of rationalisation. We've managed to sell off some of the hotel's grounds where we used to operate a restaurant, bar and night club. This has had a positive impact on our return on capital employed. Further increases in return on capital employed may be possible as we may be able to phase out other below average rate of return activities.

Required:
In light of Viking's cost of capital, which is 12 per cent, explain whether the actions of the two hotels give cause for any concern. (Helpful hint: consider the return on capital employed of the assets acquired at the Birmingham hotel and also the return on capital employed of the assets sold at the Manchester hotel.)

Problem 14.10

Len, the head of general stores in a large Australian hotel complex has been asked to defend his "gut feel" that an upgrade in the currently used stores' computerised information system is warranted. He has visited a company operating the recently developed "Super store" software and has returned very favourably impressed. He now needs to prepare an investment proposal in a manner that will find favour with the finance group that closely scrutinises all capital expenditure proposals.

Len has determined that the upgrade will cost the hotel $40,000 in new computer hardware. An annual software operating licence fee would also have to be paid. Len recommends that the licence agreement be entered into for 5 years, as the software company is providing an introductory special of "sign up for 5 years and pay a fee of only $5,000 per annum – a saving of 10 per cent off the standard fee charge". Due to computer technology advancement, it is widely believed that the hardware will be worthless after five years. For this reason, the company's policy will be to view the investment as having a life of five years.

Len believes that the new system will enable him to reduce clerical time associated with inputting data on the old computer system by 25 hours per week. This clerical work has been performed by a casual employee who cost the hotel $15,000 in wages last year. He also believes that the greater accuracy resulting from the improved record keeping that would be achieved will reduce the investment in average stock held by $10,000.

Required:

a) Ignoring tax, determine the payback of this investment.
b) Assuming a 40 per cent tax rate and that computer hardware capital expenditure is written off straight line over a five-year period for tax purposes, use NPV to determine whether the proposed computer upgrade is justified. The hotel has a 10 per cent cost of capital.

Problem 14.11

The General Manager of Eating Extravagance Ltd has approached you seeking advice on two competing investment opportunities that he has under consideration. Each investment requires an initial investment of $40,000 and will result in the following annual cash inflows over a six-year period.

Year	Alternative 1	Alternative 2
1	$ 2,000	$ 16,000
2	8,000	13,000
3	10,000	11,000
4	12,000	8,000
5	16,000	6,000
6	24,000	4,000

Required:

a) Calculate the payback for each of the investment alternatives. Based on the payback method, state which is the preferred investment.
b) Calculate the net present value of each of the alternatives, assuming the general manager uses a discount rate of 10 per cent in all NPV calculations.
c) Based on your calculations, comment on which, if either, of the investment alternatives should be taken.

Problem 14.12: The Stellar Views' chapel case study

Introduction

This is a case that draws on a real investment opportunity that was under consideration in a large Australian hotel. The numbers stated in the case have been modified and also the name of the hotel changed in order to provide anonymity to the hotel concerned. The case is presented partly as an illustration of the difficult nature of estimating future cash flows when a hotel is considering an investment in a new activity that is significantly different from its existing activities. Textbooks that provide an overview of capital budgeting too frequently give extensive consideration to the different appraisal techniques that can be used, but give little attention to the problem of generating a proposed investment's cash flow estimates.

Case description

The Stellar Views Hotel is located in a popular tourist region of Australia. The hotel comprises two adjoining buildings located near a beach. The main building is 25 storeys high, and the second is six storeys high. The smaller of the two buildings has a large flat roof with easy pedestrian access available from the large building. A small tennis facility comprising two courts has occupied this roof for the last ten years and the courts are now in need of a major overhaul. The tennis facility has been provided as a free service to hotel guests.

Stellar Views' management is considering dismantling the tennis facility and replacing it with a small 100-seater wedding chapel. The management believes there is considerable potential demand for this service, especially in light of the photo opportunities that the chapel's position would offer. In addition to catering to the local market, the chapel would be targeted towards the many Japanese visitors that come to the region to get married. Part of the rationale for the strong anticipated demand relates to a change in the type of wedding/reception/accommodation mix currently sought in the market for weddings. In earlier years it was typical for separate venues to be used for the wedding service, wedding reception and also the accommodation booked before and after the wedding. Following consultation with a Japanese tourist operator, Stellar Views' management has determined that couples are increasingly seeking a facility that can enable the wedding service, reception and accommodation to be provided at a single site. Convenience and cost issues are the main factors that lie behind this change. A single venue signifies that couples can benefit from packaged prices and also save on additional costs such as limousine hire and church decorators.

The hotel's management has commissioned a consulting group to develop estimates of the initial costs of building the chapel and also the demand for wedding ceremonies. It has been estimated that the chapel will cost $1,000,000 to build. The schedule below presents the consulting company's demand estimates. The demand estimates are based on a ceremony fee of $550. This ceremony price also covers the provision of floral arrangements, pew bows, topiary trees and a red carpeted aisle.

| | Projected demand for ceremonies* | | | | | | |
	Jan. & Feb.	Mar. & April	May & June	July & August	Sept. & Oct.	Nov. & Dec.	Total
Local Market							
Friday	0	0	2	0	4	1	7
Saturday	6	16	14	7	40	10	93
Sunday	0	2	4	0	8	1	15
Sub-total	6	18	20	7	52	12	115

	Projected demand for ceremonies*						
	Jan. & Feb.	Mar. & April	May & June	July & August	Sept. & Oct.	Nov. & Dec.	Total
Japanese inbound market							
Monday	0	1	2	0	2	0	5
Tuesday	0	3	10	0	8	3	24
Wednesday	0	3	10	0	8	3	24
Thursday	0	3	9	0	8	3	23
Friday	0	1	1	0	2	0	4
Sub-total	0	11	32	0	28	9	80
Total ceremonies held	6	29	52	7	80	21	195

* The projected demand for ceremonies is based on a proposed ceremony fee of $550.

The hotel has also projected that each ceremony will have a variable cost of $100 and that annual fixed costs associated with maintaining the chapel and surrounding gardens will be $10,000. Further, it has been estimated that 90 per cent of the Japanese inbound market ceremonies will result in a reception held at the hotel and extra guests staying at the hotel. It has been estimated that each Japanese reception held at the hotel will generate a contribution of $2,000. For the 90 per cent of Japanese ceremonies that will result in extra guests staying at the hotel, it has been estimated that each ceremony will result in an additional $1,000 of accommodation profit earned by the hotel.

With respect to the wedding ceremonies booked by locals, it is estimated that 20 per cent will result in a reception at the hotel and these receptions will contribute $5,000 per reception. Further, it is estimated that the average local market ceremony will result in 15 extra room sales which will generate an additional contribution of $100 per room. The hotel's financial controller has determined that the viability of this chapel investment will be assessed using a 14 per cent discount rate.

Required:

a) Prepare an NPV analysis of the proposed chapel investment for Stellar Views' management. Assume that the hotel's management feels that the projected demand schedule presented above will apply for the first five years following the chapel's construction. In addition, it feels the contributions earned from receptions and accommodation associated with ceremonies will be constant in the chapel's first five years. When calculating NPV, the management has a policy of not looking at cash flow estimates beyond a five-year period.

b) Describe whether you see the proposed chapel investment as risky. With respect to the discount rate that should be used when calculating the chapel's NPV, do you feel Stellar Views should use its cost of capital?

c) What sources of information do you feel the hotel might use with respect to developing its initial estimate of the cost of building the chapel?

Chapter 15

Other managerial finance issues

Learning objectives

After studying this chapter, you should have developed an appreciation of:

1. the most appropriate financial objective for companies to pursue,
2. what is meant by "agency theory",
3. problems surrounding the way that a manager's goals can differ to the goals of a shareholder,
4. how goal incongruence can arise when hotel owners engage the services of a hotel management company,
5. the basic workings of share markets and the nature of a stock market index,
6. how to value a share based on the projected earnings stream that will be provided by the share,
7. the procedure taken by companies in paying dividends,
8. distinct dividend payment policies that a company can choose to pursue,
9. how fixed costs contribute to a company's operating and financial leverage,
10. how higher levels of leverage signify greater risk for a company.

1) Introduction

This chapter provides a broad sweep across several financial management topics that are not addressed elsewhere in this book. It will demonstrate how managers pursuing a goal of maximizing earnings per share may well not be serving the best interests of shareholders. Associated with this, it will also show how managers may well have personal career goals that do not align well to the goals of shareholders. The distinctiveness of shareholder and manager goals will be examined using a conceptual approach that is widely referred to as "agency theory". Agency theory will also be employed to demonstrate goal incongruence issues that can arise when a hotel owner engages the services of a hotel operator.

We will also briefly explore the nature of share trading and factors that affect a share's value. Related to these factors, we will examine the procedure taken by companies when paying dividends and also what alternative dividend payment policies they may adopt. Finally, the concept of leverage will be introduced. Leverage concerns the way that a greater proportion of fixed costs lead to a greater volatility in earnings provided to shareholders. As volatile shareholder earnings represent a manifestation of risk, we can see that a company's level of leverage carries implications for its share value (higher risk levels are perceived negatively by the stock market). We then consider what steps a company can take should it wish to increase or decrease its level of leverage.

2) What should be the over-riding business objective in financial management?

Maximize profit (EPS)?

Many managers think that the over-riding financial objective of companies is to maximize profit. It is common to measure a company's profit performance in terms of **earnings per share** (EPS). EPS is calculated by taking a company's earnings (profit) available to shareholders and dividing it by the company's number of shares. This EPS calculation could be done for any period of time; however, it is most usually calculated quarterly (for a three month period), or a year.

As EPS is a widely quoted company performance indicator, it is understandable that many managers will hold the maximization of EPS as their number one financial management objective. We will now see, however, several reasons why this objective is inappropriate. Three factors signifying that pursuit of EPS maximization is an inappropriate goal are: 1) EPS fails to tightly capture the timing of financial returns; 2) EPS fails to capture cash flows; and 3) EPS fails to recognize risk. Each of these EPS failings are now explained in turn.

With respect to EPS's shortcoming that stems from the **timing of financial returns** issue, note that EPS indicates the earnings per share (profit) earned by a company over a period of time. For any period of time, there is scope for the earnings to be made early or late within the period. This issue of EPS timing is explained via a worked example in Box 15.1.

The second EPS shortcoming concerns the **failure of EPS to capture cash flows**. EPS is based on an accounting system's calculation of profit; it is not based on an accounting system's measurement of cash flow. We saw in Chapter 13 how profit is not the same as cash flow when we developed a cash flow budget for the BackWoods Retreat, and found that in a January–March period, the business was projected to earn a profit of $92,800, while at the same time suffering a bank balance decline of $85,300.

How can cash flow depart from profit? Well, a significant factor contributing to the difference between profit and cash flow is the way accountants account for fixed assets. If we pay $500,000 for a fixed asset, cash will immediately decline at the time we pay for the fixed asset; however, the reported profit in the year the asset is purchased will not be affected by nearly as much. If it is determined that the cost of the asset is to be depreciated over ten years, in the year that the asset is purchased, reported profit will only be reduced by the $50,000 annual depreciation charge for the asset (assuming the asset was purchased at the beginning of the year), not the $500,000 asset cost. This signifies that in the year the asset is purchased, a $450,000 discrepancy arises between reported profit (affected by a $50,000 depreciation charge) and actual cash flow (affected by a $500,000 payment to the fixed asset supplier).

Box 15.1

The importance of EPS return timing

This worked example shows the importance of the time when earnings per share (EPS) returns are achieved by a company.

Imagine that the Fortress Hotel Group and the Soft Pillow Hotel Group are similar sized hotel management companies with the same number of shares outstanding. Based on the following data, which of the two hotel management companies do you feel has performed better in terms of EPS?

Company	Year 1	Year 2	Year 3	Year 4	Total
		Earnings per share			
Fortress Hotel Group	$1.70	$2.00	$2.40	$2.80	$8.90
Soft Pillow Hotel Group	$2.85	$2.40	$2.00	$1.60	$8.85

In raw terms, clearly the Fortress Hotel Group has a better EPS performance, as the final column shows us that its overall EPS over the four-year period is $0.05 greater than the EPS achieved by the Soft Pillow Hotel Group.

Note, however, that the Soft Pillow Hotel Group provides higher EPS in the early years. Now, remember the time value concept of money that was covered in the previous chapter. This concept holds that $1 received today is worth more than $1 received in a year's time. Imagine two investors own the same number of shares in the two companies and the companies paid out their entire earnings as dividends. If both shareholders reinvested these amounts in a bank account earning 5 per cent interest, the one who had invested in the Soft Pillow Hotel Group would have accumulated a greater wealth following the payment of the fourth dividend. This signifies that a rational investor would prefer the stream of returns provided by the Soft Pillow Hotel Group over the stream of returns provided by the Fortress Hotel Group.

This clearly shows that high returns received early are preferable to high returns received late. This simple example highlights the importance of considering EPS timing, not just the absolute size of EPS.

So, which should be held as the more important financial management objective: the maximization of cash flow or the maximization of profit? A hint of an answer lies in the fact that in the previous chapter we noted that maximizing net present value is the theoretically preferred investment appraisal technique. Fundamental to the net present value investment appraisal approach is the principle that we should maximize today's value of the expected future cash flows (not profits!) resulting from a capital expenditure. While an increased profit projection might suggest that better times are ahead, the realization of a better time occurs only once operating cash inflows increase. The real return that shareholders earn from their investment is the cash dividends that they receive. In concrete terms, it is not profits that finance the payment of cash dividends, it is a company's operating cash flow that funds the payment of dividends. Remember, profit is no more than a "performance story" in which arbitrary factors such as depreciation play a significant part. There is no arbitrariness when determining cash flow, however. Money at the bank is very real in the sense that it can be objectively verified, and it is the money in a company's bank account that a company uses to pay dividends. In light of this, it is widely agreed that in order to best serve shareholders, companies should focus on maximizing the present value of their projected cash flows.

The third EPS shortcoming concerns the fact that **EPS fails to recognize risk**. A fundamental principle in finance theory concerns the risk/return trade-off. This principle generally holds that greater returns can only be made by taking on more risk. If you ever seek personal financial investment advice, invariably your financial advisor will ask you what degree of risk you can live with. In the world of finance, greater risk stems from more uncertain returns, i.e. greater variability in returns and a greater downside of potentially losing money (a greater chance of experiencing a negative return in any given year). The more risk you are willing to accept in your investment portfolio, however, the greater the return you can expect to earn over the long term. An investment held over the last 100 years in an interest bearing account (low risk) would have earned much less than an average risk portfolio investment held on the stock market (higher risk than an interest bearing account). However, while a share investment earns more over the long term, it will also provide much greater variability in returns, with more years providing negative returns compared to an interest bearing investment.

Return and risk have conflicting impacts on the price of a share. If a company starts to make more risky investments as part of an effort to increase returns, two competing factors affecting its share price will result. Any increased cash flows resulting from the greater risk strategy will have a positive impact on share price. The increased uncertainty associated with the greater risk, however, will have a negative impact on share price, as investors are risk averse (i.e., they do not like risk). A hotel company may manage to increase its EPS following its diversification into the spa sector of the hotel market. The share market may see this as increasing the risk profile of the company, however, if it sees spa operations as more risky than the company's conventional operations. If the negativity associated with greater perceived risk outweighs the positivity resulting from increased EPS, the company's share price will drop during a period in which its EPS increases. This clearly shows that the maximization of EPS does not necessarily work in the interest of shareholders.

In addition to the above shortcomings with EPS, you should also be aware that there is a particular problem in any attempt to use EPS as part of a cross-company comparison. Imagine that in a particular year, EPS for the ABC company is $4, and EPS for the XYZ company is $2. We cannot conclude from this that the ABC company is more profitable than the XYZ company. Firstly, note that if the ABC company has 100 issued shares and the XYZ company has 1,000 shares, net profit for ABC must be only $400 (100 shares × $4) compared to XYZ's $2,000 profit (1,000 shares × $2). Secondly, imagine that during 20X1, shares in ABC traded for around $50 while shares in XYZ traded for $10. The earnings when stated as a return on the owner's investment (this is sometimes called the earnings yield and is calculated by dividing EPS by the share price) is 8 per cent for the ABC company (4 ÷ 50 × 100), and 20 per cent for the XYZ company (2 ÷ 10 × 100). EPS can be usefully used, however, as part of a trend analysis of a single company (assuming the number of shares issued remains constant), and EPS is particularly useful when combined with share price to give us the **price earnings ratio** (PE ratio).

The PE ratio is computed as follows:

Price/Earnings (P.E.) ratio = *Market price per share ÷ Earnings per share*

Unlike EPS, the PE ratio can be used as part of a cross-company analysis. A high PE for a company relative to its competitors in the same industry can be caused by either of the following two factors:

1. The investing community expects an increase in the company's EPS in the future and this has resulted in increased demand for its shares which, in turn, has increased the share price (past earnings are only of interest to the investor to the extent that they provide an indication of expected future earnings),
2. The investing community perceives relatively low risk in the company. As investors are averse to risk, increasing levels of risk will result in decreasing demand for the share, which, in turn, results in a decreased share price.

Shareholder wealth maximization?

It is widely held by managerial finance commentators that the goal of a company's managers should be to maximize the wealth of shareholders. Shareholder wealth is maximized when share price is maximized. This signifies that managers need to strike an optimal balance in managing their company's risk/return trade-off that has just been described, as both risk and return carry implications for a company's share price.

While the maximization of shareholder wealth has generally been accepted as the most appropriate corporate financial goal, recent years has seen greater recognition given to other company stakeholders. These other stakeholders include employees, customers and also the broader society. Broader society has in particular become a more significant stakeholder group in light of a groundswell increase in environmental awareness. Companies are now being held much more accountable for any damage that they may inflict on the physical environment. This broadening of responsibility to stakeholders other than shareholders has seen the rise of a broader accounting initiative that has become widely referred to as "triple bottom line" reporting. While a company's annual reports have traditionally focused primarily on financial performance reporting, a growth in triple bottom line reporting has seen a broadening of the focus to also include social performance and environmental performance reporting. Social performance reporting focuses on a company's impact on society, which includes customers, employees, suppliers and the broader community. Environmental performance reporting focuses on a company's impact on the environment, which includes land, water, air, ecosystems and also people.

This broader stakeholder perspective should not be seen as displacing the shareholder wealth maximization objective, rather it can be viewed as highlighting other factors that need to be considered by managers as they pursue shareholder wealth maximization. Considered in this manner, the corporate world's increased importance attached to a range of stakeholders, beyond shareholders, has placed some constraints on the actions a company's managers can take when seeking to maximize share price.

3) Agency issues

In this section we will review agency theory in general and then consider the particular agency relationship that arises when a hotel owner engages the services of a hotel management company to manage its hotel.

Agency theory

The discussion above has led us to the idea that managers should pursue objectives that are in the interests of a company's shareholders. The extent to which managers actually manage companies in ways that are truly in the interests of their company's shareholders is questionable, however, and is an issue that has been the subject of much financial research. Much of this research has been built around the **agency theory** model. Agency theory concerns the relationship between one party that wants to have a job done and a second party that is engaged by the first party to perform the job. The party engaging the second party is generally referred to as the "principal", and the party that is engaged to perform the job is called the "agent". Examples of principal/agent relationships include:

- shareholders (acting as principals) appointing a board of directors (acting as agents) to run a company;
- a board of directors (acting as principals) employing a hotel general manager (acting as an agent) to run a hotel;
- a hotel general manager (acting as principal) appointing an F&B manager (acting as an agent) to run an F&B department.

From these three examples, it can be seen that a large organisation comprises a multitude of agency relationships. Many of these relationships mirror what we find in a standard organisational hierarchy. This signifies that a depiction of many organisational agency relationships is captured in an organisational chart (e.g., see Figure 9.1 in Chapter 9). You should now read through Box 15.2 to develop your appreciation of how you encounter agency relationship challenges in your everyday life.

Box 15.2

Everyday agency relationship challenges

In your everyday life, you experience many agency relationships. If you have a job, you will likely have a boss. Your boss is concerned with the fundamental agency issue of finding ways to monitor your performance in order to ensure you are performing the job to an appropriate standard. Although you might not appreciate it, you have also likely had experiences of acting as a principal. Whenever you engage someone to provide you with a service, the service provider is acting as an agent and you are cast as the principal.

Interesting agency issues arise for you every time you go to see a doctor or a dentist. Most of us tend to think of our doctor or dentist as in a superior position; after all, they are well qualified and have a position that is held in high standing by society. Despite this high standing, both doctors and dentists are acting as agents for their patients as they are providing a paid-for service. This is where we come to the interesting aspect of this agency relationship. Are you in a strong position to make a judgement on the quality of the service provided to you by your doctor or dentist? Do you know whether you

---

should change your medical or dental service provider due to the quality of the service that they provide? Your likely answer to both of these questions will be "No". Now, when we recognize that there are bound to be some doctors and dentists who provide an above average level of medical or dental service, what can you do to ensure you have a doctor or dentist who falls into this above average category? Here lies the classic agency problem. The principal can have trouble determining the quality of the service provided by their engaged agent.

It is because of this agency problem that occurs when engaging the services of highly trained professionals that considerable agency costs are expended in an attempt to inculcate professionals with a conscientious approach to their work, and steps are taken by medical and dental professional associations to promote ethical behaviour amongst their respective memberships. Expending resources on recruiting "the right people" for medical and dental training, then expending resources on promotion of a conscientious ethic followed by on-going monitoring of whether professionals are maintaining suitably high ethical standards are all highly costly activities that society, as a whole, has to bear. These costs can be described as "agency costs", as they are incurred in an effort to protect you and I from the dangers of being incapable of effectively monitoring the performance of our medical and dental service-providing agents. Society has determined that these are appropriate costs to incur in order to achieve greater assurance over the quality of medical and dental service provision.

Just so you can see that this agency problem is much less in many other contexts, consider the situation that arises if you decide to employ someone to spend three hours per week cleaning your house. There are several things you can do to appraise the quality of the house cleaning service that you are purchasing. At the end of the three-hour cleaning shift, you can look around the house to assess how well it has been cleaned. You could also arrange to be home when the house cleaner is doing their work and you could keep an eye on how busy they seem to be and assess what exact activities they engage in during the three-hour period. In light of the fact that you can fairly effectively gauge the quality of the service provided by a house cleaner, it is a working relationship that does not present significant work monitoring agency challenges.

In the company context, the agency relationship that is of particular interest to us concerns the role of managers, acting as agents, in serving the interest of shareholders, acting as principals. There is a fundamental agency problem here, as many managers may well be more focused on pursuing their own personal goals rather than the shareholder wealth maximization goal. Personal goals of managers that do not necessarily align well with company goals include seeking to increase personal wealth, leisure time and job security and avoiding stressful job assignments. Box 15.3 provides an elaboration of how attitude to risk can be a source of different objectives pursued by managers and shareholders.

Box 15.3

Misalignment of manager and shareholder goals

The issue of risk provides us with a clear-cut example of how the interests of the managers and shareholders of a company can be misaligned. Let's return to the example of a company considering the merits of broadening its operations into the spa sector of the hotel market. Imagine that two companies have decided to diversify their operations into this potentially lucrative sub-sector of hotel operations. Imagine that Company A is successful in managing this diversification and that, as a result, its value increases by $1.5 million. Imagine also that Company B does not manage the diversification as successfully and, as a result, its value declines by $1 million.

Now, let's imagine that you own 1 per cent of the outstanding shares in both companies. Should both companies make the investment and commitment necessary to diversify into spa operations, your share portfolio will increase in value by $5,000 (1 per cent of Company A's $1.5 million increased value minus 1 per cent of Company B's $1 million decline in value). As, in advance of the diversification, it would have likely been impossible to tell whether one, both or neither of the two companies would be successful in making the diversification, with the benefit of hindsight you should be satisfied that both made the diversification decision, as it has resulted in a $5,000 increase in your wealth. But note that you have managed to lessen the risk of your total investment by investing in more than one company. You have benefited from what financial commentators refer to as the elimination of "diversifiable risk". Diversifiable risk refers to that portion of an investment risk that can be eliminated by holding a portfolio of shares. Diversifiable risk relates to randomly occurring, company specific events such as a labour strike, a law suit or loss of a key account. Your willingness for a company you have invested in to take on risk would be greatly diminished if it was the only share that you owned, as you would then have "all your eggs in one basket". It is safer and less risky to have two or more baskets.

Now, imagine you are a manager working in one of these two companies. In advance of making the decision to diversify into the spa sector, you would know that there is some downside risk involved, as the diversification may prove to be unsuccessful. Unlike the rational shareholder who reduces risk by holding a portfolio of shares, you cannot diversify away company specific risk by holding a portfolio of jobs. For most of us, we can only hold down one full time job at a time. If the company where you work were to suffer a major downturn, you might lose your job, lose your capacity to pay your mortgage and severely damage your career prospects. The fact that you have one job signifies that you have all your eggs in one basket, and as a result you are particularly careful not to take any steps that might result in your basket tipping and the loss of your eggs.

This example shows how many managers can be expected to be more averse to taking on risky investments than shareholders. To lessen the propensity of managers acting in a risk-averse manner, some companies reward their managers for pursuing successful new initiatives by providing them with performance-based bonus shares. The issuance of company shares to a manager is a clever strategy, as it draws managers closer to a perspective that is reflective of the perspective held by shareholders.

Hotel management contracts – an agency issue particular to the hotel industry

Many large hotels are not managed by their owner. Worldwide, many hotel owners engage the services of a specialist hotel management company to manage their hotel. Research reveals that in many countries there are now more hotels that are managed by way of a contractual arrangement between the owner and a hotel operating company than there are hotels that are managed by their owners (Turner and Guilding 2010). Examples of well-known hotel management companies that manage hotel chains worldwide include the Accor, Hilton, Marriott and Sheraton companies. These companies specialize in operating, but not owning, hotels.

Where a hotel management company is engaged to manage a hotel for an owner, we can see that an agency relationship arises between the owner (acting as principal) and the management company (acting as agent). Under the typical contractual arrangement, the owner retains ownership of all of the hotel's assets and earns any profits made by the hotel, after deduction of the hotel operator's fee. Fees earned by hotel operating companies are generally linked to the level of sales and profit achieved by the hotels that they operate. More specifically, the fee received by an operator is typically:

- about 3 per cent of the revenue earned by the hotel that the operator manages (widely referred to as the "base fee"), plus
- about 10 per cent of the operating profit earned by the hotel that the operator manages (widely referred to as the "incentive fee").

Turner and Guilding (2010) show that this basis for determining the management fee to be paid to the hotel manager can create particular agency problems. These problems appear to be most evident in connection with capital budgeting decision making. As the hotel operating company is closely involved in the operations of a hotel, management in the operating company will be particularly aware of what hotel assets are most in need of major refurbishment or replacement. Accordingly, the hotel operating company will play a key role in identifying to the owner aspects of a hotel that are most in need of capital expenditure. Given that a hotel management company will be motivated by a desire to maximize their fee, we need to explore whether the capital expenditure ideas that they are motivated to promote are actually consistent with maximizing net present value (NPV) for the owners.

Factors suggesting that the way operators' fees are determined might cause operators to promote capital expenditure projects that are not necessarily consistent with maximizing an owner's NPV include:

1. The revenue-determined "base fee" represents an encouragement to operating companies to promote large capital expenditures, which result in large increases in revenue, regardless of a project's predicted profitability.
2. The revenue-determined "base fee" provides a hotel operating company with no incentive to recommend capital expenditure projects that will trigger large cost savings but have no impact on revenue. An example of such a capital expenditure project would be the decision to upgrade a hotel's air conditioning system. A hotel's old air conditioning system may have become inefficient and consume large amounts of electricity relative to the amount of cool air produced. This old air conditioning system may also be proving costly

to maintain due to frequent breakdowns and system malfunctioning. This suggests that replacement of the old system will result in a considerable saving in electricity and maintenance costs. These cost savings may be sufficiently large to signify that a new air conditioning system capital expenditure outlay would provide a high positive NPV for the hotel owners. Yet the revenue determined "base fee" that is paid to hotel operators provides them with no incentive to identify and promote capital expenditure projects that provide cost savings but no increases in revenue. Accordingly, when a hotel owner asks its hotel operating company to draw up a wish list of suggested capital expenditure project proposals for its property, a potential high NPV air conditioning system up-grade capital expenditure idea may stay in the bottom of a drawer and never be brought to the owner's attention. The likelihood of such a scenario occurring is heightened by the fact that an owner's funds available for capital expenditure are generally limited.

3. The profit-determined "incentive fee" will encourage hotel management companies to promote projects that will generate a high profit, in an absolute sense, without giving due consideration to the amount of investment necessary to generate the profit. Consider the case of a hotel appraising two mutually exclusive projects (mutual exclusivity signifies the hotel owner cannot invest in both projects). Project A is projected to provide an annual profit of $100,000 and will require an initial investment of $2,000,000. Project B is projected to provide an annual profit of $90,000 and will require an initial investment of $1,000,000. If an operating company earns a profit-determined incentive fee, it will prefer Project A, as it provides $10,000 more profit than Project B. However, Project B provides a 9 per cent ROI ($90,000 ÷ $1,000,000 × 100) which is higher than Project A's 5 per cent ROI ($100,000 ÷ $2,000,000 × 100). Based on ROI, the hotel owner would prefer Project B. This highlights the problem of attempting to interpret a profit number in isolation of the investment amount required to earn the profit.

These three distinct examples of how a potential divergence can arise between the interests of a hotel owner and a contracted hotel operator highlight the extent to which hotel management contracts provide incentives for hotel operators to promote capital expenditure projects that do not necessarily optimize the interests of hotel owners. Clearly there are deficiencies with respect to the extent that conventional hotel management contracts promote goal congruency between hotel owners (the principal) and hotel management companies (the agent). Goal congruency refers to the extent that the goals of one party are well aligned and consistent with the goals of another party. The significance of this problem becomes particularly apparent when we recognize that a hotel operator is in a powerful position to influence what capital expenditure projects will be invested in by a hotel owner, as a hotel operator can decide not to submit to a hotel owner those capital expenditure ideas that fail to maximize the operator's interests.

This goal congruency deficiency between hotel owners and operators with respect to capital budgeting decision making is a good example of a widespread hotel industry agency challenge. Box 15.4 demonstrates that the combination of a revenue-determined "base fee" with a profit-determined "incentive fee" does not solve this goal congruency problem. As explained in Box 15.4, it appears this agency problem would be lessened if, instead of a hotel operator's fee being determined by revenue and profit, it was based on ROI or residual income (the calculation of "residual income" was explained in Chapter 9).

> ## Box 15.4
>
> # Problem with management contract fee determination
>
> Imagine a hotel operator is considering which of two mutually exclusive potential investment opportunities, Project A or Project B, it will promote to the owner of a hotel it manages. Project A will require an initial investment of $1,000,000 and Project B will require an initial investment of $4,000,000. The projected revenue and profit projections associated with the two investment alternatives are outlined below.
>
> | | Project A | | Project B | |
> |--------|-----------|------------------|-----------|------------------|
> | | Revenue | Operating profit | Revenue | Operating profit |
> | Year 1 | $500,000 | $200,000 | $800,000 | $320,000 |
> | Year 2 | $500,000 | $200,000 | $800,000 | $320,000 |
> | Year 3 | $500,000 | $200,000 | $800,000 | $320,000 |
> | Year 4 | $500,000 | $200,000 | $800,000 | $320,000 |
> | Year 5 | $500,000 | $200,000 | $800,000 | $320,000 |
>
> Based on a typical traditional fee incentive of 3% of revenue and 10% of operating profit, we find that the operator would prefer Project B as it would result in an increase in the operator fee revenue of $56,000 (3% of $800,000 + 10% of $320,000) per annum for the five years of Project B's life. This is more than the $35,000 (3% of $500,000 + 10% of $200,000) projected incremental fee revenue that would result if Project A were pursued.
>
> On an ROI and RI basis, it can be seen that project A provides the higher return, however. Project A provides an ROI of 20% ($200,000 ÷ $1,000,000 × 100) per annum and Project B provides an ROI of 8% ($320,000 ÷ $4,000,000 × 100) per annum. If the hotel owner imputes a 10% required rate of return (based on its cost of capital) charge when calculating RI, we see that Project A has a positive RI of $100,000 ($200,000 − (0.1 × $1,000,000)) per annum and Project B has a negative RI of $80,000 ($320,000 − (0.1 × $4,000,000)) per annum.
>
> If the operator were to be paid an incentive that is set at (say) 40% of RI, pursuit of Project A would result in an increase in the operator's fee revenue of $40,000 (40% of $100,000) per annum and pursuit of Project B would result in a decrease in the operator's fee revenue of $32,000 (40% of −$80,000) per annum.
>
> A comparison of the projected ROIs for the two projects and the fact that Project B fails to satisfy the owner's 10% required rate of return provides a persuasive case that the hotel owner would prefer to take

Project A. Capital expenditure goal congruency is promoted if the operator is remunerated based on RI (Project A has the higher RI), but it is not promoted if the operator is remunerated based on a revenue and profit incentive, as the operator would have an incentive to promote Project B.

4) Trading shares in publicly listed companies

When a company is first being established, it can raise its initial share capital by either making a public offering that involves selling new shares to the public, or making a private placement that involves selling new shares to a single investor or a group of investors. When making an initial public offering of shares, the new company develops a prospectus, which is a document that describes the details of the offering, key dates associated with the offering and also its key financial statements. So purchasing newly issued shares is one way for you to buy shares in a company. The market for new shares is called the primary market.

You can then sell the shares on a stock market, which is, in effect, a second hand market for portions of equity ownership in companies. We don't tend to refer to "equity portions", however, as you are much more used to hearing such portions of equity ownership referred to as "shares". So a second way for you to acquire shares in a company is for you to buy them on a stock market. Some of the largest stock markets in the world are the London, NASDAQ, New York and Tokyo stock exchanges.

You have most likely heard of a **stock market index**. This can be thought of as an indicator of the average price of all shares (or a particular set of shares) on a stock market. Imagine we select 100 companies as being reflective of all the companies on a particular stock market. We could then identify a base day and say that on this day, the price of these 100 companies' shares, in combination, is going to be represented by an index that we chose to set at 1,000. Now, if at the end of the following year, half the shares represented by the index have increased by 10 per cent and the share price for the other half is unaltered, on average the shares will have increased by 5 per cent. This will result in a 5 per cent increase in the stock market index, i.e. over the year it will have risen from 1,000 to 1,050. You will hear financial commentators sometimes say something like "the local stock market's index increased by 50 points today which represents an increase of 1 per cent". This means that at the end of the day, on average, the value of shares on the stock market is 1 per cent more than what they were trading for at the end of the previous day. The reason that we have stock market indexes is simply to enable stock market commentators to refer to a single number when describing the average movement in share prices of all companies on a particular stock exchange during a particular time period.

5) Share valuation

From a theoretical perspective, we can say that the value of a share is equal to the present value of all future benefits that the share will provide to its owner. The most obvious financial benefit that shareholders receive is the stream of dividends that a company pays to its shareholders. Using the "PVIF" notation that was introduced in the last chapter, this valuation approach can be stated as an equation in the following way:

$$\text{Share value} = D_1 \, (\text{PVIF}_{r,\,1yr}) + D_2 \, (\text{PVIF}_{r,\,2yr}) + D_3 \, (\text{PVIF}_{r,\,3yr}) + \ldots \ldots \text{etc.}$$

where:

D_1 = dividend expected in year 1; D_2 = dividend expected in year 2; etc.
r = required rate of return for shares in the company being valued.

It is widely accepted by stock market analysts that investors are risk averse. This factor lies behind the inclusion of "r" (required rate of return) in the equation above. Shareholders have a higher required rate of return for a share that is perceived to be relatively risky. In effect, investors need to be compensated if they purchase a share that is perceived to be risky. Greater levels of risk will increase "r". If "r" is increased, but everything else in the equation is kept the same, the share value (share price) will decrease. This signifies that all other things being equal, shares with higher risk will command a lower price.

Imagine it has been projected that Company A and Company B will provide the same dividends per share into the foreseeable future. This statement, considered in isolation, suggests that the two companies' shares should have the same value. Now imagine that Company B has a greater proportion of debt in its long-term capital, compared to Company A. This higher debt will make likely returns to Company B shareholders more volatile (see leverage discussion below) and also increase the likelihood of Company B facing bankruptcy. This signifies that Company B will be perceived as more risky and, as a result, shareholders will require a higher expected rate of return if they are to invest in Company B. The higher "r" in the valuation model for Company B's shares will have the effect of reducing the value of Company B's shares relative to Company A's shares. As you will therefore be able to purchase Company B's shares for a lower price than Company A's shares, the return on your investment will be greater if you purchase Company B's shares (don't forget that it has been predicted that Company A and Company B will provide the same dividends per share into the foreseeable future). You may wonder why wouldn't all investors buy Company B's shares if it will provide a relatively higher return on its shares' purchase price? This question takes us back full circle – it is because investors do not like the greater risk that they perceive in Company B.

Now you might be thinking that the share valuation formula provided above will not work for a share that you plan to sell in two years' time. This will mean that after two years you will not be receiving the dividends any more. In this situation, the cash flows that are relevant to you are the dividends that you will receive in the next two years, plus the share's sale price in two years time. The valuation model still works for this situation. This is because the share valuation in two years' time will be determined by discounting the future dividends that share purchasers will be expecting at that time. Stated in another way, your share in two years' time will have the same value as the present value of the projected dividends at that time. So, whether you plan to hold a share for the next 20 years or just two years, the present value of the inflows you can expect from owning the share are the same, i.e. the present value of all future dividends projected for the share.

A technique that enables you to value a share that is projected to continue providing a constant annual dividend well into the future is described in Box 15.5.

Box 15.5

Valuing a share that provides a consistent annual dividend

There is a simple formula (often referred to as the "perpetuity formula") that can be applied if it is estimated that a share will continue providing the same annual dividend every year indefinitely into the future.

An investment that provides a series of cash flows that are expected to go on forever is referred to as a "perpetuity". The formula for finding the value of a financial investment that will perpetually provide the same cash flow return every year simply involves dividing the annual cash flow return by the per cent required rate of return for the investment (stated as a decimal). Applying this formula to a share valuation situation gives us the following formula:

Value of share that provides perpetual annual return =
Annual return ÷ per cent required annual return (stated as a decimal)

Imagine the shares of the SteadyHotel Management company have been paying annual dividends of $2 for many years and analysts believe this dividend pattern will continue indefinitely into the future. Also, imagine SteadyHotel's shareholders' required rate of return is 10%. This suggests SteadyHotel's shares represent a perpetuity and we can provide a valuation of the SteadyHotel Management company's shares by applying the above formula as follows:

Steady Hotel's share value = $2 ÷ 0.1 = $20

Now you may be asking that with these valuation approaches, why is it that share prices are constantly moving and can even move as far as 10 per cent or more in a single day when a stock market crash occurs. Significant stock market crashes occurred on 29th October 1929, 19th October 1987 and 29th September 2008. The reason that share prices constantly change is investors' outlook on risk is constantly evolving as it is affected by events occurring around the world at global and local levels. If a company announces the redundancy of 100 employees, this newsworthy event can be expected to affect the investing communities' expectations with respect to future dividends in that company and maybe also the dividends of competing companies. This would also likely affect investors' assessment of the risk associated with the company and, as a result alter the "r" (required rate of return) for the company. News of an unexpected increase in unemployment in a large economy such as the US can trigger a ripple effect that can have tsunami-like implications. This ripple can run a long way, affecting investor confidence around the world and carrying a quick negative impact on share prices quoted on stock markets internationally.

6) Dividends

In this section we will explore the dividend payment procedure and also how the declaration of a dividend impacts on a company's share price. We will then examine issues surrounding the development of a company's dividend payment policy.

Dividend payment procedure

The stages involved in a company paying a dividend are:

1. The company announces the per share dividend amount and the date when investors must be registered as owning shares (referred to as the "date of record") in order to be entitled to receive the dividend payment.
2. Following the company's announcement of the dividend payment intention, the share enters a period of being traded "cum-dividend", which means "with dividend". If you purchase a share during the time that it is trading cum dividend, you will be entitled to receive the per share dividend payment that has been announced.
3. Shares will start trading "ex-dividend" four days before the date of record. As shares are constantly being bought and sold, this four-day period is required to provide the company with time to update its record of share owners. Investors purchasing a share during an ex-dividend period will have purchased it too late to be entitled to receive the declared dividend. On the day that a share starts trading ex-dividend, we can expect the share price to drop by the value of that dividend. In effect, on the last day that a share trades cum-dividend, anyone purchasing a share not only becomes a share holder, they also acquire the right to shortly receive a known cash flow, i.e., the dividend. On the following day, when the share enters its ex-dividend period, the share purchaser no longer receives the dividend receivable benefit, they only receive the share. At the time the "dividend receivable" benefit is lost from the share (i.e., the day that it starts trading ex-dividend), it is logical to expect that the cost of acquiring the share will drop by the value of the dividend.
4. Shareholders receive their dividend payments. At that time there is no longer a need to refer to the share as trading "ex-dividend", as the term is only used to help share traders determine whether acquisition of a share will carry the entitlement of receiving a forth-coming dividend payment that has been declared.

Box 15.6 provides a worked example of this dividend payment procedure and also the accounting implications arising.

Box 15.6

Dividend payment – accounting implications and timeline

The MagnificentHotel Company has 50,000 shares outstanding. Following a meeting on 15th July, its board of directors announced that the company would be paying a cash dividend of $1.20 per share to investors recorded as owning MagnificentHotel Company shares on 8th August (date of record) and that the dividend would be paid on 7th September.

The company's relevant accounts prior to the dividend declaration were:

Cash	$400,000	Dividends payable	$0
		Retained earnings	$800,000

On 15th July, following the declaration of the dividend, the company's commitment to pay the dividend was recorded in its accounts by taking $60,000 out of "Retained earnings" (total dividend = 50,000 shares × $1.20 dividend per share) and recognizing the amount as a liability by putting it in the "Dividends payable" account. This resulted in the following revised balances in the relevant accounts:

Cash	$400,000	Dividends payable	$60,000
		Retained earnings	$740,000

The MagnificentHotel Company's shares will start trading ex-dividend four days before the 8th August date of record. This signifies that anyone buying a share in the company on 3rd August or before will be entitled to receive a dividend. All things being equal, we would therefore expect to see a $1.20 drop in the price of the share when it starts trading on 4th August.

Payment of the $1.20 per share dividend to shareholders on 7th September would signify a cash outflow of $60,000 for the company. Accordingly, on that date $60,000 would be deducted from the "Cash" account and removed from the "Dividends payable" account, resulting in the following revised account balances:

Cash	$340,000	Dividends payable	$0
		Retained earnings	$740,000

Dividend declaration and payment timeline

Dividend declaration	Ex-dividend date	Date of record	Dividend payment
15th July	4th August	8th August	7th September

Dividend policy

Dividend payments represent a cash allocation of profits to a company's shareholders. Such payments can be seen as representing the delivery of a return on the investment in shares made by a shareholder. A second source of return for shareholders arises when a shareholder sells their shares at a price that is greater than the price that they paid to purchase the shares. Such a share price gain is widely referred to as a "capital gain". If shares are sold for a price that is below their purchase price, a "capital loss" arises.

An issue that finance theorists have debated over for many years concerns what policy a company's board of directors should pursue when determining the size of dividend payments. Some talk of an **information effect dividend theory**. According to this view, a decision to pay an increased dividend to shareholders carries a positive impact on share price. This is because the decision to pay a higher dividend can be seen as a signal that flags a company's intent to pay higher dividends in years to come. Conversely, a decrease in dividends is believed to provide a negative signal, as it suggests that dividends might decrease in years to come. This view results in many companies pursuing a policy of only raising dividend levels if they are confident that the increased dividend level can be maintained in years to come. In effect, companies seek to avoid the negative impact on share price that would result should they drop the amount of dividends paid in any given year.

A very different view is provided by the **residual dividend theory**. According to this theory, a company should use all its funds not needed for operations investing in positive net present value (NPV) projects, until no further positive NPV project opportunities remain. Following this line of thinking, once a company has invested in all available positive NPV projects, any remaining excess long-term capital (i.e., residual funds) should be distributed as a dividend to its shareholders. This theory is built on the view that a shareholder should be happy to forgo receiving dividends, so long as the company that they own shares in is investing in projects that, over the long term, will generate profits that will enable shareholders to be provided with returns that exceed their required rate of return (see the cost of capital calculation in Box 14.5). If a company can provide returns to shareholders that exceed their required rate of return, all things being equal, demand for the company's shares will rise, causing an increase in the share price.

Closely associated with the residual dividend theory is the idea that when financing investments in positive NPV projects, it is cheaper to use retained earnings rather than raising new equity finance. This is because a company has easy access to funds retained in the business, especially when compared to raising new equity capital. The raising of new equity will result in considerable expenditure associated with administering the new share issue process. Accordingly, using retained earnings to fund capital expenditures is preferable to using new equity funding, as retained earnings represent a cheaper source of equity capital.

Application of the residual dividend theory will result in volatile dividend payments. There will be low dividend payments in years when a company has many high NPV projects to invest in, and high dividend payments in years when a company has no, or only a few, positive NPV projects to invest in. As already noted in this chapter, investors do not like uncertainty and dividend volatility represents a source of uncertainty. Accordingly, some financial commentators argue that rather than pursuing the residual dividend theory, companies should seek to provide their shareholders with a steady stream of dividends. Some have gone so far as to argue that in low profit years, new equity capital should be raised in order to finance dividend payments at a rate that is consistent with dividend payments made in previous years.

The difference in the residual dividend theory and the "information effect" dividend theory is quite stark. If applying the residual dividend theory, a low payment of dividends would be consistent with the company investing in many positive NPV project opportunities. From a high number of positive NPV opportunities perspective, we should expect share prices to rise, due to the enhanced company value that should derive from making the positive NPV investments. However, from an "information effect" dividend theory perspective, we would expect share prices to decline due to the negative signal associated with a drop in dividends.

Research has found that in practice the behaviour of financial managers and shareholders suggest that the market does perceive an information effect. It has been found that many companies pursue a dividend policy that sees slow and consistent growth levels, or the payment of a consistent dividend that is only raised should the company have confidence it can maintain the higher dividend payment level.

There is also a **clientele effect** that argues that companies should not alter their established dividend policy. Imagine hotel company A has a tradition of paying out a high proportion of its profit as dividends and hotel company B has pursued a low dividend payout policy. Hotel company A will have attracted shareholders that like a high dividend payout. If they did not want high dividend payouts, they would not have bought hotel A's shares. Hotel company B's shareholders can be expected to be interested in getting their investment ROI in the form of share price capital gains rather than dividends, otherwise why would they have purchased hotel company B's shares? If either company were to change its dividend payout policy, it might alienate its existing shareholders which would cause them to sell their shares, which in turn would result in a drop in share price.

7) Operating and financial leverage

Leverage arises when a company incurs fixed costs. Fixed costs can be divided into two main categories. The first category relates to a company's operating activities (e.g., salaries, insurance, etc.). The second category concerns fixed costs arising from a company's long-term capital financing (e.g., interest payable on long-term debt).

As will be seen below, fixed costs have the effect of magnifying returns (or losses) earned by a company's shareholders. Fixed costs can therefore be seen to lever up, or down, shareholder returns, and it is this levering characteristic that has resulted in the term "leverage" being widely used to describe the extent to which a company's cost structure contains fixed costs.

As leverage has the effect of magnifying shareholder returns, it triggers greater shareholder return volatility. This greater shareholder return volatility signifies that higher leverage signifies higher risk. Or, stated differently, higher fixed costs signify higher risk.

We will examine a company's leverage according to the three leverage levels depicted in Figure 15.1. The three leverage levels are:

- **Operating leverage** which concerns the relationship between movements in a company's sales and the resulting movement in its earnings before interest and tax (EBIT).
- **Financial leverage** which concerns the relationship between movements in a company's EBIT and the resulting movement in its earnings per share (EPS).
- **Total leverage** which spans operating and financial leverage. It concerns the relationship between movements in a company's sales and the resulting movement in its earnings per share.

Figure 15.1 Different spans of leverage

Operating leverage

Operating leverage results when a company has some fixed operating costs (e.g., salaries, rent and insurance). The presence of fixed operating costs results in a percentage change in sales triggering a larger percentage change in EBIT. A worked example showing the effect of operating leverage in the WateryWillow Hotel is presented in Table 15.1.

The WateryWillow Hotel case shows us that operating leverage is in evidence for a decrease as well as an increase in sales. From Table 15.1, we can see that a 20 per cent increase in WateryWillow's sales from its current 10,000 room nights per annum sold level would result in a 52 per cent increase in the hotel's EBIT. We can also see that a 20 per cent decline in sales would result in EBIT decreasing by 52 per cent. The sole reason accounting for EBIT's percentage change being greater than the percentage change in sales is the presence of fixed costs. If the $800,000 of operating fixed costs present in the WateryWillow Hotel's cost structure were to be removed and we were to recalculate the numbers in Table 15.1, we would find that a given percentage change in sales would result in the same percentage change in EBIT. This highlights the way that fixed costs act as a lever causing a change in sales to trigger an amplified change in EBIT.

Table 15.1 Operating leverage – impact of sales increase on EBIT

	WateryWillow Hotel		
	20% sales decrease	Current sales level	20% sales increase
Annual room night sales	8,000	10,000	12,000
Sales revenue	$1,200,000	$1,500,000	$1,800,000
Less: Variable costs	160,000	200,000	240,000
Contribution	1,040,000	1,300,000	1,560,000
Less: Fixed costs	800,000	800,000	800,000
EBIT	$240,000	$500,000	$760,000
	52% EBIT decrease		52% EBIT increase

We can calculate a numerical indicator of a company's degree of operating leverage (DOL). As operating leverage concerns the extent to which a changed level of sales becomes amplified in a resulting change in EBIT, it follows that the DOL can be measured by comparing a percentage change in sales to the resulting percentage change in EBIT. Accordingly, DOL can be measured by applying the following equation:

$$\text{Degree of operating leverage index} = \frac{\text{Percentage change in EBIT}}{\text{Percentage change in sales}}$$

Plugging the numbers from the WateryWillow example into this formula (regardless of whether we take the case of increased or decreased sales) we find WateryWillow's DOL to be 2.6 (52 ÷ 20).

If the WateryWillow Hotel were to take a step that increased its fixed costs relative to variable costs (e.g. replace a casual staff member who worked in a café with a coffee vending machine), then its fixed costs would rise, causing an increase in its DOL. As a high DOL index signifies high EBIT volatility relative to any changes in sales, we can view the DOL index as an indicator of risk. A high DOL index signifies high risk with respect to a company's operating cost structure.

If it is possible to obtain unit cost data for a company, an alternative approach to calculating the DOL index can be taken. Imagine that we have been able to determine that the WateryWillow Hotel sells its room nights for $150, incurs $20 in variable costs for each room night sold and has fixed operating costs of $800,000 per annum. Using this data (derived from Table 15.1), we can apply the following formula as an alternative approach to determining the DOL index:

$$\text{DOL index at current level of sales} = \frac{Q(P-V)}{Q(P-V) - F}$$

Where: Q = quantity of sales; P = unit selling price; V = unit variable cost; and F = fixed costs. Substituting WateryWillow Hotel's data in this formula we get:

WateryWillow Hotel's DOL index =

$$\frac{10,000\,(\$150 - \$20)}{10,000\,(\$150 - \$20) - \$800,000} = \frac{\$1,300,000}{\$500,000} = 2.6$$

Note that this 2.6 DOL index is consistent with the index we computed earlier when we divided WateryWillow Hotel's percentage change in EBIT by its percentage change in sales.

Financial leverage

As already noted, financial leverage concerns the relationship between movements in a company's EBIT and the resulting movement in its earnings per share (EPS). Financial leverage results when a company has some fixed financing costs. The main example of a fixed financing cost is interest paid on debt. Similar to the approach we took to examine operating leverage, we will explore the nature of financial leverage by considering the WateryWillow Hotel. The relationship between changes in EBIT and the resulting changes in EPS for

Table 15.2 Financial leverage – impact of EBIT increase on EPS

	WateryWillow Hotel		
	20% EBIT decrease	*Current EBIT level*	*20% EBIT increase*
EBIT	$400,000	$500,000	$600,000
Less: Interest	100,000	100,000	100,000
Net profit before tax	300,000	400,000	500,000
Less: Tax (40%)	120,000	160,000	200,000
Earnings available to shareholders	$180,000	$240,000	$300,000
	÷ 20,000	÷ 20,000	÷ 20,000
Earnings per share (EPS)	$9	$12	$15
	25% EPS decrease		**25% EPS increase**

the WateryWillow Hotel is provided in Table 15.2. It is assumed that the WateryWillow Hotel has 20,000 shares, pays $100,000 per annum in interest and is subject to 40% tax.

Consistent with the workings of operating leverage, Table 15.2 shows us that financial leverage is in evidence for a decrease as well as an increase in EBIT. We can see that a 20 per cent increase in WateryWillow's current EBIT of $500,000 would result in a 25 per cent increase in its EPS. We can also see that a 20 per cent decline in EBIT triggers a 25 per cent EPS decrease. The factor causing EPS to change by a greater percentage than the percentage change in EBIT is the presence of fixed costs, which in the case of financial leverage is interest on debt capital.

Similar to the case of operating leverage, we can calculate a degree of operating leverage index by comparing the percentage change in EPS with the percentage change in EBIT that has caused the altered level of EPS. The degree of financial leverage (DFL) can be measured by applying the following equation:

$$\text{Degree of financial leverage index} = \frac{\text{Percentage change in EPS}}{\text{Percentage change in EBIT}}$$

Plugging the numbers from Table 15.2 into this formula (regardless of whether we take the case of an increased or decreased level of EBIT) we find WateryWillow's DFL index to be 1.25 (25 ÷ 20). As the index is greater than 1, we know that financial leverage must be present.

Again we can use an alternate formula that is not reliant on having data relating to differing levels of performance. The alternate formula for computing the DFL index is:

$$\text{DFL index at current EBIT level} = \frac{EBIT}{EBIT - I}$$

Where: EBIT = earnings before interest and tax; and I = interest

Substituting WateryWillow Hotel's data in this formula we get:

WateryWillow Hotel's DFL index =

$$\frac{\$500,000}{\$500,000 - \$100,000} = \frac{\$500,000}{\$400,000} = 1.25$$

Total leverage

Total leverage simply represents the combination of operating and financial leverage. It captures the effect that fixed operating and financial costs have on the relationship between changes in sales and EPS. A high total leverage stems from a high degree of fixed operating and financial costs and will result in changes in sales levels triggering relatively high EPS changes.

In a manner consistent with the approaches taken for DOL and DFL, a company's degree of total leverage (DTL) index could be computed by applying the following formula:

$$\text{DTL index} = \frac{\text{Percentage change in EPS}}{\text{Percentage change in sales}}$$

Alternatively, consistent with the alternate formulae provided above for calculating an index for DOL and DFL, we can compute a DTL index as follows:

$$\text{DTL index at current level of sales} = \frac{Q(P - V)}{Q(P - V) - F - I}$$

Where: Q = quantity of sales; P = unit selling price; V = unit variable cost; F = fixed costs; and I = Interest.

Finally, the DTL index can also be determined by multiplying the DOL index by the DFL index. This signifies that WateryWillow Hotel's DTL index =

$$\text{DOL} \times \text{DFL} = 2.6 \times 1.25 = 3.35.$$

This 3.35 DTL index signifies that if WateryWillow Hotel's current level of room nights sold were to increase by 10 per cent from 10,000 to 11,000, then its EPS would increase by 33.5 per cent (i.e. a percentage increase that is 3.35 times more than the percentage increase in sales).

Leverage implications for management decision making

Imagine the WildHotel company has a relatively high total leverage compared to its competitors. This would result in it having greater EPS volatility, signifying a relatively high uncertainty held by shareholders with respect to their likely investment returns. This high EPS volatility may be sufficient to negatively impact on the WildHotel's share price. As a result of this, the company's management may well be wanting to reduce the company's DTL. This strategy can be pursued by seeking to:

a. reduce operating leverage,
b. reduce financial leverage, or
c. reduce both operating and financial leverage.

Options to reduce operating leverage can be limited by the nature of technology required to undertake operational activities. For instance, in a hotel context it is not likely to be feasible to stop using a lift (which may have high maintenance and running costs) and require hotel guests to use the stairs. Nevertheless, in many hotels there are likely to be some options for reducing operating fixed costs, especially over the longer term. Imagine that laundry equipment in the WildHotel is approaching the end of its life and management is considering when to replace the equipment. This would be an opportunity to reduce operating leverage by deciding not to purchase new laundry equipment, but to outsource laundry cleaning to a laundry specialist provider that is willing to charge on the basis of the volume of laundry cleaned. If the WildHotel decided to take this laundry outsourcing option, it would be replacing some significant fixed costs with variable costs. The fixed costs that it would be losing would include any salary paid to the head of laundry, laundry equipment maintenance costs, cleaning of the laundry area, etc. The new outsourcing laundry costs would be all variable if WildHotel entered into an outsourcing arrangement with fees paid based on the volume of laundry cleaned.

While many businesses experience technologically based constraints on the degree to which they can replace operating fixed costs with operating variable costs, such a constraint does not apply to modifying financial leverage levels. If the WildHotel company has a high degree of financial leverage, it can either raise new equity capital or retain a greater proportion of its profit and use retained earnings to fund the retirement of debt capital. In effect, the company would be replacing debt funding with equity funding.

Alternative financing options and impact on shareholder returns

From the above discussion concerning the way that debt financing will cause greater EPS volatility, it will be evident that a decision to raise debt or equity capital should be taken by considering the impact the debt capital will have on shareholder earnings levels. Financial decision making in action case 15.1 provides an example of a company considering the likely impact on shareholder earnings resulting from a decision to raise equity or debt capital.

FINANCIAL DECISION MAKING IN ACTION CASE 15.1

The Financial Controller and financial leverage

Imagine Nottingham's RobinHood hotel chain has £2 million of assets and a debt to assets ratio of 40 per cent (£800,000 in debt and £1,200,000 of equity). It pays 10 per cent annual interest on its debt, currently achieves an EBIT of 15 per cent on assets employed, and pays company tax at the rate of 40 per cent. The management of RobinHood is considering a £1 million expansion in capital, which, consistent with existing assets, is projected to earn a 15 per cent return. The management is deliberating whether to fund the £1 million expansion through arranging a further loan at 10 per cent annual interest or to finance the expansion through raising more equity capital. Management believes that issuance of debt will not result in insolvency problems and is primarily focusing on its desire to maximise the hotel owners' return. The impact on the owners' return resulting from the issuance of debt (financing option 1) versus the issuance of further equity capital (financing option 2) are detailed in the schedule presented below.

	Financing option 1 (debt)	Financing option 2 (equity)
	£	£
Projected return on assets: 15% of £3 m.	450,000	450,000
Less interest on debt[a]	180,000	80,000
Profit before Tax	270,000	370,000
Less 40% Tax	108,000	148,000
Profit after Tax	162,000	222,000
% Return on owners investment[b]	13.5%	10.1%

a For financing option 1: 10 per cent of £1,800,000; for financing option 2: 10 per cent of £800,000.
b For financing option 1: £162,000 ÷ £1,200,000 × 100; for financing option 2: £222,000 ÷ £2,200,000 × 100.

From this example, it is apparent that a greater return on owners' investment results from taking the debt financing option. This highlights how the hotel finance function can use debt financing to "lever" or "gear" up returns to equity holders.

The Financial Controller must be careful not to raise too much debt, however, due to risk implications. High perceived risk will reduce the value of the hotel's equity. Relative to many other industries, the hotel sector has fairly high business risk due to relatively volatile sales and a relatively high proportion of fixed operating costs. As a result, hotel financial controllers tend to be averse to taking on high levels of financial leverage.

8) Summary

In this chapter we have looked at several different financial management topics. The chapter commenced with a consideration of what represents an appropriate financial objective for companies. We reviewed agency theory and goal congruency problems that can arise when hotel owners engage hotel operators.

We explored the nature of share trading, stock market indices and how shares can be valued. We reviewed what steps have to be taken by companies when paying dividends and also issues surrounding a company selecting its dividend payment policy.

Finally, we examined the nature of leverage. We noted that leverage can be examined at the level of operating fixed costs or financing fixed costs. Greater levels of leverage result in greater EPS variability, and therefore greater perceived company risk.

Having read this chapter you should now know:

- managers should pursue the financial objective of maximizing shareholder wealth, not EPS
- that agency theory concerns the relationship between one party that wants to have a job done (the principal) and a second party (the agent) that is engaged by the first party to perform the job
- that the way fees for hotel operators are widely calculated can create goal congruency problems between hotel owners and operators
- that a share can be valued by calculating the present value of its expected dividends
- that there are conflicting theories with respect to what approach should be taken when setting a company's dividend policy
- that more operating leverage signifies greater EBIT variability
- that more financing leverage signifies greater EPS variability.

References

Gitman, L.J., Juchau, R. and Flanagan, J. (2011) *Principles of Managerial Finance*, 6th edition, Frenchs Forest, NSW: Pearson Education Australia (Chapters 1, 12 & 13).

Moyer, R.C., McGuigan, J.R., Rao, R. and Kretlow, W.J. (2012) *Contemporary Financial Management*, 12th edition, Mason, OH: South-Western (Chapters 1, 7 & 15).

Petty, J.W., Keown, A.J. Scott, D.F. and Martin, J.D. (2009) *Financial Management*, 5th edition, Frenchs Forest, NSW: Pearson Education Australia (Chapters 1, 15 & 17).

Turner, M. and Guilding, C. (2010) "Hotel management contracts and deficiencies in owner-operator capital expenditure goal congruency", *Journal of Hospitality & Tourism Research*, Vol. 34, No. 4, 478–511.

Problems

Problem 15.1

Provide three reasons why pursuit of shareholder wealth maximization is preferable to pursuing EPS maximization.

Problem 15.2

a. With respect to setting dividend payment policy, explain the difference between the residual dividend and information effect theories.
b. In practice, do companies tend to adhere to the residual dividend theory or the information effect theory when setting dividend policy?
c. What does the clientele effect tell us with respect to dividend payment policy making?

Problem 15.3

What three dimensions of reporting are captured in triple bottom line reporting?

Problem 15.4

For each of the following agency relationships, identify which party is the principal and which party is the agent.

1. Board of directors' relationship with a company's shareholders.
2. Food & Beverage Manager's relationship with a Restaurant Manager.
3. Doctor's relationship with a patient.
4. Stockbroker's relationship with a share investor.
5. Member of Parliament's relationship with voters in his electorate.

Problem 15.5

You have predicted that you will be able to sell your 100 shares in the Sydney-based BlissfulEscape hotel company in three years' time for $25 each. Prior to selling the shares, you believe the company will pay you a $2 per share dividend at the end of each of the next two years. Shareholders in the BlissfulEscape hotel company have a 10 per cent required rate of return. Based on this information, provide an estimate of the current value of your total share investment in the BlissfulEscape company (present value factors are presented in Table 14.1 and 14.2).

Problem 15.6

New York's Reliable Hotel Management Company has been consistently paying an annual dividend of $6.00 for many years and all indications suggest that this behaviour will continue for many years to come. Analysts attribute a required rate of return of 12 per cent for shareholders in the company. Use the perpetuity formula to develop a valuation of the Reliable Hotel Management company's share.

Problem 15.7

Imagine a hotel operator is considering which out of two potential investment opportunities, Project A or Project B, it will promote to the owner of a hotel it manages. Project A will require an initial investment of $500,000 and Project B will require an initial investment of $2,000,000. The projected revenue and profit projections associated with the two investment alternatives are outlined below.

| | Project A | | Project B | |
	Revenue	Gross operating profit	Revenue	Gross operating profit
Year 1	$250,000	$100,000	$400,000	$160,000
Year 2	$250,000	$100,000	$400,000	$160,000
Year 3	$250,000	$100,000	$400,000	$160,000
Year 4	$250,000	$100,000	$400,000	$160,000
Year 5	$250,000	$100,000	$400,000	$160,000

The operator's fee is determined as 3 per cent of gross revenue (base fee) and 10 per cent of gross operating profit (incentive fee).

Required:

a) Calculate the impact on the annual operator's fee that would result from investing in Project A vs Project B. Based on this calculation, indicate which of the two projects the hotel operator would likely prefer.
b) Calculate the annual ROI of the two projects. Based on this calculation, which project would you expect the hotel owner to prefer?

Problem 15.8

Your cousin purchased shares in the French Utopia hotel group two years ago. He tells you that the earnings per share are currently €2 and that the share price has performed strongly over the last two years, rising by 25 per cent to €40. Hotel groups with an international profile similar to Utopia currently have price earnings ratios averaging around 16. Your cousin is questioning how well Utopia is performing relative to its competitors and asks if the EPS and share price can provide any insights into Utopia's performance.

Required:
Use the information provided to comment on Utopia's relative financial standing and performance.

Problem 15.9

Hotel A's degree of operating leverage index is 2 and Hotel B's degree of operating leverage is 4.

Required:

a. If Hotel A's room nights sold were to double, by what percentage would you expect its EBIT to increase?
b. Which of the two hotels is more risky with respect to its operating cost structure?
c. If management in the hotel with the more risky operating cost structure would like to reduce this risk, what steps could it take?

Problem 15.10

Two hotel chain companies that provide only room accommodation services are competing in the same market. Historically they have provided similar rates of return to their shareholders. Information on the two hotel companies follows:

● Swanky Hotel sells 45,000 room nights per annum, has a $160 average room rate, its variable costs are $15 per room night sold and it has operating fixed costs of $540,000 per annum. The Swanky hotel's long-term capital comprises 10,000 shares and debt capital of $4,000,000 that carries a 7 per cent interest rate.
● Swish Hotel sells 40,000 room nights per annum, has a $155 average room rate, its variable costs are $10 per room night sold and it has operating fixed costs of $1,040,000

per annum. The Swish hotel's long-term capital comprises 5,000 shares and debt capital of $5,000,000 that carries an 8 per cent interest rate.

Required:

a. A friend who is considering buying shares in one of the two companies has approached you and asked you to provide a degree of operating leverage, degree of financial leverage, and degree of total leverage analyses for the two companies.
b. Based on your leverage analyses, comment on which of the two companies appears to be the more risky investment.

Problem 15.11

The Singapore Tiger hotel's degree of operating leverage index is 8 and its degree of financial leverage is 1.25. The Singapore's Lion hotel's degree of operating leverage index is 2.5 and its degree of financial leverage is 4.

Required:

a. Which of the two hotels has the higher degree of total leverage?
b. If both of the hotels have an objective of halving their degree of total leverage, which of the hotels do you believe is better placed to achieve this objective?

Problem 15.12

Canada's FrozenIce hotel chain has $3 million of assets and a debt to assets ratio of 30 per cent ($900,000 in debt and $2,100,000 of equity). It pays 7 per cent annual interest on its debt, currently achieves an EBIT of 20 per cent on assets employed, and pays company tax at the rate of 40 per cent. The management of FrozenIce is considering a $500,000 expansion in capital which, consistent with existing assets, is projected to earn a 20 per cent EBIT return. FrozenIce's management is trying to decide whether to fund the $500,000 expansion through arranging a new loan at 7 per cent annual interest or to finance the expansion through raising more equity capital. Management believes that issuance of debt will not result in insolvency problems and is primarily focusing on its desire to maximise the hotel owners' return.

Required:

a. Compare what the FrozenIce's owners' return on investment is if they raise the new finance through debt funding as opposed to equity funding.
b. Based on your answer to a), provide a recommendation to the company's management with respect to which financing approach they should use.

Chapter 16

Revenue management

Learning objectives

After studying this chapter, you should have developed an appreciation of:

1. what business characteristics are conducive to revenue management's application,
2. how revenue management is focused on striking an appropriate balance between minimising lost revenue resulting from rooms not sold and lost revenue resulting from selling rooms at prices below what that they could have been sold for,
3. how to appraise a hotel's need for improved revenue management decision making,
4. how rate categories can be used in combination with demand forecasts to increase total revenue,
5. how length of stay controls can be implemented to increase total revenue,
6. how changing the timing and size of group bookings can increase a hotel's revenue.

1) Introduction

Revenue management is a facet of hotel management that has become much more prominent in recent years. In large hotels it is now common for a senior manager to have the functional title "Revenue Manager".

Put simply, "Revenue Management" is concerned with maximising total revenue by using **demand forecast** information to determine what **price** to charge and **length of stay** to grant for a class of rooms at a particular time. When demand forecasts indicate that room night demand for a particular day is strong, we should hold out for a high price. When forecasts indicate that demand for room nights on a particular day is weak, we should consider discounting room prices in an effort to increase occupancy levels. The potential for a well-run revenue management system to affect profit is considerable. Cross (1997) suggests that a sales expense decrease of 5 per cent can raise profit by 3 per cent, a sales volume increase of 5 per cent can raise profit by 20 per cent, and a sale price increase of 5 per cent has the potential to increase profit by 50 per cent.

This philosophy of adjusting prices in accordance with demand is apparent in a range of business settings. For instance, theatre tickets are frequently discounted for matinee performances. Tickets to soccer matches are discounted when a fixture involves a team that has a small following, but marketed at a premium rate when the likes of Manchester United are coming to town. Airline ticket prices are much higher during school holiday periods than they are outside school holidays.

Following deregulation of the US airline industry, the 1980s saw a rapid growth of several "budget airlines" and their extensive application of revenue management techniques. These budget airlines employed rapidly evolving computing technology to inform seat price setting across a growing number of flight fare categories. Factors affecting quoted prices included: how far in advance a flight reservation was booked, whether the booking coincided with a peak demand period, and prices offered by competing airlines. Computing capacity is significant in this exercise, as the airline seat price setting decision is highly fluid. As there are many evolving factors such as a competitive airline announcing a new discounted price for an equivalent flight journey, seat price setting should not be viewed as a static "one-off" exercise, but rather as an on-going exercise that constantly reacts to unfolding market demand information.

During these early years, "yield management" was the term generally used to describe this demand-based flexible approach to pricing. Today, however, the term "revenue management" is more common, especially in hotels.

Hotel revenue management can be applied to the broad range of services sold by a hotel e.g., room accommodation, restaurant, bar and conferencing. The discounting of restaurant prices during lunchtime sittings, the provision of happy hour prices in a bar and the discounting of convention facility prices during quiet times can all be viewed as manifestations of revenue management decision making. To assist the development of your understanding of the nature and workings of revenue management, we will simplify matters by only considering revenue management in the context of decisions concerning the sale of room nights. This focus is particularly appropriate as, in reality, in most hotels it is room sales that receive the greatest amount of revenue management attention.

Revenue management is a highly inter-disciplinary activity, as marketing, accounting and operations management are all involved in its application. Due to this book's focus, we will be taking a financial perspective on revenue management decision making. In this chapter we will examine what types of business stand to benefit most from applying a well-designed revenue management system and how demand forecasting is fundamental to the workings of a revenue management system. Following a review of techniques that can be applied to appraise an organisation's need for revenue management, we will explore a range of specific revenue management applications that include the establishment of room rate categories and length of stay controls as well as group booking management approaches.

2) Business characteristics conducive to revenue management application

Revenue management is not equally applicable to all business settings. In this section we review the range of factors that make some business settings more conducive to revenue management application than others.

Fixed capacity

In many business situations, companies can relatively easily adjust their output in line with fluctuating levels of demand. For instance, a ski manufacturer will increase its level of production as the busy winter sales period approaches, maybe by working more shifts, and then decrease production as the summer season approaches. In this situation, it is evident that the manufacturer is clearly changing the volume of skis it is supplying to shops in line with changing levels of demand over the course of a year.

Now consider the case of a 200-room ski resort hotel that experiences a high demand for room nights during the winter months, but relatively low demand during the summer months. The hotel cannot vary the supply of room nights from one season to another. The hotel was built several years ago, signifying that its number of rooms available for sale are fixed. During the peak winter period, each day the hotel can sell 200 room nights, just as it can sell 200 room nights on any day in the summer. Its capacity is fixed. Because its capacity is fixed, there is an obvious incentive for the hotel to seek to charge higher room rates during its busy season, but then drop its room rates during its quiet season in an effort to sell off its excess capacity of rooms.

Ability to segment markets

The capacity to segment customers into distinct categories that are based on buying behaviour is a key feature of revenue management. For instance, we might be able to identify key buying behaviour differences between a hotel's guests who travel on business relative to vacationing family guests. Due to families needing to plan and coordinate their vacation ahead of time, it is customary for this market segment to book their accommodation well in advance. Business travel tends to be arranged more spontaneously with much shorter booking lead-times. Other typical buying behaviour differences between these two market segments include the fact that business guests have a greater propensity to dine in at a hotel's restaurant and also purchase drinks from in-room mini bars. Guilding et al. (2001) demonstrate how knowledge of such buyer behaviour differences can inform a decision to set different room rates for different market segments.

If a hotel is projecting low room night demand in six months' time, it could develop a room discounting strategy targeted to its family guest vacation market segment. To access this market segment, it could inform vacation booking agents that a temporary special discount is being offered for room nights booked in six months' time. This revenue management strategy would carry minimal negative implications for the room rates paid by business guests booking last minute accommodation, as these guests would not be making room bookings six months in advance through a vacation agent. This is a small example designed to demonstrate how different pricing structures can be offered simultaneously to distinct market segments.

Perishable inventory

If a car manufacturer's sales are slow on a particular day, there is no particular need for the manufacturer to drop the prices of its cars in an effort to sell more on that day. Cars not sold today can simply remain in the car manufacturer's finished goods inventory in readiness to be sold tomorrow or at some other time in the future. This is because cars represent a non-perishable inventory item.

This is not the situation for a hotel's room inventory, however. If tonight's right of occupancy in a particular hotel room is not sold today, the opportunity to sell that occupancy right will be lost forever, as an unsold room night today cannot be placed into inventory for sale at a later date. This heightens the incentive for hotels to consider a strategy of discounting room rates as the time of an unsold block of room nights approaches. As an unsold room night cannot be sold at a future date, it is described as being highly "perishable".

Product sold in advance

Some transient hotels (such as a roadside motel) sell the majority of their room inventory no more than a week in advance and have a substantial number of "same day" room bookings. For hotels that have a large volume of group sales, however, room reservations tend to be made several months in advance.

Revenue management is more relevant to hotels that have a high proportion of long lead-time bookings (i.e. bookings made well in advance of room night occupancy). In hotels that have a high proportion of long lead-time bookings, hotel managers are often having to decide whether to accept a reservation from a group booking agent who is seeking a block of rooms in several months time at a heavily discounted price. The manager has to decide whether to: 1) take the booking and face the possibility of having to turn away guests who would have booked late and paid a higher room rate, or 2) turn away the booking and face the possibility of the hotel achieving low occupancy for the nights in question and therefore lose the revenue that had been on offer from the group booking agent. A good revenue management system can help inform a manager confronted by this type of decision-making situation.

Fluctuating demand

If demand for whatever product or service a business is selling is constant, there is little need for a revenue management system, as there is little reason to change prices over the course of a year. Many hotels, however, confront highly fluctuating demand over the course of a week, month and year.

Revenue management is all about adjusting prices in line with fluctuating demand levels. When demand for rooms is low, an attempt can be made to increase total revenue by discounting room rates in an effort to increase occupancy levels. When demand for rooms is high, total revenue can be increased by setting higher room rate levels. A revenue management system can help inform a manager who is seeking to determine when, and by how much, room rates should be lowered or raised.

Low variable costs

The primary variable cost arising when a hotel sells an additional room night is the cost of cleaning and preparing the room for a new occupancy. In most hotels, this cost is small relative to the room rate paid by a hotel guest. As a contribution to profit results so long as the room rate charged is greater than the variable cost of cleaning the room, from a "covering cost" standpoint, a hotel manager has considerable discretionary scope to discount room rates.

In Chapter 12's Figure 12.1, it was noted that the percentage price discretion range applying to the sale of a bottle of wine is much smaller than the percentage price discretion range price for a room night sale. This is because, compared to a room night sale, the bottle of wine's variable cost represents a much larger proportion of its selling price. The high price discretion range associated with setting room rates signifies there is considerable scope for a hotel manager to modify room rates in light of information provided by a revenue management system.

3) Demand forecasting

It is helpful to think of a hotel revenue management system as focused on two goals:

- Goal 1: Minimising lost revenue resulting from rooms not sold.
- Goal 2: Minimising lost revenue resulting from rooms sold at prices below what they could have been sold for.

If a hotel is able to simultaneously minimise these two sources of lost revenue, it will be maximising its room sales revenue and, by implication, maximising its Revpar (revenue per available room).

An obvious tension arises, however, between these two goals. Pursuit of "Goal 1" causes us to focus on room rate discounting in an effort to sell more of our room inventory. This focus raises the prospect of damaging our pursuit of "Goal 2", however, as the dropping of room rates increases the likelihood of losing revenue as a result of selling some room nights at rates that are below what the rooms could have been sold for. Similarly, a hotel focusing on "Goal 2" will be trying to keep room rates high. Keeping room rates high will increase the likelihood of not achieving "Goal 1", as higher room rates will cause some potential guests to seek out alternative accommodation at a competing hotel. This signifies that the best Revenue Managers and the best revenue management systems will have a strong track record in striking an appropriate balance between the pursuit of Goals 1 and 2. They will ensure that too much emphasis on pursuing Goal 1 does not damage the pursuit of Goal 2, and vice versa.

Fairly obviously, a key factor in striking an appropriate balance between the pursuit of Goals 1 and 2 is knowing the nature of the demand for rooms on a particular night. Demand forecasting is fundamental to revenue management. Decisions on what rate to set for a room night can only be made if we have an understanding of the nature of demand for that room night. This underscores the fact that the quality of revenue management decision making can only be as good as the quality of the forecasting system on which it is based.

It is important to appreciate the distinction between forecasts and budgets. Budgeting was examined in Chapter 9. Once a budget is developed, based on forecast information available at the time of budget-setting, it does not tend to be altered. It is then used as a basis for gauging performance, through the comparison of actual financial results to budgeted financial performance. Forecasts, however, are not so static, as they are constantly evolving and being updated. It is on the basis of updated demand forecast information that room rates to be charged several months in the future can be changed on a daily, or even hourly, basis.

A forecast of room sales in a year's time cannot be expected to have the same accuracy as a forecast of sales in a week's time. This is simply because there is much greater scope for unanticipated events and developments to occur over the course of the forthcoming year than over the forthcoming week. As a result, longer-term forecasts are typically less detailed. They are intended to provide broad indications of likely demand and will be based on relatively generalised information such as projected tourism demand and the projected disposable income of people in a hotel's key markets. If one market's segment demand is expected to decline relative to another market segment, this needs to be considered by a revenue manager and room rate adjustments made accordingly.

4) Gauging a hotel's need for revenue management

There are three approaches that can be taken to gauge a hotel's need to employ revenue management, or stated differently, to guage its revenue management performance. The three approaches are:

a) Internal analysis of lost revenue;
b) Conducting a "competitive set" Revpar comparative performance analysis;
c) Conducting a comparative Revpar analysis based on purchased competitor data.

Each of these three approaches to gauging a hotel's revenue management performance will now be considered in turn.

Internal analysis of lost revenue

An internal analysis of lost revenue can be made by focusing on the two goals that were stated above, i.e.:

- Goal 1: minimising lost revenue resulting from rooms not being sold.
- Goal 2: minimising lost revenue resulting from selling room nights at prices below what they could have been sold for.

With respect to "Goal 1", for the previous year, we could develop an estimate of how much low rate category business our hotel turned away for dates when the property did not sell out. With respect to "Goal 2", we could develop an estimate of the number of potential rack rate (full price) sales that were lost due to rooms sold at a discount, on nights when our property achieved 100 per cent occupancy. These two estimates could then be added together to provide an estimate of lost revenue due to sub-optimal revenue management. The relationship between these Goals 1 and 2 and the measures required to gauge their achievement are depicted in Figure 16.1.

Gauging the dollar value of these two lost sources of revenue is bound to involve a degree of estimation. The relative accuracy of the estimate will likely depend on the quality of pertinent record keeping and also the knowledge of key managerial staff such as the room sales manager.

Despite the fact that this exercise will never rise above being an estimate, the insights deriving from conducting the estimation exercise and the impact it can have on raising staff appreciation of revenue management's importance should not be underestimated. "What gets measured is what gets managed" is a widely cited adage in management. In order for staff to attach a high priority to revenue management, they need to be alerted to the $ value of lost revenues associated with not achieving Goals 1 and 2.

Revenue Management Goals	Goal achievement measurement
1. Minimise lost revenue from rooms not sold.	For dates when the property has not sold out, estimate how much low rate category business was turned away.
2. Minimise lost revenue resulting from selling room nights at prices below what they could have been sold for.	For 100 per cent occupancy dates, develop an estimate of the number of potential rack rate sales that were lost due to rooms sold at a discount.

Figure 16.1 Internal analysis of lost revenue

Conducting a "competitive set" Revpar comparative performance analysis

Another approach to gauging whether a hotel needs to improve its revenue management performance can be taken by examining how its Revpar compares to the Revpar achieved by its closest competitors. To do this, a hotel will first need to identify the set of hotels operating within its close proximity, and then determine which of these hotels provide comparable levels of service. A group of hotels that are in close proximity and provide similar standards of service is referred to as a **"competitive set"**. Imagine that we are involved in the management of the Imperial Hotel and that we have determined that we have three other hotels in our competitive set (Hotels A, B and C). Revenue performance for this competitive set of hotels for the last 30 days is provided in Table 16.1. If a hotel seeks to develop the type of data reported in Table 16.1 it is bound to undertake some estimating. It is notable, however, that a distinguishing feature of the hotel sector concerns the extent to which it has a strong information sharing culture. Information sharing on factors such as occupancy levels is widespread between competing properties (Anderson and Guilding 2006).

In Table 16.1, the "market share capacity" column reflects the percentage of the competitive set's total number of rooms provided by each of the hotels. "Room nights sold" reflects the total room nights sold by each of the hotels during the 30-day period. The "room nights share" column reflects the proportion of the competitive set's total number of room sales accounted for by each individual hotel. "Room revenue" simply records the total room revenue generated by each hotel. In the final column, the "room revenue share" reflects the proportion of the competitive set's total revenue generated by each of the hotels.

From Table 16.1 we can see that the Imperial Hotel is underperforming with respect to its share of room nights sold (23.58 per cent) as this falls below its share of the competitive set's number of rooms (25.7 per cent). With respect to revenue, however, the Imperial is punching above its weight, as it is earning 27.05 per cent of the competitive set's revenue, which is above its proportion of the competitive set's number of rooms (25.7 per cent).

We can take this analysis further by calculating a set of penetration indices that capture each hotel's relative performance with respect to occupancy, average daily rate (ADR) and Revpar. To do this we first need to compute the average occupancy for the whole market (first formula below), the ADR achieved by the whole market (second formula below) and the Revpar achieved by the whole market (third formula below).

Table 16.1 Competing hotels revenue comparison

Hotel	Number of rooms	Market share capacity	Room nights sold	Room nights share	Room revenue	Room revenue share
Imperial	180	25.7%	3,240	23.58%	$609,120	27.05%
A	150	21.4%	2,835	20.63%	$493,290	21.90%
B	170	24.3%	3,468	25.23%	$561,816	24.94%
C	200	28.6%	4,200	30.56%	$588,000	26.11%
Total	**700**	**100%**	**13,743**	**100%**	**$2,252,226**	**100%**

Revenue management

Market occupancy %	=	Market room nights sold ÷ Room nights available × 100	
	=	$13{,}743 ÷ (700 × 30) × 100$	
	=	65.44%	
Market ADR	=	Market room nights sold revenue ÷ Room nights sold	
	=	$\$2{,}252{,}226 ÷ 13{,}743$	
	=	$\$163.88$	
Market Revpar	=	Market room nights sold revenue ÷ Room nights available	
	=	$\$2{,}252{,}226 ÷ (700 × 30)$	
	=	$\$107.25$	

OR: Occupancy (as a decimal) × ADR:

$0.6544 × \$163.88 = \$107.24$ (difference due to rounding error)

The occupancy penetration index is calculated by dividing each hotel's occupancy percentage by the market occupancy percentage. If this index is greater than 1, it signifies that a hotel has outperformed its competitive set with respect to the occupancy levels it has achieved. Occupancy penetration indices are provided in the third column of Table 16.2. The fact that the occupancy penetration index for the Imperial hotel is less than 1 signifies that it has underperformed compared to its competitive set of hotels with respect to occupancy levels it has achieved.

The ADR penetration index is calculated by dividing each hotel's ADR by the market ADR. ADR penetration indices are provided in the fifth third column of Table 16.2. The ADR penetration index for the Imperial Hotel is greater than 1. This signifies that it has outperformed its competitive set with respect to room rates charged.

Finally, the Revpar penetration index is calculated by dividing each hotel's Revpar by the market Revpar. Revpar penetration indices are provided in the final column of Table 16.2. The Revpar penetration index for the Imperial Hotel is greater than 1. This signifies that it has outperformed its competitive set with respect to Revpar. From a revenue management perspective, Revpar represents the most complete indicator of a hotel's revenue management performance. This is because, as was noted in Box 5.1 in Chapter 5, Revpar represents the combination of a hotel's occupancy performance and its ADR achievement. As the Imperial Hotel's Revpar penetration index is the highest of its competitive set, this analysis suggests that overall the Imperial Hotel is outperforming all of its most immediate competitors with respect to revenue management.

Table 16.2 Competing hotels occupancy, ADR and Revpar penetration

Hotel	Occupancy %	Occupancy penetration	ADR	ADR penetration	Revpar	Revpar penetration
Imperial	60	0.92	$188	1.15	$112.80	1.05
A	63	0.96	$174	1.06	$109.62	1.02
B	68	1.04	$162	0.99	$110.16	1.03
C	70	1.07	$140	0.85	$98.00	0.91

The analysis provided in Table 16.2 suggests that Hotel C is the poorest performing hotel as it has the lowest Revpar penetration index. The analysis provided in this table also provides us with a clue with respect to which aspect of its revenue management it should address. Hotel C performs strongly on the occupancy penetration index. This suggests that its main immediate focus should not be Goal 1 of revenue management, i.e. minimising the loss of revenue resulting from rooms not being sold, as compared to its competitors it is achieving a high proportion of rooms sold. Hotel C is performing very weakly, however, on the ADR penetration index. This suggests its main immediate focus should be on Goal 2 of revenue management, i.e., minimising the loss of revenue resulting from selling rooms at prices that are below the price that they could have been sold for. It appears Hotel C may have got the balance in simultaneously pursuing Goals 1 and 2 too slanted towards seeking low room vacancies, and as a result, it has dropped its room rates too low.

Conducting a comparative Revpar analysis based on purchased competitor data

There are several companies that collect and distribute performance data for hotels and hotel companies on a commercial basis. Companies that provide such a service include Horwath Consulting, PricewaterhouseCoopers and Smith Travel Research (in the USA). Such performance data can be categorised according to hotel characteristics such as size and star rating. Equipped with such information, a revenue manager can quickly determine her hotel's occupancy, ADR and Revpar performance relative to comparable hotels and use this information as an indicator of her hotel's revenue management performance.

5) Revenue management system requirements

It has already been noted that having a well-developed demand forecasting system is fundamental to revenue management. More specifically, an effective revenue management system requires historical data concerning booking patterns, the price elasticity of demand and the nature of demand across different market segments in order to develop room sale forecasts. In addition, a hotel's overbooking policy has to be fed into a revenue management system.

Reservation booking pattern information

The nature of a hotel's market can have a major impact on its average booking lead-time (i.e., the time between date of room occupancy and the date the occupancy was reserved). It is important that a hotel has an understanding of its average booking lead-time, as this information is critical when determining whether a period of high or low occupancy is approaching.

Imagine that a hotel's reservation system indicates that 60 per cent of its accommodation rooms have been booked for a particular night in one month's time. If the hotel operates primarily in the group booking market, it may be justified in introducing a discount for the room night in question, as prior experience could indicate that high occupancy tends to only be achieved when 80 per cent of rooms have been booked one month in advance. However, if the hotel operates primarily in the business traveller market, it may be justified in raising the price of the room night in question, as prior experience could indicate that a room night typically sells out if it is 50 per cent booked up one month in advance.

Price change effects

Also fundamental to a revenue management system is historical information concerning the impact that a change in price has on the volume of sales. If we drop the price of a room night by 10 per cent, by how much do we expect room sales to increase?

The relationship between price and demand is generally referred to as the price elasticity of demand. This concept was introduced in Chapter 12 where it was noted that a product or service is viewed as being price elastic if a percentage change in price results in a greater percentage change in demand. For example, imagine that a hotel has found that at a room rate of $120 it maintains an average sales level of 500 room nights per week. In addition, it has also found that if it increases its room rate by 10 per cent to $132, a 15 per cent reduction in demand will result, i.e., sales will drop to 425 room nights per week. As the percentage change in demand is greater than the percentage change in price, the rooms can be described as price elastic. The price elasticity of demand is generally measured using the following formula:

$$\textit{Price elasticity of demand} \; = \; \frac{\textit{\% change in quantity demanded}}{\textit{\% change in price}}$$

If this formula yields a value greater than 1, then the product or service in question is price elastic. If the formula yields a value less than 1, the product or service in question is price inelastic.

Demand patterns by market segment

Many hotels serve more than one market. As distinct sales distribution channels frequently apply to these different markets, hotels can simultaneously offer different room rates to different market segments. Financial decision making in action case 16.1 demonstrates how different price elasticity of demand indices can apply to different market segments. Equipped with such information, the revenue manager can tailor different price offerings to different market segments.

FINANCIAL DECISION MAKING IN ACTION CASE 16.1

The Revenue Manager and price elasticity of demand

The Revenue Manager in Hong Kong's EasternTemple Resort Hotel is discussing with colleagues a room night pricing decision. The EasternTemple has 249 rooms and serves two distinct markets: domestic vacationers and overseas vacationers. The hotel's Revenue Manager is exploring ways to increase its projected occupancy during the first week in the up-coming August. Presently 135 of the hotel's rooms have been sold for the week at the currently advertised nightly room rate of $100. The Revenue Manager has proposed the introduction of a substantial discount off the usual room rate for the week in question.

If no change is made in the room rate, the revenue management system predicts that 50 further room nights will be sold to the domestic vacationer market and

20 further room nights will be sold to the overseas vacationer market. The system also indicates that for the week in question, the price elasticity of demand for room night accommodation is 2.2 for the domestic vacationer market and 1.5 for the overseas vacationer market. Equipped with this information, the revenue manager has determined that the introduction of a 40 per cent discount for the domestic vacationer market represents an optimal solution to this particular revenue management issue. He has supported this view by providing the following information to the hotel's General Manager. In this analysis, the Revenue Manager has limited his focus to room nights that have yet to be sold, i.e., he has ignored the bookings that have already been made, as these cannot be changed.

Incremental daily room night revenue = Additional domestic vacationer room revenue + Additional overseas vacationer room revenue.

Incremental daily room night revenue if no room rate discounting is introduced:

$$(50 \times \$100) + (20 \times \$100) = \$5,000 + \$2,000 = \$7,000$$

Incremental revenue if 40 per cent discount is introduced for the domestic vacationer market:
Room sales to the domestic vacationer market segment will increase by 88 per cent (2.2 × 40 per cent) as the price elasticity of demand is 2.2. This signifies that projected rooms purchased by the domestic market will increase from 50 to 94 if the room rate drops by 40 per cent to $60.
Therefore, incremental daily room night revenue if 40 per cent domestic vacationer market room rate discount is introduced = (94 × $60) + (20 × $100) = $5,640 + $2,000 = $7,640.

If 40 per cent discount is introduced for the overseas vacationer market:
Room sales to the overseas vacationer market segment will increase by 60 per cent (1.5 × 40 per cent) as the price elasticity of demand is 1.5.
Incremental daily room night revenue if 40 per cent overseas vacationer market room rate discount is introduced = (50 × $100) + (32 × $60) = $5,000 + $1,920 = $6,920.

As revenue is maximised if the 40 per cent discount for the domestic vacationer market is introduced, this represents the preferred course of action.

Overbooking policy

Due to the frequency of last minute cancellations and also guest "no-shows", many hotels operate an overbooking policy. This means taking more bookings for a particular night than a hotel is able to meet, for instance, a 500-room hotel may accept 505 bookings for a particular night. As the application of an overbooking policy effectively increases the number of room bookings that a hotel is willing to accept, this factor needs to be incorporated into a hotel's revenue management system.

While application of an overbooking policy will likely increase occupancy rates, it also carries obvious risks. On an overbooked day when no guest cancels and there are no "no-shows", a hotel will have to deal with irate guests for whom it cannot find a room. Strategies that can be applied in such a situation include having arrangements with neighbouring hotels to accommodate displaced guests, providing a displaced guest with alternative accommodation, paying for the displaced guest's accommodation or offering displaced guests with some other compensation. Managing such a situation can be highly stressful for front office staff. Particular care should be taken not to alienate a guest who is a loyal customer. These issues highlight the fact that prior to adopting an overbooking policy, careful consideration should be made of the risk and downside implications.

6) Using rate categories and demand forecasts

Most revenue management systems are built upon a framework of price categories. For rooms in a hotel, we talk of room rate categories. We might establish a room pricing system whereby rate category 1 refers to rooms sold with no discount, rate category 2 refers to rooms sold at a 1–10 per cent discount, rate category 3 refers to rooms sold at a 11–20 per cent discount, etc. Box 16.1 illustrates how room rate categories can be used when attempting to maximise a hotel's revenue for a particular night. It also illustrates the on-going monitoring of whether room bookings are in line with projected sales levels and how failure to reach originally anticipated booking levels for a particular night can result in the opening up of initially withheld rate categories.

Box 16.1

Using rate categories and demand forecasts to maximise revenue

The 300 room Emerald Hotel has broken up its customer base into several distinct market segments. For most of the year, it operates four distinct room rate categories. On 2nd January, based on prior years' data, the hotel developed the following segmented sales projection for room sales on 1st November.

Rate category	Discount off rack rate	Available rooms	Demand forecast
1	None	300	90
2	1–10%	210	110
3	11–20%	100	130
4	21–35%	0	150

To make sense of this data, we should move down the 4 rate categories. The hotel projected that on 1st November it would sell 90 rooms with no room

---

discount applied (rate category 1). This leaves 210 of the hotel's 300 rooms available for sale to rate category 2 (1–10 per cent rate discount). The hotel's revenue management system predicted that it would sell 110 rooms at rate category 2, leaving 100 rooms available for rate category 3 customers. The projected rate category 3 level demand was 130 rooms, signifying no rooms left to be allocated to rate category 4. If, however, rooms had been released at the rate category 4 level, on 2nd January the system predicted 150 further room nights would be sold.

Now imagine that today is 1st October and the hotel's reservation system is indicating that the following room reservations have been made for the night of 1st November.

Rate Category	Rooms sold	Originally expected sales 30 days out
1	40	80
2	86	82
3	123	126
4	–	–

This schedule's middle column reflects the number of rooms already sold and the final column reflects the 1st November room bookings that the revenue management system had originally projected would be sold by 1st October. The schedule shows that while rate categories 2 and 3 have performed approximately as expected, rate category 1 room bookings are 50 per cent below their originally forecast level.

Analysis implications: The fact that rate category 1 room sales are well below expectation signifies that if management does nothing, there is likely to be a significant shortfall in the originally projected 1st November room night sales. Emerald's management should therefore seriously consider releasing some rate category 1 rooms to some of the lower revenue rate categories. A case might even be made for now offering some 1st November room nights at the rate category 4 level.

7) Length of stay controls

Rate category control focuses on the idea of having a room night available for occupancy at a future date and deciding whether to sell it at a discounted rate today or to hold out with the hope of selling it at a higher rate in the future. Length of stay issues have a distinctly different focus. Revenue management systems not only have to deal with the fact that room bookings differ with respect to the room rate paid, they also differ with respect to guests' length of stay. An example of how a revenue management becomes involved with length of stay management issues is described in Box 16.2.

> ### Box 16.2
>
> ## Length of stay revenue management
>
> Imagine that our hotel has one remaining room to be booked for the night of 20th June which coincides with a major local sporting event. Immediately following the event, on the 21st June, we are anticipating a large exodus of guests, and that our hotel will be running at 60 per cent occupancy on the nights of 21st, 22nd and 23rd June. Our revenue manager knows that we will have little problem selling the one remaining room night on 20th June for its rate category 1 price of $200. He also projects that if we hold this last remaining single room night sale back, there is a high likelihood that we can sell it as the first night of a "four room nights at $150 per night" package deal. Should we sell the 20th June room night as a stand-alone sale for $200, or should we sell it as the first night of a "four room nights at $150 per night" package?
>
> If the 20th June room night is sold as a stand-alone, our hotel's revenue will increase by $200. If the 20th June room night is sold as part of the four room night package, however, our hotel's revenue will increase by $600 (4 × $150). This signifies that the total positive impact on revenue is $400 greater ($600 – $200) if we sell the room as part of a "four room nights at $150 per night" package instead of the stand-alone 20th June room night sale option.
>
> This revenue analysis misses one important issue, however. The sale of the room for four nights would trigger room cleaning costs for three more days than if we were to sell the room as a stand-alone room night. Imagine that we have determined that the variable cost of daily room cleaning is $30. If this is the case, a $310 positive impact on profit results from using the room as part of a "four room nights at $150 per night" package instead of a $200 stand-alone room night sale (increased revenue of $400 minus three days extra room cleaning costs at $30 per day). This analysis signifies the hotel should sell the last 20th June room night as part of a "four room nights at $150 per night" package and not as a stand-alone room night sale, as the four night package sale will generate $310 more in profit.

Length of stay management requires prior data concerned with how many guests are likely to book for what length of stay periods throughout the year. The complexity of this information underscores the importance of having a computer-based revenue management system.

A Revenue Manager needs to know the projected number of check-ins on a particular day for 1 night, 2 night, 3 night stays, etc. Consistent with the type of analysis provided in Box 16.2, this will help in determining if there is a justification in turning away a 1 night booking (or maybe a 2 or 3 night booking). Armed with this information, the revenue management system will enable a manager to prevent short length of stay reservations from starting on a key date. For instance, a manager may wish to prevent 1, 2 and 3 day bookings starting on the 25th June. He would be motivated to do this if he felt that these shorter period bookings would displace yet-to-be-reserved one week bookings starting on 25th June.

8) Managing group bookings

Too many managers think that revenue management revolves exclusively around using forecast data to determine when discounted group bookings should be turned away. There is a more subtle side to revenue management, however. Instead of turning away undesirable sales, it can pursue a philosophy of converting undesirable room sales into desirable room sales.

We will now explore two ways that undesirable room sales can be converted into desirable room sales. Firstly, we will examine the financial implications arising if a tour operator can be enticed to change the dates of a proposed group booking, then we will look at the financial implications that can result if a tour operator is enticed to reduce the size of a proposed group booking. Box 16.3 provides an example of how a hotel can profit from persuading a tour booking agent to change the date of a planned group booking.

Box 16.3

Changing the timing of a group booking

The 250-room GraciousGrounds Hotel has been approached by a tour operator who wants to book 60 rooms at the per room group room rate of $100 on a particular night in six months' time. The hotel's revenue management system projects that for the night in question, if it does not take the group booking, it will sell 225 rooms at $140 each.

GraciousGrounds' revenue manager provides the following analysis to determine whether the hotel should accept the group booking:

Revenue without the group booking: 225 rooms × $140 = $31,500

Revenue with the group booking:
Revenue from non-group bookings: 190 rooms × $140 = $26,600
Revenue from group booking: 60 rooms × $100 = $6,000
Total revenue with the group booking = $32,600 ($26,600 + $6,000).

Based on this analysis, it appears that the group booking should be accepted, as it will provide $1,100 more revenue ($32,600 – $31,500). It is of concern, however, that acceptance of the $6,000 group booking (60 rooms at $100) has resulted in revenue increasing by only $1,100 above what it would have been had the group booking not been accepted.

The GraciousGrounds' Revenue Manager is smart and decides to try a different approach to dealing with this situation. Based on her awareness that a 60 per cent occupancy is projected at the hotel one week following the date that the tour operator is wishing to book, she says to the agent "As you have always been a very good client of ours, I want to give you an extra 5 per cent room rate discount, if you make your booking one week later". The tour operator likes what he hears and takes up the offer.

Now, for the later date, let's determine the incremental revenue resulting from the group booking:

Revenue without the group booking (60 per cent occupancy): 150 rooms × $140 = $21,000

Revenue with the group booking:
Revenue from non-group bookings = 150 rooms × $140 = $21,000
Revenue from 5 per cent discounted group booking = 60 rooms × $95 = $5,700
Total revenue for the night with the group booking = $26,700 ($21,000 + $5,700).

By deferring the group booking by one week, the Revenue Manager has managed to raise the revenue from the night in question by $5,700 (from $21,000 to $26,700). This means that the group booking provides a $4,600 ($5,700 − $1,100) greater beneficial impact on revenue if the booking is made a week later. This provides justification for the Revenue Manager deciding to give the tour operator a 5 per cent room rate discount incentive to accept the later group booking date.

The analysis provided in Box 16.3 provides a comprehensive overview of the changed impact on revenue that results from moving a group booking from a high occupancy period to a low occupancy period. The key to the issue described in Box 16.3 is the fact that if the group booking is made during the high occupancy period, 35 potential premium rate paying guests will be displaced by lower "group rate" paying guests. The analysis provided in Box 16.3 can actually be simplified by taking the following approach:

Incremental revenue impact if group booking is made on the earlier date:
Incremental revenue from group booking: 60 rooms × $100 = $6,000
Lost revenue from displaced premium room rate guests: ($140 × 35) = $4,900
Net incremental revenue impact from early group booking = $1,100 ($6,000 − $4,900)

Incremental revenue impact if group booking is made on the later date:
60 rooms × $95 = $5,700.

As the incremental revenue impact of the later booking is $4,600 more ($5,700 − $1,100) than if the early booking is made, the later group booking is the preferred option.

Box 16.4 provides an example of how revenue can be increased by changing the number of rooms allocated to a group booking. This box demonstrates that incremental revenue can be increased if the number of higher rate room night sales displaced by lower rate room night sales can be reduced by lowering the number of rooms allocated to the cheaper rate group booking.

Box 16.4

Changing the size of a group booking

Imagine now that for the case described in Box 16.3, the tour operator turned down the offer of making the group booking a week later. He explained that he has no date flexibility, as the timing of all of the tour's activities are already finalised. Still motivated by a desire to avoid the prospect of the group booking displacing 35 premium rate paying guests, GraciousGrounds' Revenue Manager plays another card. She says to the agent "OK, I think I know of a way that I can double that room rate discount offer. I will discount the room rate by 10 per cent if you can find a way to reduce the number of rooms that you need in your group booking from 60 rooms to 25 rooms". The tour operator then takes a day to work out whether he can reduce the size of his group booking and then comes back to the Revenue Manager indicating that he is happy to take her up on the 25 rooms at $90 per room offer.

Let us now see how much the hotel's incremental revenue increases as a result of reducing the group booking reduction from 60 to 25 rooms.

Total room revenue if the 60 room group booking is made:
Revenue from non-group bookings: 190 rooms × $140 = $26,600
Revenue from group booking: 60 rooms × $100 = $6,000
Total revenue for the night = $32,600 ($26,600 + $6,000).

Total room revenue if the 25 room discounted group rate booking is made:
Revenue from non-group bookings: 225 rooms × $140 = $31,500
Revenue from group booking: 25 rooms × $90 = $2,250
Total revenue for the night = $33,750 ($31,500 + $2,250).

This analysis demonstrates that $1,150 more revenue results ($33,750 − $32,600) if the 25 room $90 group booking is made relative to the 60 room $100 group booking. The higher net incremental revenue resulting from the 25 room group booking financially justifies GraciousGrounds' Revenue Manager's decision to offer the $10 room rate discount as an incentive for the tour operator to reduce the number of rooms booked.

9) Revenue management implementation issues

Avoid alienating customers

Customers may be more accepting of revenue management in some industries relative to others. For instance, airline customers appear to have grown accustomed to the notion that airlines charge different rates for equivalent seats on the same flight. Hotel customers may be not as accustomed to the application of revenue management in the hotel sector. Hotels will need to establish procedures for dealing with an irate customer who arrives at the registration desk and starts complaining that following a poolside chat with another guest, they have just discovered that they are paying 20 per cent more per night, and would like a hotel manager to explain this inequity.

Minimise negative staff morale issues

Revenue management systems greatly reduce the guesswork associated with decisions concerning room rate levels and the release of group bookings. This can frustrate a manager who has been used to exercising discretion in making such decisions. It can therefore be important to view a revenue management system more as a resource than as a finite decision maker.

Staff reward and incentive systems

Many staff in group-sales departments have been rewarded based on the volume of group sales achieved. Such a reward system should be modified, however, if a revenue management system is being implemented. This is because a revenue management system can result in the acceptance of a reduced number of group bookings. Also, no managers should be rewarded based on occupancy levels or average room rates achieved. Staff should be rewarded on Revpar performance, as this is the measure that will most closely align them to a revenue management system's focus.

Training of staff

As with all new systems, the introduction of a revenue management system will necessitate staff training, if the system is to deliver to its potential. Generally, the staff most closely involved in this training are the sales, reservations and front office personnel.

Organisation of the revenue management function

While a revenue management system needs to have a property level focus, it obviously needs to be integrated with a hotel chain's central reservation system.

Senior management commitment

As with any system, in order for a revenue management system to run smoothly and achieve its potential to raise a property's revenue level, it needs to have strong support from senior management. It is only when a revenue management system has strong "buy-in" from senior hotel management, that it will be embraced as an important tool and philosophy.

10) Words of caution in applying the revenue management philosophy

While this chapter has highlighted approaches that can be taken to maximise revenue on any particular day, care should be taken not to inflict long-term damage as a result of maximising a particular night's revenue. Examples of ways that maximising revenue on a particular day might damage long-term performance include:

- Extensive room rate discounting can tarnish the image of an up-market resort.
- Maximising the inventory of rooms sold can result in no rooms retained for last minute loyal guest bookings. If a loyal guest who travels extensively for business, with little notice provided, finds he has not been able to make a late booking at a hotel on a couple of occasions, his loyalty may be diverted to a competitor.
- If an agent who has brought much group-booking business to a hotel is denied the opportunity to make a group booking, he may in the future take his business elsewhere.

It is also worth noting that revenue management may not be an appropriate philosophy to apply in all hotels. For some hotels it may be appropriate to adopt a very simple pricing approach. Take the example of a roadside motel, located close to a highway exit and with no competing hotels in close proximity. Such a motel may experience little demand seasonality and primarily deal with guests who do not make reservations and generally stay for only one night. In this case, it might be quite appropriate for the motel manager to set the price of the first room night sold at the same level as the price of the last room night sold, as potential guests are not shopping around for the best price they can find. If guests are not "price-shopping", the motivation for applying a revenue management approach to setting room rates is largely eliminated.

In exploring the application of revenue management, we have exclusively focused on the setting of room rates. It should be noted, however, that a room sale does not only trigger a contribution to hotel profitability from the room rate received. Many guests will eat at the hotel's restaurant, drink at the bar, make purchases from their mini-bar, etc. These "supplementary purchases", which add to a hotel's profitability, all derive from room night sales (Guilding et al. 2001). If a hotel has strong data indicating that one market segment has a greater propensity to make "supplementary purchases" than another market segment, a strong case can be made to include market segment differential supplementary purchasing propensities in revenue management decision making. This issue need not represent a major stumbling block for revenue managers, however, as the "total yield" facet of a guest's stay can be easily dealt with by most sophisticated revenue management computer systems.

11) Summary

This chapter has described the nature of revenue management systems and how revenue management approaches can be used in a range of ways to increase revenue. We noted that a fundamental concept of revenue management concerns the striking of an appropriate balance between minimising revenue lost as a result of unsold rooms and minimising lost revenue resulting from selling rooms at prices below what that they could have been sold for.

Having read the chapter you should now know:

- how to appraise a hotel's need for improved revenue management decision making,
- how rate categories can be used in combination with demand forecasts in an attempt to increase total revenue,
- how length of stay controls can be implemented in an attempt to increase total revenue,
- how attempts can be made to change the timing of group bookings in an attempt to increase total revenue,
- how attempts can be made to change the size of group bookings in an attempt to increase total revenue.

References

Anderson, S. and Guilding, C. (2006) "Competitor focused accounting applied to a hotel context", *International Journal of Contemporary Hospitality Management*, Vol. 18, No. 3, 206–18.

Cross, R. (1997) "Launching the Revenue Rocket: How Revenue Management can work for your business", *Cornell Hotel and Restaurant Quarterly*, Vol. 38 (2), 32–43.

Forgacs, G. (2010) *Revenue Management: Maximizing Revenue in Hospitality Operations*, East Lansing, MI: American Hotel & Lodging Educational Institute.

Guilding, C., Kennedy, D. and McManus, L. (2001) "Extending the boundaries of customer accounting: applications in the hotel industry", *Journal of Hospitality & Tourism Research*, Vol. 25 (2), 173–94.

Kimes, S.E. (1989) "The basics of yield management", *Cornell Hotel and Restaurant Quarterly*, Vol. 30 (3), 14–19.

Quain, W.J. and LeBruto, S. (2007) "Yield management: choosing the most profitable reservations," in Rutherford, D.G. and O'Fallon, M.J., *Hotel Management and Operations*, Hoboken, NJ: John Wiley & Sons.

Problems

Problem 16.1

Explain why the existence of low variable costs is a business characteristic that is conducive to the application of revenue management.

Problem 16.2

Identify five industry factors that are conducive to the application of revenue management.

Problem 16.3

Identify three ways that a hotel can assess its revenue management performance and gauge whether it needs to implement revenue management.

Problem 16.4

The following table provides an analysis of the rooms division revenue earned by the Classic Hotel in the last 30 days, relative to its three closest competitors.

Classic Hotel: Competing hotels revenue comparison						
Hotel	Number of rooms	Market share capacity	Room nights sold	Room nights share	Room revenue	Room revenue share
Classic	160	25.00%	3,840	28.26%	$460,800	23.38%
A	140	21.87%	3,150	23.18%	$472,500	23.97%
B	160	25.00%	3,360	24.72%	$487,200	24.71%
C	180	28.13%	3,240	23.84%	$550,800	27.94%
Total	640	100%	13,590	100%	$1,971,300	100%

Required:

a) Calculate the occupancy, ADR and Revpar penetration indices for the Classic Hotel.
b) Based on this analysis, how well does the Classic Hotel appear to be performing with respect to revenue management.
c) Based on your answer provided in a), which aspect of revenue management do you believe provides greatest scope for improved performance for the Classic Hotel: 1) minimising the loss of revenue resulting from rooms not being sold, or 2) minimising the loss of revenue resulting from selling rooms at prices below what they could have been sold for.

Problem 16.5

Over the last year, the Regal Hotel has achieved an occupancy rate of 68 per cent and a $140 average daily rate (ADR) for room nights sold. The Regal Hotel competes closely with three other hotels. During the last year, this four hotel competitive set has achieved a market occupancy percentage of 72 per cent and a market ADR of $124.

Required:

a) Calculate the occupancy, ADR and Revpar penetration indices for the Regal Hotel.
b) Based on this analysis, how well does the Regal Hotel appear to be performing with respect to revenue management.
c) Based on your answer provided in a), which dimension of revenue management do you believe provides greatest scope for improved performance by the Regal Hotel: 1) minimising the loss of revenue resulting from rooms not being sold, or 2) minimising the loss of revenue resulting from selling rooms at prices below what they could have been sold for.

Problem 16.6

Barcelona's BullFighter Hotel has 198 rooms and serves two distinct markets: business travellers and tourists. The hotel is considering trying to raise its occupancy in a particular week in four months' time. Presently 120 of the hotel's rooms have been sold for the week at the advertised nightly room rate of (120). If no change is made in the room rate, the revenue management system predicts that 32 further room nights will be sold to the business traveller segment and 20 further room nights will be sold to the tourist market. The system also indicates that for the week in question, the price elasticity of demand for room night accommodation is 2.5 for the business traveller market and 1.6 for the tourist market.

The hotel's Revenue Manager has recommended that a 30 per cent discount should be introduced for bookings made by the business traveller market. He warns, however, that dropping the room rate for this market to €84 will signify some lost revenue as the business guests who are currently intending to book a room will now be able to purchase their room nights for €36 less.

Required:
Prepare a financial analysis to determine if the Revenue Manager's 30 per cent discount for business travellers recommendation is well justified.

Problem 16.7

The LeafyLodge Hotel has one remaining room to be booked for the night of 1st August. The hotel is expecting a relatively low occupancy, however, during the subsequent six days. LeafyLodge's Revenue Manager is confident that the last room to be booked on 1st August could be sold for $250. As an alternative, the room could be booked as the first night of a "three room nights at $120 per night" package. Variable room cleaning costs are $25 per room night sold.

Required:
Demonstrate whether the LeafyLodge Hotel should sell the 1st August room night as a single night sale for $250, or as the first night of a "three room nights at $120 per night" package.

Problem 16.8

The 400-room LuxuriousLayback Hotel has been approached by a tour operator who is seeking to book 80 rooms at the per room group room rate of $75 on a particular night in six months' time. The hotel's revenue management system projects that for the night in question, if it does not accept this group booking, it will sell 360 rooms (90 per cent occupancy) at $120 each.

The hotel's manager has asked you to assist in providing an analysis to determine whether the hotel should try to get the tour operator to move the room booking into its low season, which is projected to commence three weeks after the tour operator's requested booking date. During the low season, LuxuriousLayback seldom surpasses a 70 per cent occupancy rate. The hotel manager feels that if the tour operator were to be offered a discounted group room rate of $70 for the later booking date, he would likely take the offer.

Required:
Provide a financial analysis to determine if it is financially justifiable to provide the tour operator with a $5 room rate discount to encourage him to move his 80-room block booking from the projected 90 per cent occupancy period to a 70 per cent occupancy period.

Problem 16.9

The 300-room GreatWall Hotel in Beijing has been approached by a tour operator seeking to book 70 rooms at the group room rate of Y300 per room on a particular night in 22 weeks' time. The hotel's revenue management system projects that for the night in question, if it does not take the group booking it will sell 260 rooms at Y450 each.

The hotel's revenue manager is aware that two weeks after the proposed group booking date, the hotel will be operating at a 70 per cent occupancy and is considering offering the tour operator a lower room rate if he is willing to move the group booking back by two weeks. He knows that a large room rate discount will have to be offered to entice the agent to move the block booking back by two weeks, but is uncertain how much of a room rate discount is financially justifiable.

Required:
Prepare an analysis to determine the maximum room rate discount that the revenue manager can financially justify in seeking to move this room block booking back by two weeks.

Problem 16.10

Osaka's PowderSki Hotel has been approached by a tour operator wanting to book 30 rooms for one week at the group rate of ¥70,000 per room. The hotel has 110 rooms. The hotel's Revenue Manager has predicted that if the booking is not accepted, the hotel will be able to achieve an 80 per cent occupancy with all guests paying a weekly room rate of ¥100,000. PowderSki's Revenue Manager is concerned about the displacement of higher rate paying guests if the group booking is accepted and is thinking about cutting the weekly room rate to ¥60,000 if the tour operator can find a way to reduce the size of his room allocation request to 22 rooms.

Required:
Prepare a financial analysis to determine whether PowderSki's Revenue Manager can be justified in offering the ¥60,000 discounted room rate to the tour operator.

Problem 16.11

The MightyAllBlacks Hotel in Wellington has 200 rooms and specialises in hosting guests attending sport events at the Wellington Regional Stadium. The hotel's Revenue Manager has just received an email from a tour operator client who is indicating that he would like to book 50 rooms for a Friday and Saturday night in four months' time at $100 per room night. The hotel's revenue management system is predicting that the hotel will achieve 88 per cent occupancy for the two nights in question if the 50-room group booking is not accepted. This occupancy level would comprise guests who are paying a non-discounted room rate of $150. Knowing that many rugby tour guests are not averse to sharing a room if rates are discounted, the hotel's Revenue Manager is considering providing the tour operator with the following two options:

- Nightly room rates discounted to $95 if the tour operator can consolidate the group booking down to 40 rooms.
- Nightly room rates discounted to $90 if the tour operator can consolidate the group booking down to 25 rooms.

Required:

a) Prepare a financial analysis to demonstrate whether the MightyAllBlacks Hotel's Revenue Manager would be justified in offering the room rate discounts that are under consideration.
b) If the manager is justified in offering these discounted room rate options, which one is preferred from the hotel's perspective?

Problem 16.12

Rio de Janeiro's BeachView Hotel is considering a group booking opportunity to sell 50 rooms on a particular night in four months' time at a room rate of R$200. The hotel has 250 rooms. The hotel's revenue management system is predicting that if the group booking is not accepted, the hotel will sell 225 room nights on the night in question, with all rooms sold at the hotel's rate category 1 level which is R$250. The hotel's Revenue Manager is concerned that if the group booking is accepted, some high rate paying guest bookings would be displaced. As a result, the Revenue Manager is considering providing the following two options to the group booking agent:

- Discounting the group room rate to R$170 if the agent would move the booking date to two weeks later. If the group booking could be moved to the later date, it would signify that no hotel guests paying a higher rate would be displaced.
- Discounting the group room rate to R$190 if the agent would consolidate the group booking down to 25 rooms.

Required:

a) Prepare a financial analysis to demonstrate whether the two room rate discounting options that the Revenue Manager is considering are financially justifiable.
b) If the manager is justified in offering these discounted room rate options, which one is preferred from the hotel's perspective?

Solutions to first three problems in each chapter

CHAPTER 1

Introduction

Problem 1.1: Solution

a) Functional interdependency exists when the performance of one functional area is affected by the performance of a separate functional area. For example, in a hotel complex that is dominated by a casino, the success of the rooms and food and beverage departments will be affected by the success of the casino operations in attracting clients to the complex.

b) Functional interdependency is an important issue for the designers of a hotel's system of accountability because care should be taken to hold a manager accountable for only those aspects of the hotel's performance that he or she can influence. For example, the heads of rooms and food and beverage departments should not be held accountable for a decrease in their room sales if it is caused by reduced casino activity.

Problem 1.2: Solution

a) The four main dimensions of sales volatility in the hotel industry are:
1. economic cycle induced sales volatility,
2. seasonal sales volatility,
3. weekly sales volatility,
4. intra-day sales volatility.

b) The implications that these dimensions of sales volatility carry for hotel accounting systems are as follows:
1. *Economic cycle induced volatility*: Hotel sales' high susceptibility to general economic conditions highlights the importance of hotels carefully forecasting economic cycles as part of the annual budgeting process.
2. *Seasonal sales volatility*: Three accounting implications arise:
   - Seasonal sales volatility can be so severe to warrant temporary closure for some resort properties. This possibility of having to make a closure decision signifies that cost and revenue data should be recorded in a manner that will enable a well informed financial analysis of the pros and cons of closing.
   - Seasonal sales volatility can also pose particular cash management issues. During the middle and tail-end of the busy seasons, surplus cash balances are likely to result, while in the off-season and the build up to the busy season, deficit cash balances are likely to result. Careful cash budgeting will therefore need to be conducted.

- Seasonal sales volatility will also affect price discounting decisions. To ensure such decisions are well informed, careful forecasting as part of the annual budgetary process will have to be conducted.

3. **Weekly sales volatility**: Accurate forecasting of weekly sales volatility will inform management's decision making with respect to the amount and timing of room rate discounting, staffing needs as well as restaurant purchasing needs.

4. **Intra-day sales volatility**: Intra-day demand volatility has led to widely used pricing strategies such as "early bird specials" in restaurants and "happy hours" in bars. Records concerning demand at different times of the day will have to be maintained in order to inform such hotel pricing issues.

Problem 1.3: Solution

Examples of business decisions requiring the use of financial accounting data include:

(a) A bank manager deciding whether to lend money to a company.
(b) A shareholder deciding whether to sell her shares due to a fear that the company she has invested in might go bankrupt.
(c) A potential shareholder thinking about purchasing shares in a company and interested in determining if the company is profitable.

Examples of business decisions requiring the use of management accounting data include:

(a) Determining whether accounts are being collected on time.
(b) Determining whether the business will have sufficient cash over the next year to avoid the need to arrange a line of credit.
(c) Determining whether a drinks vending machine or a confectionery vending machine should be installed in a hotel's foyer area.
(d) Determining what room rate to charge to achieve a target level of profit.
(e) Determining whether a seasonal hotel should be closed down during the quiet season.
(f) Determining whether a restaurant manager is performing well.

CHAPTER 2

Analysing transactions and preparing year-end financial statements

Problem 2.1: Solution

a) Simply defined, assets are things that are owned by a business. Typical hotel assets include: cash, accounts receivable, prepayments, inventory, cars, china, silver, glass, linen, uniforms, equipment, land and buildings.

b) Simply defined, liabilities comprise financial obligations of the organisation. Typical liabilities include: wages and salaries payable, accounts payable and bank loans.

c) Simply defined, owners' equity represents the residual claim that owners have on the assets of an organisation subsequent to the acquittal of all liabilities. Owners' equity increases when owners introduce more funds to the organisation and when the organisation makes profit.

Problem 2.2: Solution

The balance sheet equation relates to the fact that assets minus liabilities equals owners' equity. The equation can also be stated as assets equal liabilities plus owners' equity.

Underlying the first equation is the notion that the value of the owners' equity in a business equals the surplus assets that would remain following acquittal of all liabilities. Sense can also be made of the second equation as a business raises money and then invests the money in various assets.

Problem 2.3: Solution

Analysis of SerenitySleep Hotel's financial transactions in first 10 days of June

June	Cash at Bank	Accounts Receivable	Inventory	Office equipment	=	Accounts Payable	Loan Payable	+	Capital	Profit or Loss
		Assets			=	Liabilities		+	Owners' Equity	
1	+20,000								+20,000	
2	−3,000			+3,000						
3	−900		+900							
4			+1,400			+1,400				
5	−1,500			+6,000			+4,500			
6		+1,000								+1,000
7	−800								−800	
8	+1,300									+1,300
9			−400							−400
10	−240									−240
	14,860	1,000	1,900	9,000		1,400	4,500		19,200	1,660
		$26,760			=	$5,900		+	$20,860	

CHAPTER 3

Double entry accounting

Problem 3.1: Solution

No, it is inappropriate and misleading to suggest a debit to an account represents a good or a bad thing. It is true that a debit to the cash or bank account may be seen as beneficial as it signifies that an inflow of money has occurred. However, a debit to an expense account signifies an increase in the expense account and not many businesses would regard an increase in an expense as beneficial. We can conclude that we can only say that a debit to an account is a good thing if we know what type of account we are talking about.

Problem 3.2: Solution

No, in double entry accounting we cannot say that a debit represents a plus and a credit represents a minus. Debiting an asset account will usually represent a plus as asset accounts generally have a debit balance (the bank account can be an exception, however, if it is overdrawn). Liability accounts (e.g., accounts payable), however, generally have a credit balance, therefore a debit entry will have the effect of reducing the account's credit balance.

Problem 3.3: Solution

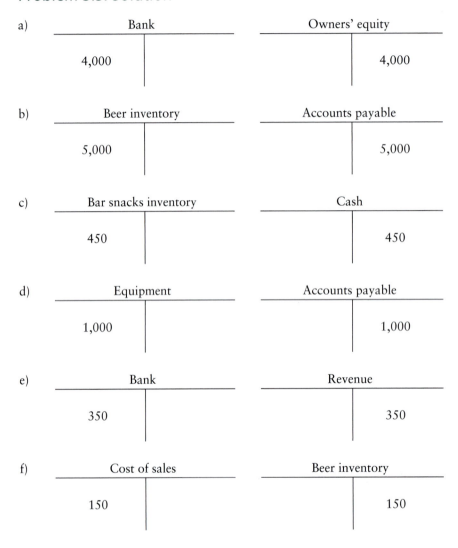

a)

Bank		Owners' equity	
4,000			4,000

b)

Beer inventory		Accounts payable	
5,000			5,000

c)

Bar snacks inventory		Cash	
450			450

d)

Equipment		Accounts payable	
1,000			1,000

e)

Bank		Revenue	
350			350

f)

Cost of sales		Beer inventory	
150			150

CHAPTER 4

Adjusting and closing entries

Problem 4.1: Solution

"Adjusting entries" is the term used to describe the set of bookkeeping entries that need to be made in order to update some accounts prior to the preparation of the accounting year-end income statement and balance sheet. This "tidying up" of accounts, which is really what the adjusting entries represent, has to be completed prior to closing entries. In many cases, the need for adjusting entries arises because the timing of cash flows (either receipts or disbursements) does not coincide with the period in which it is appropriate to recognise the revenue or expense. This distinction between the timing of a cash flow and the timing of the recognition of a revenue or an expense item stems from the accrual concept of accounting which holds that:

- revenue is recognised when it is earned and certain, rather than simply when cash is received,
- an expense is recognised in the period when the benefit derived from the associated expenditure arises.

Closing entries involve rolling all the accounts that feed into the income statement (plus the drawings account) back to zero at the end of the accounting year. For this reason, these accounts are sometimes referred to as temporary accounts. Accounts that feed directly into the balance sheet are sometimes referred to as permanent accounts as they are not rolled back to zero at the end of the accounting year. The revenue, expense and drawings accounts have to be wound back to zero at the end of the accounting year, otherwise they would carry amounts that relate to the business since its inception, rather than the current accounting year.

Problem 4.2: Solution

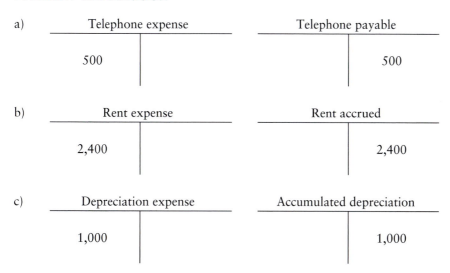

a)

Telephone expense		Telephone payable	
500			500

b)

Rent expense		Rent accrued	
2,400			2,400

c)

Depreciation expense		Accumulated depreciation	
1,000			1,000

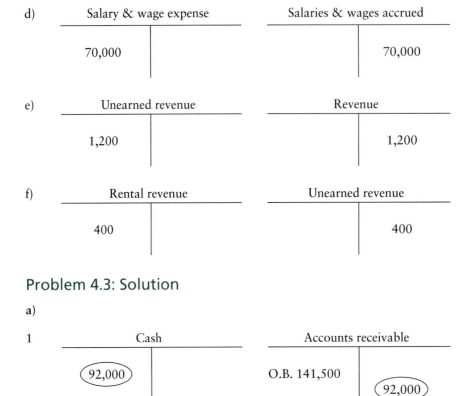

d)

Salary & wage expense			Salaries & wages accrued	
70,000				70,000

e)

Unearned revenue			Revenue	
1,200				1,200

f)

Rental revenue			Unearned revenue	
400				400

Problem 4.3: Solution

a)

1

Cash			Accounts receivable	
92,000			O.B. 141,500	
				92,000

2

Accounts receivable			Revenue	
141,500				O.B. 1,320,000
101,000	92,000			101,000

b) The first entry is to record the write down of the accounts receivable for the 180 days due balance:

Allowance for doubtful accounts			Accounts receivable	
4,500	O.B. 2,400		141,500	92,000
			101,000	4,500

Following the review of the accounts receivable ledger, it has been determined that the allowance for doubtful accounts should have a credit balance of $2,080 [($84,000 × 0.0075) + ($44,000 × 0.0125) + ($18,000 × 0.05)].

An inspection of the balance on the "allowance for doubtful accounts" account reveals that following the above debit entry of $4,500, it has a debit balance of $2,100. In order to achieve the requisite closing credit balance of $2,080, an adjusting credit entry of $4,180 has to be made to the "allowance for doubtful accounts". This adjusting entry signifies that the allowance for doubtful accounts entries made throughout the year were insufficient to reflect the doubtful account reality at the year-end. It is presumed that through the year, when the monthly entry has been made to allow for doubtful accounts, the "bad debts expense" account has been debited. Accordingly, we need to increase the bad debts expense account at the year-end, i.e., make an adjusting debit entry of $4,180 to the "bad debts expense" account.

Allowance for doubtful accounts		Bad debts expense	
4,500	2,400	O.B. 12,400	
	(4,180)	(4,180)	

CHAPTER 5

Financial statement analysis

Problem 5.1: Solution

a)

Dupont (ROI)	$\dfrac{\text{EBIT}}{\text{T.A.}}$	=	$\dfrac{\text{EBIT}}{\text{Revenue}}$	×	$\dfrac{\text{Revenue}}{\text{T.A.}}$
HoJo:	50 ÷ 250	=	50 ÷ 500	×	500 ÷ 250,
	0.2	=	0.1	×	2
EasyRest	15 ÷ 75	=	15 ÷ 300	×	300 ÷ 75,
	0.2	=	0.05	×	4

b) Both companies' F&B activities have achieved a 20 per cent return on total assets. However, their methods of achieving this return have been quite different. HoJo has earned a 10 per cent profit margin and a 200 per cent turnover of sales to total assets, whereas EasyRest has had a much higher sales turnover (4 or 400 per cent) with a smaller profit margin (5 per cent).

The companies appear to have different pricing policies. HoJo's mark-up on cost of sales is 150 per cent (300/200), whereas EasyRest only marks up cost of sales by 36 per cent (80/220).

Problem 5.2: Solution

a) Cost of sales = 0.6 × £28,750,000 = £17,250,000

$$\text{Average inventory} = \frac{£400,000 + £800,000 + £900,000 + £200,000}{4} = £575,000$$

$$\text{Inventory turnover} = \frac{£17,250,000}{£575,000} = 30$$

$$\text{Average age of inventory} = \frac{365}{30} = 12.17 \text{ days}$$

b) Enwad appears to have less liquid inventory than the average firm in the industry. Enwad's inventory is converted into a sale after 12 days while the average firm in the industry is taking approximately 9 days (365 ÷ 40).

Problem 5.3: Solution

a. Year ending 20X1 working capital:
($10,800 + 27,000 + 7,500 + 10,400 + 1,500) – ($8,400 + 3,600 + 4,500 + 700 + 10,700)
= $57,200 – $27,900 = $29,300
Year ending 20X2 working capital:
($14,300 + 26,000 + 7,500 + 12,000 + 1,600) – ($12,200 + 5,600 + 3,400 + 400 + 9,500)
= $61,400 – $31,100 = $30,300

b. Year ending 20X1 current asset ratio: $57,200 ÷ $27,900 = 2.05
Year ending 20X2 current asset ratio: $61,400 ÷ $31,100 = 1.97

c. Year ending 20X1 acid test ratio: ($57,200 – 10,400 – 1,500) ÷ $27,900 = 1.62
Year ending 20X2 acid test ratio: ($61,400 – 12,000 – 1,600) ÷ $31,100 = 1.54

d. The working capital shows a marginal increase; however, both the current asset ratio and the acid test ratio have decreased marginally. It appears the increase in the working capital has largely been accounted for by an increase in the size of the business (all things being equal, as a business doubles in size, so its working capital needs to double in order to maintain the same level of liquidity). Overall, we can conclude that there has been a marginal decrease in the restaurant's level of liquidity.

e. Accounts receivable turnover = Credit sales ÷ average accounts receivable
Credit sales = $500,000 × 0.55 = $275,000
Average accounts receivable = ($27,000 + $26,000) ÷ 2 = $26,500
Accounts receivable turnover = $275,000 ÷ $26,500 = 10.38

f. Accounts receivable collection period = 365 ÷ A.R. turnover:
365 ÷ 10.38 = 35.16 days

g. Inventory turnover = Cost of sales ÷ average inventory
Cost of sales = $150,000
Average inventory = ($10,400 + $12,000) ÷ 2 = $11,200
Inventory turnover = $150,000 ÷ $11,200 = 13.39

h. Inventory collection period = 365 ÷ inventory turnover:
365 ÷ 13.39 = 27.25 days

CHAPTER 6

Internal control

Problem 6.1: Solution

1) Safeguard assets
This objective concerns the protection of an organisation's assets from theft, ensuring that fixed assets are maintained so that they can be used efficiently and safely (e.g. appropriate hotel lift maintenance), and ensuring inventory items are appropriately stored to avoid waste and spoilage.

2) Promote efficient operations
In a labour-intensive business such as a hotel, ensuring appropriate recruitment and training can go a long way towards promoting efficiency. Adoption of technological advancements, such as providing all banquet staff with earpiece communication devices, can also greatly facilitate efficient operations. A system that monitors the adoption of technological advance-

ments in the sector can ensure a hotel is at the forefront of reaping technology-based operating efficiencies.

3) Maintain accurate and reliable accounting records

This objective requires that procedures are established to ensure the production of reliable annual reports to outside parties such as shareholders. Users of external financial reports need assurance that the reports provide a fair reflection of the economic events that have affected an organisation. Managers also need reliable accounting information to assist their operational management decision making and control.

4) Promote the pursuit of business policies

It is not worth having internal control procedures if they are not followed. Many organisations conduct internal audits that provide several internal control roles, including an appraisal of the extent to which document procedures are being correctly adhered to. Other ways to ensure business policies are adhered to include appropriately training staff and video recording staff as they conduct their work (video recording is an extensively used internal control device in casinos).

Problem 6.2: Solution

Examples of particular internal control challenges arising in hotels include:

- Hotels have a high volume of cash transactions.
- Hotels experience high employee turnover.
- Many activities within hotels are conducted as relatively small independent units. For instance, if a bar is staffed by two individuals, economies of scale that can facilitate the development of segregated roles consistent with strengthening internal controls are absent.
- In hotels many employees work in close proximity to inventory items that can be easily pilfered.

These characteristics signify that hotel managers need to have a sound appreciation of internal control system design.

Problem 6.3: Solution

HarbourView Hotel
Bank Reconciliation
as at 31 December 20X1

		$
Balance as per bank statement	Cr	34,290
Add: outstanding deposits		1,240
		35,530
Less: unpresented cheques		2,170
Balance as per cash at bank account	Dr	$33,360 *

* Workings
HarbourView's double entry accounting system bank account record

		$
Cash at bank balance – 31 December 20X1	Dr	33,376
Less: Bank fees		32
		33,344
Add: Bank account interest received		16
Adjusted cash at bank balance – 31 December 20X1	Dr	$33,360

CHAPTER 7

Cost management issues

Problem 7.1: Solution

The range of cost classifications arise due to the wide diversity of management decision making and control situations that can arise. In the text of the chapter it was noted that the cost classifications that can arise include the following:

a) outlay vs. opportunity costs,
b) direct vs. indirect costs,
c) variable vs. fixed costs,
d) controllable vs. non-controllable costs,
e) incremental vs. sunk costs.

An opportunity cost can be a significant issue if management is considering taking an action that will result in a lost opportunity. The issue of direct versus indirect costs is an issue when attempting to determine the profitability of revenue-generating departments, as calculation of each departments' net profit would necessitate the allocation of indirect costs. Many issues arise that necessitate a distinction between fixed and variable costs; one significant issue addressed in this chapter concerns the aggressive pricing strategy of setting prices over the short term at a level designed to cover variable costs. In responsibility accounting it is important that managers are only held accountable for costs that they can control. Finally, sunk costs are irrelevant in decision making; the decision maker need only focus on costs that will be affected by whatever decision is at hand.

Problem 7.2: Solution

a)

Variable costs:	£
Food and drink	7.0
Conference materials	6.0
Fixed costs (£360 ÷ 80)	4.5
	£17.5

b)

Variable costs:	£
Food and drink	7
Conference materials	6
Fixed costs (£360 ÷ 120)	3
	£16

c) The cost per attendee declines with more attendees because the fixed cost is spread across more attendees.

d) If 120 people attend, the cost per attendee is £16.

If profit is to be 20 per cent of revenue, then cost must be 80 per cent of revenue. As cost = £16 per person when 120 people attend, revenue per person must be £16 ÷ 0.8 = £20.

e) The lowest price that does not result in the conference adversely affecting this year's profit is the variable cost, i.e., £13 (£7 + £6).

Problem 7.3: Solution

a) *Determination of variable cost function:*
   When 20,000 kgs of laundry was processed (highest level of activity), cost = $22,000.

   When 18,000 kgs of laundry was processed (lowest level of activity), cost = $20,400.

   It therefore costs an extra $1,600 ($22,000 – $20,400) to process an extra 2,000 kgs of laundry (20,000 – 18,000).

   Therefore, the variable cost per kg is $1,600 ÷ 2,000 = $0.80 per kg.

   Determination of fixed cost function:
   Calculation based on July's performance:
   HighFlyer's laundry costs for July are $22,000, and their variable laundry costs are $16,000 ($0.80 × 20,000 kgs). Fixed laundry costs must therefore be $6,000 ($22,000 – $16,000).

b) Total laundry costs if 25,000 kilograms of laundry are processed:
   (25,000 × $0.80) + $6,000 = $26,000

CHAPTER 8

Cost-volume-profit analysis

Problem 8.1: Solution

The contribution margin format enables us to quickly answer questions such as "What will happen to profit if our hotel's revenue increases by $100,000?". If variable costs are 20 per cent of revenue, then the contribution margin ratio is 80 per cent. This signifies that a $100,000 increase in revenue will result in an $80,000 increase in profit (0.8 × $100,000).

The contribution margin format can also be seen as helpful to management's understanding of cost structure as it places revenue alongside those costs that are affected by the level of revenue achieved.

Problem 8.2: Solution

Cost-volume-profit analysis can be helpful if a manager is considering questions such as:

1. "How many units will we need to sell in order to breakeven?"
2. "How much will we need to sell in order to achieve our target profit level?"
3. "What will happen to profit if we manage to increase sales volume by 10 per cent?"

4. "By what volume of sales are we currently surpassing our breakeven point?"
5. "If fixed costs increase by $20,000, how much more would we have to sell in order to maintain our current level of profit?"

Problem 8.3: Solution

a)

The Hulsey Restaurant
Income statement for the year ending 31 December 20X1
(Contribution margin layout)

	$	Percentage
Sales revenue	500,000	100.0
Variable costs		
Variable cost of sales	100,000	20.0
Variable operating expenses	16,000	3.2
Contribution margin	384,000	76.8
Fixed costs		
Salaries and wages	144,000	28.8
Marketing	10,000	2.0
Rent	48,000	9.6
Maintenance	5,000	1.0
Other	10,000	2.0
	217,000	43.4
Net profit	$ 167,000	33.4

b) Breakeven point = Fixed costs ÷ Contribution per cover =
    $217,000 ÷ (25 − [5 + 0.8]) = $217,000 ÷ $19.2 = 11,302 meals per annum.
c) From the income statement prepared using the contribution margin layout, it is evident that the contribution margin is 76.8 per cent.
    An increase in sales of 10 per cent represents a $50,000 sales increase ($500,000 × 0.1). As the contribution margin ratio is 76.8 per cent a 10 per cent increase in sales will result in a $38,400 increase in profit ($50,000 × 0.768).
d) Profit = Contribution margin − Fixed costs.
    ($600,000 × 0.768) − $217,000 = 460,800 − 217,000 = $243,800.
e) A 10 per cent increase in revenue would signify that profit would increase by $50,000 ($500,000 × 0.1).
    Alternately stated, profit would increase by $2.5 for each cover served. As there are 20,000 covers sold, profit would increase by $50,000 ($2.5 × 20,000).

CHAPTER 9

Budgeting and responsibility accounting

Problem 9.1: Solution

Responsibility accounting involves sub-dividing an organisation into units of accountability. It is fundamental to control as it involves holding managers accountable for the performance of their respective units. Budgeting is closely associated with responsibility accounting because budgeting involves allocating resources to an organisation's sub-units. In addition, the budget highlights benchmarks that are used when appraising a unit manager's performance. As the budgeting system sets targets for all of an organisation's sub-units, it is difficult to conceive of any meaningful budgeting occurring in the absence of a responsibility accounting system.

Problem 9.2: Solution

There is no single "easy" answer to this question.

Issues that might be addressed in a well-reasoned answer include:

- So long as Bromwich provided the requisition to Joe in reasonable time (i.e., sufficient purchasing lead time), it would be inappropriate to hold the head of banqueting and conferences responsible for the part not arriving. Despite this issue, it would appear that the head of banqueting and conferences was responsible for the refund decision and therefore justification could be given for charging at least a portion of the lost revenue to her department. One could also argue that given the importance of the part, Maxine should have followed up with Joe more times.
- The following rationale could be developed for charging all of the lost revenue to the purchasing department:
  1. In the whole organisation, the purchasing manager is the one who is most closely associated with the role of ensuring timely delivery.
  2. Joe could be criticised for not getting another staff member or Maxine to follow up on the order while he was away on holiday.
  3. Joe could have requested that a copy of the consignment be faxed when told that the delivery was underway.
  4. Joe should have informed Maxine earlier of the potential problem with the delivery.
  5. By requiring Joe's department to carry the loss, he may take greater care when ordering one-off special parts in the future.
- It could also be argued to be inappropriate to attach blame to Joe (it was really the supplier's fault), as it appears he may well have made reasonable efforts to ensure timely delivery.
- Joe and Maxine could attempt to recoup some of the loss from the supplier. At the very least, this would inform the supplier of the cost of their mistake.
- This case appears to be a situation highlighting how it can be very inappropriate to use the responsibility accounting system as an apportioning blame system rather than a "determining who should have the opportunity to explain" system.

Problem 9.3: Solution

1) The first thing to note is that the responsibility accounting system appears to be perceived as an "apportioning blame" system. This is highly undesirable as it is likely to give rise to ill-feeling that is more damaging than helpful. A properly used responsibility system emphasises information rather than blame. If managers feel they are beaten around the head when unfavourable variances occur, they are likely to view the system as a tool of bureaucracy and start conjuring up ways to undermine the system. When the numbers are used in a manner that emphasises the informational role of the responsibility system, managers are more likely to be open to discussion with colleagues in a quest for gaining improved performance. Scheduling an inter-departmental management meeting following the receipt of monthly performance reports may be one way of focusing on the information aspect of the responsibility accounting system.

2) The accountant could agree that in the future "pastry cutters" wages will be charged to Maintenance at the rate of $9 per hour and that a correction will be made for last month's entry. The $4.50 premium could be charged to a "Loss from unused capacity" account which is charged back to the F&B department because it was the F&B director who elected to retain these staff. The Maintenance Manager should be told that it is up to him to get $9 of work per hour out of the staff placed under his direction. The fact that these are non-preferred personnel could be recognised in a note to the monthly report.

3) Theoretically, the accountant could argue that the $4.50 (or even the whole $13.50) represents investment in an asset as:

   a) It is an investment today that will yield a benefit in the future (i.e., retention of preferred kitchen staff),

   b) It is an investment today that will result in a saving in the future (i.e., no need to expend resources recruiting and training new skilled kitchen staff).

Due to conservatism, accountants would not tend to take this view, however. The distinction is nevertheless important. An "expense" tends to be viewed in a negative light, while an "investment" tends to be viewed in a positive light.

CHAPTER 10

Flexible budgeting and variance analysis

Problem 10.1: Solution

In a static budgeting system, a budget is rigid in the sense that it is not modified once the actual volume of sales is known. While this approach is used extensively, some managers find it helpful to flex budgets up or down in line with the actual volume of sales achieved. Failure to accurately predict the volume of sales is a major factor causing many significant differences between the static budget and actual performance. Under flexible budgeting, however, the effect of a hotel selling more or less than was originally projected is eliminated from differences between the actual and budgeted performance. Elimination of this factor is significant because, by definition, managers in cost centres exert little influence on sales volumes.

A shortcoming of isolating variances between actual performance and the static budget is that much of a variance may be attributable to the fact that it is practically impossible to correctly estimate the volume of sales that will occur in a forthcoming accounting period. Variances occurring as a result of an organisation being busier or quieter than expected are not really reflective of the performance of many managers. If we were to take static budget variances to the extreme, we can see that very favourable variable cost variances can be achieved if we have no one staying at our hotel! To remove the effect of actual volume of sales being different to the budgeted volume of sales, we can produce a flexible budget. In a flexible budget, the static budget figures are restated as if the actual volume of sales achieved had been known at the time the budget was set.

Problem 10.2: Solution

The $1,200 unfavourable materials price variance signifies that the materials used in the kitchen in the previous month cost $1,200 more than what budget data indicates they should have cost.

The $800 favourable materials efficiency variance signifies that in the previous month, kitchen materials were used more efficiently than was budgeted for. For instance a reduction in food scrapped due to poor quality, or a reduction in food thrown away as a result of staleness would be two factors contributing to a favourable materials efficiency variance. Such efficiencies achieved in the previous month have caused the kitchen to beat the budget by $800 in terms of materials efficiency.

The unfavourable materials flexible budget variance is simply the net of the materials price variance and the materials efficiency variance. The fact that we have a $400 unfavourable efficiency variance in the previous month signifies that for the volume of sales that we actually achieved in the kitchen, materials used cost $400 more than they should have done as per budgeted data.

Problem 10.3: Solution

a) As the lodge has made 15 per cent more room sales than was budgeted for ([12,420 – 10,800] ÷ 10,800 × 100), we can produce a flexible budget by increasing the revenue and variable cost figures stated in the static budget by 15 per cent. A simple way to achieve this is to multiply them by a factor of 1.15.

The Curbside Motor Lodge
Flexible Budget Performance Report
For the Quarter Ended 30 September 20X1

	Actual	Budget	Flexible budget	Flexible budget variances
Room nights sold	12,420	10,800	12,420	
	£	£	£	£
Revenue (sales)	1,179,900	1,080,000	1,242,000	62,100 (U)
Variable costs:				
Labour	84,456	75,600	86,940	2,484 (F)
Room amenities	5,216	5,400	6,210	994 (F)
Contribution margin	1,090,228	999,000	1,148,850	58,622 (U)
Fixed costs	241,000	235,000	235,000	6,000 (U)
Operating profit	£ 849,228	£ 764,000	£ 913,850	£ 64,622 (U)

b) A shortcoming of isolating variances between actual performance and the static budget is that much of a variance may be attributable to the fact that it is practically impossible to correctly estimate the volume of sales that will occur in a forthcoming accounting period. Variances occurring as a result of an organisation being busier or quieter than expected are not really reflective of the performance of many managers. If we were to take static budget variances to the extreme, we can see that very favourable variable cost variances can be achieved if we have no one staying at our hotel! To remove the effect of actual volume of sales being different to the budgeted volume of sales, we can produce a flexible budget. In a flexible budget, the static budget figures are restated as if the actual volume of sales achieved had been known at the time the budget was set.

The flexible budget performance report provides very different management insights to those provided by the static budget variances computed by Curbside's conventional performance report. The extent of these differences is highlighted by the following table.

Curbside: Comparison of static budget and flexible budget variances		
	Static budget variances	Flexible budget variances
Revenue (sales)	(F)	(U)
Variable costs:		
Labour	(U)	(F)
Room amenities	(F)	(F)
Contribution margin	(F)	(U)
Fixed costs	(U)	(U)
Operating profit	(F)	(U)

- The unfavourable flexible budget variance for revenue signifies that rooms must have been sold below the rate budgeted for. This fact was not evident from the static budget variance.
- The favourable flexible budget variance for labour signifies that labour worked efficiently or the labour rate was below the rate budgeted for. This fact was not evident from the static budget variance.
- The size of the unfavourable revenue flexible budget variance is sufficient to have turned the favourable static budget contribution margin variance into an unfavourable flexible budget variance. This impact is also apparent at the operating profit level.

CHAPTER 11

Performance measurement

Problem 11.1: Solution

There appears to be considerable validity in the adage that "what gets measured is what gets managed". Consideration of students' approach to studies supports this view. Students tend to put much more effort preparing assignments that carry a mark relative to homework problems that do not carry a mark. It appears people have a great tendency to attach more importance to those things that are measured. This close association between what gets measured and what gets managed highlights the importance of carefully thinking through what should be measured in a hotel's performance measurement system.

Problem 11.2: Solution

1. Many hotels engage the services of a specialist hotel operating company. Many large hotels operate in this manner, with a management contract struck between the hotel owner and hotel operator. The tension that can arise between the focus of a hotel's operating company and its owner highlights an additional complexity factor heightening the importance of careful performance measurement system design.
2. The underlying diversity of the activities conducted in a hotel that were described in Chapter 1 (i.e., the service orientation evident in the provision of accommodation, the retail orientation evident in bar sales and the production orientation evident in restaurant

kitchens) requires the development and application of a range of performance measures that move well beyond traditional financial performance measures.

Other challenges arising include the fact that hotel groups have to manage highly geographically dispersed operating units (i.e., hotels) and operate in a sector where very high turnover rates prevail for operating staff.

Problem 11.3: Solution

(a) **Financial performance measures focus on results not causes.** If a hotel's financial performance measurement system indicates a declining level of sales, we know that all is not well. We would not know, however, what factors account for this bad financial result. We would have no sense of what corrective action should be taken because the sales account represents a highly aggregated performance indicator and there are many factors that could account for a changed level of sales. A broader-based performance measurement system will have a greater capacity to highlight factors that lie behind a declining level of sales.

(b) **Financial performance measures suffer from a backward-looking orientation.** Financial performance measures tend to focus on performance in a specific period of time that has past. A more valuable performance measurement system is one that can provide pointers towards likely future performance. For instance, increasing levels of customer satisfaction suggests future strong performance due to an increase in return guests and positive word of mouth promotion. Similarly, improved employee morale points towards a likely reduction in future staff turnover and an increase in the care and quality of service provided.

(c) **Financial performance measures focus on a limited performance dimension.** Financial performance measures are obviously limited to measuring those things that can be measured in money terms. Marketing managers in hotels recognise that customer loyalty is an exceedingly important factor contributing to a hotel's overall performance. Human resource managers recognise that employee morale is very important, particularly as hotel customers come into contact with many hotel employees. Computers and information systems are key integral components contributing to the effective operation of any large hotel (just consider the drastic implications of a one-week failure in a hotel's computerised reservation system). Despite the undoubted importance of factors such as customer loyalty, staff morale and information system support, none of these aspects of a hotel's operation can be monitored using a financial measure.

(d) **Financial performance measures can promote short-term focused behaviour.** If managers focus too much on the short term, they may be taking steps that can damage a hotel's long-term success. This issue is a particularly apparent problem in the hotel industry because of the frequency with which General Managers (GMs) experience relocation within a chain of hotels. In many chains, it is not unusual for a GM to average around three years at each property. If a hotel chain operates such a management policy and attaches major emphasis on financial performance indicators, there is an incentive for managers to take steps that will result in increasing reported profit for the three years they are with a hotel, with limited concern given to the hotel's longer-term performance. This could mean that the GM cuts back on those financial outlays where no immediate downside is apparent. For example, a GM could reduce property preventative maintenance expenditure, cut back on staff development and training, and reduce expenditure associated with the hotel's local customer loyalty programme that was established by the preceding GM. All of these steps can be expected to result in an immediate cost saving. The negative implications of these expenditure reductions may not begin to be felt until three years after they have been implemented. This signifies that the GM initiating the expenditure can appear to have performed well, due to the increased reported profit associated with the time he was GM. He could well look even better once he is replaced and the deferred negative implications of the steps he has taken start to be realised following his departure.

CHAPTER 12

Cost information and pricing

Problem 12.1: Solution

Contribution pricing is concerned with covering variable costs to ensure a positive contribution results. It is particularly appropriate with perishable stock such as rooms. If a room is not sold for a particular night and the night in question elapses, that particular room night can never be sold in the future. The contribution pricing philosophy holds that it is better to receive some contribution to profit rather than no contribution, before an unsold room night elapses. As a result, contribution pricing can be seen as a "last minute" mentality that can come into play as the time for a room night elapsing approaches. Viewed in this way, contribution pricing represents an attempt to secure a contribution from stock that is about to be sacrificed (either because of the passage of time or, in the case of food, if the stock is becoming too old to sell).

Yield management is not a "last minute" room pricing philosophy. Yield management involves sales and marketing management developing pricing plans that recognise factors such as whether a reservation pertains to a quiet or busy season, weekday or weekend and also the nature of a customer's market segment (e.g., group booking vs. a single transient guest). Unlike contribution pricing that focuses on generating a price that covers variable cost, yield management focuses on maximising revenue per available room. Questions addressed in yield management include whether a discounted tour booking should be made for a future period, when most of a hotel's stock of rooms has already been sold for the period in question.

Problem 12.2: Solution

a. If a car manufacturer's sales are slow on a particular day, there is no particular need for the manufacturer to drop the prices of its cars in an effort to sell more on that day. Cars not sold today can simply remain in the car manufacturer's finished goods inventory in readiness to be sold tomorrow or at some other time in the future. This is because cars represent a non-perishable inventory item.

This is not the situation for a hotel's room inventory, however. If tonight's right of occupancy in a particular hotel room is not sold today, the opportunity to sell that occupancy right will be lost forever, as an unsold room night today cannot be placed into inventory for sale at a later date. This heightens the incentive for hotels to consider a strategy of discounting room rates as the time of an unsold block of room nights approaches. As an unsold room night cannot be sold at a future date, it is described as being highly "perishable".

b. Pricing strategies should take into account the degree to which a product or service is perishable. To illustrate, let us compare a bottle of wine and a fresh cream cake that are available for purchase from a café that adjoins a hotel's foyer. Due to differences in the perishability of the two products, a manager would be justified in implementing very different pricing strategies for the two products.

Let us assume that the unit variable cost of making the cakes is $1.20, and that immediately following production, the cakes are priced at $4 each. Let us also assume that if a cake is not sold by the end of the day following its production, it will have to be discarded as waste (i.e., the cake is highly perishable). On the day following the cake's production, if the cake is not sold by the time the café closes, its revenue earning potential will be lost forever. Accordingly, a manager might be justified in dropping the retail price of the cakes to $0.50 one hour before the café is due to close.

The bottle of wine does not suffer from the same perishability as the cream cake. The closing of the café on a particular day does not signify that the future revenue potential of the bottle of wine is lost. Accordingly, the rationale for dropping the price of cream cakes to a point that is below their variable cost does not apply to the bottle of wine.

Problem 12.3: Solution

Total costs:

	£
Bank loan (£250,000 @ 9%)	22,500
Depreciation	40,000
Other fixed costs	65,000
Operating expenses	85,000
Total costs	£212,500

After tax profit sought by owners = £450,000 × 0.15 = £67,500.

Before tax profit needed to provide after tax profit of £67,500 = £135,000 (tax is 50 per cent).

Total revenue needed to provide before tax profit of £135,000 =

Total costs + desired before tax profit, i.e., £212,500 + £135,000 = £347,500.

Room rate = Total revenue ÷ Room nights sold in a year

Room nights sold in a year = 40 × 0.55 × 365 = 8,030

Room rate = £347,500 ÷ 8,030 = £43.27

CHAPTER 13

Working capital management

Problem 13.1: Solution

A significant factor contributing to the difference between profit and cash flow is the way accountants account for fixed assets. If we pay $500,000 for a fixed asset, cash will immediately decline at the time we pay for the fixed asset; however, the reported profit in the year the asset is purchased will not be affected by nearly as much. If it is determined that the cost of the asset is to be depreciated over ten years, in the year that the asset is purchased, reported profit will only be reduced by the $50,000 annual depreciation charge for the asset (assuming the asset was purchased at the beginning of the year), not the $500,000 asset cost. This signifies that in the year the asset is purchased, a $450,000 discrepancy arises between reported profit (affected by a $50,000 depreciation charge) and actual cash flow (affected by a $500,000 payment to the fixed asset supplier).

Other factors accounting for a difference between profit and cash flow include:

- We recognise revenue at the time a service is provided, not when cash is received.
- If supplies are paid for on credit, there will be a lag between purchases and payments.
- Employees are paid following the completion of work or a working period.
- In many countries, electricity accounts are settled on a quarterly basis. This signifies at least a three month discrepancy between some of the electricity expense incurred and payment for electricity.
- Insurance and rent are paid in advance of charging the associated expense to the income statement.
- In the case of insurance, payment is made a year in advance of a portion of the expense.
- When a company arranges a loan or increases its share capital there is an immediate large positive impact on cash flow. The only income statement impact concerns the loan's annual interest expense, however.

Problem 13.2: Solution

The following issues should be appraised when considering whether to extend trade credit to a customer:

1. Character: does the customer have a predisposition towards timely payment of accounts?
2. Capacity: does the customer have the capacity to run a successful business?
3. Capital: does the customer have sufficient working and long-term capital to honour the account when it is due for payment?
4. Conditions: are there any particular economic conditions that might affect the potential customer's ability to pay? In addition, there might be particular circumstances such as low occupancy in the off season that might cause a hotel to consider extending credit to less creditworthy customers.
5. Collateral: does the customer have assets that could be liquidated relatively easily in the event of a liquidity crisis that threatened timely reimbursement of the account due.

Problem 13.3: Solution

Schedule of projected cash receipts for CrownJewel in ($ thousands)

	October	November	December	Total
Room sales	$ 540	$ 500	$ 600	
10% cash sales	$ 54	$ 50	$ 60	$ 164
50% received in month following sale	300	270	250	820
35% received 2 months following sale	231	210	189	630
5% received 3 months following sale	31.5	33	30	94.5
Total room receipts	$ 616.5	$ 563	$ 529	$ 1,708.5

	October	November	December	Total
Restaurant & bar sales	$ 70	$ 60	$ 80	
30% cash sales	$ 21	$ 18	$ 24	$ 63
70% received in month following sale	56	49	42	147
Total restaurant & bar receipts	77	67	66	210
Total all receipts	$ 693.5	$ 630	$ 595	$ 1,918.5

CHAPTER 14

Investment decision making

Problem 14.1: Solution

The payback method is intuitively appealing and is relatively simple to understand. Payback can be used as an initial screening mechanism prior to the use of more sophisticated investment appraisal techniques, particularly if a hotel is considering an investment in a high risk country that is subject to high exchange rate volatility. Such volatility can motivate a manager saying "If we don't get our money back in three years" I don't want to make this investment.

The payback technique has several shortcomings. Two major shortcomings of the payback approach are:

1. It fails to consider any cash flows occurring after the payback period. The second of the two examples presented in Box 14.2 has the faster payback; however, the first example generates the most lifetime cash inflows. In the first payback example, if the projected operating cash inflows had been $100,000 in each of the last four years of the investment's life, the payback would still be four years.
2. It fails to recognise the time value of money, i.e., $1 today does not have the same value as $1 in a year's time. Payback treats cash flows occurring in different time periods as if they have the same value.

Problem 14.2: Solution

a) The theoretically preferred investment appraisal technique is the Net Present Value approach.
b) The Net Present Value technique does not suffer from any obvious shortcomings. If a company commits itself to a project with an NPV of $5m, and the share market is working efficiently, the company's value should increase by $5m. This is because today's value of all the company's future cash flows has been increased by $5m.

　　The ARR's shortcomings include:

1. It fails to consider the period of the investment. Suppose a hotel is deciding whether to take a 40% ARR investment option with a three year life or an $8,000 investment option that has a ten year life and an ARR of 38 per cent. The ARR approach would say take the three year project as it has the highest ARR. By investing in the ten year asset that provides a 38

per cent ARR, however, the investor would be able to increase its average return on assets for seven years longer than if it invests in the three year asset that provides a 40 per cent ARR. Accordingly, it appears the ten year 38 per cent ARR investment option is preferable to the three year 40 per cent ARR option.

2. The ARR is based on accounting profits. These figures involve some apportioning of cash flows to different accounting periods (e.g., depreciation). As a result, profits are not "real" in a tangible sense. They represent nothing more than the accountant's "account" of performance. Cash flows, however, are real, and it is the commercial reality of the timing of money entering and exiting the organisation, and not the accountant's account, that we need to incorporate in the decision model.

Two major shortcomings of the payback approach are:

1. It fails to consider any cash flows occurring after the payback period. The second of the two examples presented in the book's Box 14.2 has the faster payback; however, the first example generates the most lifetime cash inflows. In the first payback example, if the projected operating cash inflows had been $100,000 in each of the last four years of the investment's life, the payback would still be four years.
2. It fails to recognise the time value of money, i.e., $1 today does not have the same value as $1 in a year's time. Payback treats cash flows occurring in different time periods as if they have the same value.

The IRR approach to investment appraisal has the following shortcomings:

1. In some cases, where a project's cash flows include future cash outflows, two different discount rates can result in an NPV of zero (i.e., two IRRs for one project).
2. In a single project, accept or reject situation, NPV and IRR will give the same indication (i.e., if IRR > required rate of return, NPV will be > 0). When ranking projects, however, NPV and IRR can give conflicting signals, i.e., the highest NPV project will not necessarily be the highest IRR project. If this situation arises, preference should be given to the NPV indication as it is the theoretically preferred technique.

Problem 14.3: Solution

Present value = $600 (PV8, 5yr) = $600 × 0.681 = $408.60

CHAPTER 15

Other managerial finance issues

Problem 15.1: Solution

Three reasons accounting for EPS being a deficient financial goal for companies are:

● The issue of EPS timing (early high EPS returns are preferable to late high EPS returns).
● The **failure of EPS to capture cash flows**. A period of high EPS may be a period of low company cash flow.

- **EPS fails to recognize risk.** A company may take on a risky project that increases its EPS; however, the resulting increased risk profile for the company may well cause a decline in its share price.

Problem 15.2: Solution

a. The **residual dividend theory** holds that a company should use all its available long-term capital investing in positive net present value (NPV) projects, until no further positive NPV project opportunities remain. Following this line of thinking, once a company has invested in all available positive NPV projects, any remaining excess long-term capital (i.e., residual funds) should be distributed as a dividend to its shareholders. Applying this approach will result in considerable volatility in the dividends paid to shareholders. The **information effect dividend theory** holds that a decision to pay dividends to shareholders carries a positive impact on share price. This is because the decision to pay an increased dividend can be seen as a signal that flags a company's intent to pay higher dividends in years to come. Conversely, a decrease in dividends is believed to provide a negative signal, as it suggests that dividends might decrease in years to come. This thinking results in many companies pursuing a policy of only raising dividends levels if they are confident that the increased dividend level can be maintained in years to come.

b. The findings of empirical research suggest that in practice companies tend to adhere to the information effect theory when setting their dividend policy.

c. The clientele effect tell us that whatever policy a company is adopting with respect to paying dividends, it should continue to apply this policy. This is because investors who have bought shares in a company must have been attracted to it, based on the dividend payment policy it is pursuing.

Problem 15.3: Solution

Triple bottom line reporting focuses on:

- financial performance reporting,
- social performance reporting, and
- environmental performance reporting.

CHAPTER 16

Revenue management

Problem 16.1: Solution

A low variable cost for a product or service signifies a high price setting discretionary range. A high price setting discretionary range signifies there is considerable scope to modify price in light of information provided by a revenue management system.

Problem 16.2: Solution

Five business characteristics making an industry conducive to the application of revenue management are:

- Fixed capacity
- Ability to segment markets
- Perishable inventory
- Product sold in advance
- Fluctuating demand
- Low variable costs

Problem 16.3: Solution

Three approaches that a hotel can take to gauge its revenue management performance are:

a) Internal analysis of lost revenue.
b) Analysing Revpar performance relative to other hotels operating within the same competitive set.
c) Gauging Revpar performance by purchasing market data concerning hotels with a similar profile.

Index